Counselling and Supporting Children and Young People

PRAISE FOR THE BOOK

'Mark Prever writes with considerable passion. He is passionately committed to the person-centred approach and all that it has to offer the worlds of education and counselling. He is also passionately concerned with the well-being of children and young people and the alleviation of their suffering. His book is permeated by this dual commitment. It is scholarly without ever becoming arid; it is enlivened by numerous case studies which demonstrate the breadth and depth of his experience; it is encouraging for all those already engaged in work with young people and for many it will be a source of inspiration when the going gets rough and problems seem intractable.'

Brian Thorne, Emeritus Professor of Counselling, University of East Anglia, Norwich and Co-founder of The Norwich Centre

' ... both interesting and stimulating ... it was enriching to see the person-centred approach in the context of working with children and young people. This book would be an excellent aid for both student counsellors and a very valuable reminder to experienced practitioners of the core principles and values of the approach. It illuminates for the reader the importance of the relationship between therapist and client within the person-centred approach.'

Carmel Mullan-Hartley, person-centred counsellor, supervisor and trainer, Open Door Youth Counselling

Counselling and Supporting Children and Young People

A Person-centred Approach

Mark Prever

Los Angeles | London | New Delhi
Singapore | Washington DC

First published 2010

SAGE Publications Ltd
1 Oliver's Yard
55 City Road
London EC1Y 1SP

SAGE Publications Inc.
2455 Teller Road
Thousand Oaks, California 91320

SAGE Publications India Pvt Ltd
B 1/I 1 Mohan Cooperative Industrial Area
Mathura Road
New Delhi 110 044

SAGE Publications Asia-Pacific Pte Ltd
33 Pekin Street #02-01
Far East Square
Singapore 048763

Library of Congress Control Number: 2009931949

British Library Cataloguing in Publication data

A catalogue record for this book is available from the British Library

ISBN 978-1-84787-934-9
ISBN 978-1-84787-935-6 (pbk)

Typeset by C&M Digitals (P) Ltd, Chennai, India
Printed in Great Britain by CPI Antony Rowe, Chippenham, Wiltshire
Printed on paper from sustainable resources

ABOUT THE AUTHOR

Mark Prever has spent over 30 years working in education as well as a substantial period in the counselling field as counsellor, trainer and supervisor, working in a person-centred way. For a period, he was seconded to Dudley Education Authority where he acted as a peripatetic counsellor, working in three secondary and a number of junior schools across the Borough. He has held a wide variety of pastoral roles in schools as well as managing a Student Support Centre for young people with mental health difficulties and social-emotional problems. He has been executive chair of a person-centred youth counselling agency in Birmingham as well as holding the role of Counselling Development Officer. He is a former chair of Counselling Children and Young People, a division of The British Association for Counselling and Psychotherapy. Mark writes regularly and is the author of *Mental Health in Schools: A Guide to Pastoral and Curriculum Provision*, also published by Sage.

CONTENTS

Acknowledgements   ix

THEORY   1

1   Introduction: why working with children and young people
    in a person-centred way is different   3

2   The person-centred approach: theoretical framework   17

3   Historical, national, ethical and legal issues in working
    with children and young people   32

4   Measuring outcomes   46

5   Why young people become unhappy: the person-centred
    approach in context   54

6   The importance of the relationship   64

PRACTICE   75

7   Working with feelings and emotions   77

8   Unconditional positive regard   86

9   Congruence   97

10 Empathy   106

11 Working creatively   120

12   Developing person-centred skills, attitudes and qualities   139

13   Key questions about working with children and young people   154

14   Training, supervision and well-being   164

Appendix   175
References   180
Useful organisations   187
Index   189

ACKNOWLEDGEMENTS

I am thankful to Sage for encouraging me to write this book which has been in my thoughts, in one form or another, for many years. In particular, I would like to thank Susannah and Alice, my editors, who have guided me through the whole process with sound advice, ideas and support; all this offered with sensitivity and kindness.

I am grateful to my partner Ruth who didn't complain when I disappeared on evenings and weekends to read, think and write.

I am indebted to The Open Door Youth Counselling Service in Birmingham where I learned my trade. It was here that I first met its Director of Services, Carmel Mullan-Hartley, who trained and supervised me as a counsellor and has continued to support me over the years, both personally and professionally. Thanks are also due to the many colleagues I have met through Open Door over the past 15 years. I have worked with some very warm, caring and supportive people whom I believe have possessed many of the attitudes and qualities so important to the person-centred approach.

Finally, thank you to all the young people I have worked with, in a variety of settings; young people who have trusted me with their innermost selves and whose influence on me has been so profound.

THEORY

1

INTRODUCTION:
Why Working with Children and Young People in a Person-centred Way is Different

INTRODUCING THIS CHAPTER

This chapter explores why working with children and young people is so rewarding. It will use case study material to examine the variety of ways in which we listen to young people and why the person-centred approach is so highly valued by the younger age group. The chapter will show how interest in working with children and adolescents has grown in recent years. It will introduce the reader to the work of Carl Rogers and the influence of his thinking and practice. Some of the criticisms and limitations of the person-centred approach will be identified and challenged, including those issues raised by the professional environments in which this kind of work takes place. The chapter begins with some discussion about the differences between counselling and helping and who this book is written for.

TO THE COUNSELLOR

Whether you are new to the profession or have been counselling for some time, I believe that there will be much to interest you in this book. The counsellor always remains a counsellor in the making, never reaching the end of learning.

(Continued)

(Continued)

Counselling is a unique and sometimes stressful profession and there are times when you may have questioned what you are doing and whether the person-centred approach was sufficient. I hope that this book will sustain your faith in the process. It may be that you are new to working with children and young people or are considering working with young clients. To you, I say read on, for there is little that is more rewarding.

TO THE HELPER

This book is deliberately directed at therapists and those who are not professionally trained as counsellors, but who want to work within the person-centred approach with children and young people. The approach set out here emphasises the qualities needed by the caring adult to establish warm and empathic relationships with young people, based upon acceptance and realness. There are of course differences between the role of helper and that of the professional counsellor and hopefully this book will highlight these. However, the essence of the person-centred approach remains the same. You may already have decided to pursue a qualification in counselling or may be happy working with children and young people outside of the profession. Either way, you are welcome.

WITH CHILDREN AND YOUNG PEOPLE IN MIND

Many of the ideas, concepts and principles, which have helped shape the person-centred approach, have been developed with adults in mind. However, I hope to show their relevance and meaning to working with children and young people. Working with this age group (8–19) does however present us with different challenges and I hope this book will explore how these can be overcome without losing the essence of the approach.

So far, I have used the words 'children and young people' interchangeably. Often, working therapeutically with young people is the same across the ages. However, where the age of a young person is significant in our work, I will draw attention to these differences.

WHAT THIS BOOK IS ABOUT AND HOW TO USE IT

This book is about working with children (aged 8–13) and young people (aged 14–19) in a very special way. It is about working therapeutically, using the person-centred approach, which is based on the writings, research and practice of the celebrated American counselling psychologist Carl Rogers (1902–1987), whose influence lives on in a wide variety of professions which offer psychological support to people in need. Many people have been helped in this way and have subsequently gone on to grow and develop in ways that Carl Rogers believed individuals had the potential to. However, this book has an ambitious goal in mind, that is, to apply the approach directly and specifically to counselling and supporting children and young people.

This book is meant to be read in its entirety. This is because the person-centred approach evolves with each new chapter. However, an experienced practitioner may wish to focus on specific sections of the book or use it for reference. Each chapter begins an **Introduction** which sets out an overview of the chapter, its content, and significant concepts or themes to be explored.

This book is designed for both the specialist and non-specialist and whilst the content is relevant to all readers, I have used boxes – **To the counsellor** and **To the helper** to speak to counsellors or helpers directly where there exist tensions in practitioner-related issues or where there is information or a particular perspective to share with this particular readership.

I have tried to weave together the person-centred approach and work with children and young people throughout the book, although all person-centred theory is applicable when working both with adults or younger clients. However, where I want to emphasise issues around working with younger people, I have used a number of 'pop-up' boxes – **With children and young people in mind**. These are designed to extend and complement the main text and draw attention to an issue of direct importance to work with children and young people. They provide relevant information, a new perspective or may simply offer an additional observation.

Finally, the chapter normally concludes with a number of **Exercises**. These can be completed alone or preferably in collaboration with others; most probably those participating on a course. I hope you find them stimulating, thought provoking and an opportunity for self-reflection and sharing thoughts, feelings and experiences with others.

WHO THIS BOOK IS FOR

This book has set itself a difficult task, that is, to be of use and interest to both the professional counsellor and non-specialist alike. Firstly, an important point needs to be made – working in a person-centred way with children and young people is less concerned with knowledge, techniques and methodology and more to do with the relationship between client and counsellor or helper, that is, between the adult and child. For this reason, the approach is relevant to all adults who want to work in this way.

It is important that the practitioner who wishes to work with the young continues with their professional and personal development. However, courses and reading alone do not make a person-centred practitioner. The emphasis of the person-centred approach rests with the practitioner, as the name suggests, as a 'person'. Mearns and Thorne (1988) tell us that: 'The person-centred counsellor knows that she cannot rely upon her diagnostic skill, her role as a provider of "treatment", or a sense of superiority at being regarded as an all-knowing: "expert"'(p. 22).

WITH CHILDREN AND YOUNG PEOPLE IN MIND

This book is relevant to the experienced counsellor, possibly turning towards specialising in work with young people; to the counsellor in training as well as the non-specialist working in a school, in the youth justice system, in social work, health or the third sector, which includes charitable organisations, charitable trusts and funded community groups and organisations.

A refreshing perspective on the relationship between counselling and helping can be found in John McLeod's (2008) discussion around the use of counselling 'skills' by non-specialists. He argues that whilst there has been a growth in the provision of counselling by specialist counsellors and therapists, most counselling takes place outside the formal counselling room, and is carried out by professionals, where therapy is an important aspect of their work, but where they are not in a specifically counselling role. Examples include teachers, nurses, GPs, career advisers, youth and community workers, youth justice workers and within those in social care or support roles.

McLeod introduces us to the concept of the 'embedded' counselling roles, which he feels more accurately reflects the idea of using 'counselling skills' but which, he argues, do not do justice to the 'complexity and reality' of this aspect of people's work. Consequently, the work of the generalist professional who attempts to work therapeutically could possibly be more challenging than that of the specialist counsellor who has the benefit of a special room set aside for a prescribed period. He provides us with an illustration of this point:

> Compare this to the situation where an upset student turns up at his or her teacher's office during the morning coffee break. Many decisions need to be made around what can be done at that moment, and whether other moments can be found later in the day to follow up the crisis – and in 15 minutes time the teacher will be standing in front of a class in a teaching mode. (2008: 14–18)

McLeod's article is forceful in its recognition that, whilst much counselling takes place in the counselling setting, a lot occurs outside, and that much good work occurs 'as fulfilment of other professional roles'.

Over the years, I have worked with highly qualified and experienced counsellors. However, some of the most effective practitioners have been in the voluntary sector and other settings, who have few qualifications but who display a passion for young people and an ability to establish the kind of relationships, which are explored in the remainder of this book.

TO THE HELPER

Whilst it is wholly appropriate and I believe desirable for the non-counsellor to work in a person-centred way, it is important for the practitioner to be aware of their role and to be clear whether the relationship they have initiated is a counselling one, established by a contract with clear understandings. This is to differentiate your helping or support role; where you are essentially working within the approach, but not in the role of counsellor. Wherever possible in this book, I will attempt to draw attention to these differences and tensions.

The specialist counsellor and non-specialist often share a commitment to children and young people and a belief in the person-centred approach, and in this sense, this book will hopefully speak to all.

Before continuing, it is important by way of introduction to place the book in some kind of counselling context. Because the approach owes its origins largely to the work of Carl Rogers, this would seem like a good place to begin.

THE INFLUENCE OF CARL ROGERS

WITH CHILDREN AND YOUNG PEOPLE IN MIND

Whilst Carl Rogers is most often associated with adult work, we will see below how much of his early thinking evolved through his work with children who were experiencing problems in their lives. There is little, if anything in the work of Carl Rogers, that is not highly relevant and transferable to work with children and young people. Indeed, his influence upon work with children and young people has been most profound and still influences much practice today. Sometimes practitioners have identified a need to interpret and develop his ideas in creative ways and these will be examined in later chapters.

Carl Rogers is widely known for his original thinking and radical ideas, which have had a profound impact on personality theory and the development of psychotherapy. That we should not understate the influence of Carl Rogers is articulated by Brian Thorne (1992), who knew Carl Rogers personally and whose own works have discussed and extended the person-centred way of working. He writes:

> Carl Rogers enabled countless people throughout the world to be themselves with confidence. His impact has been enormous through his voluminous writings, through the school of counselling and psychotherapy which he founded and through the indirect influence of his work on many areas of professional activity where the quality of human relationships is central. (Preface: vii)

David Cohen (1997), in his biography of Carl Rogers, comments on how such a famous psychologist 'was amazed his ideas should have touched and affected so many people'. He also suggests that although 'psychologists are often cynical about the greats of their discipline', Rogers was regarded as accepting, non-judgemental, with an ability to attune to another human being and hear what they were saying as an individual. It is qualities and skills such as these which form the essence of the person-centred approach.

Carl Rogers' own interest in children and young people relates to the early part of his career. Carl's father was a civil engineer but during his early teenage years, the family moved to a farm. Rogers studied for a degree in agriculture at the University of Wisconsin. Later, his career was to move in a different direction. He started studying history, which he believed would provide a better background for eventually entering the ministry, which he felt was his calling. At this time, he was one of a small group of students from the United States who were offered an opportunity to go to Beijing for the 'World Student Christian Federation Conference' for a period of six months. It was at this time that he began to question some of the more traditional doctrine he was exposed to, and after marrying Helen Elliot, they moved to New York City where he began attending the Union Theological Seminary. Rogers changed direction again, this time to studying psychology at Columbia University Teacher's College where he received his PhD in 1931.

Between 1928 and 1940, Rogers was appointed as a member of staff at the Child Study Department of The Rochester Society for the Prevention of Cruelty to Children. These 'Rochester Years' have been explored in depth by Howard Kirschenbaum. Between 1928 and 1939, Rogers worked with problem children and their parents. Kirschenbaum writes:

> And troubled children they were. Every year an average of 600–700 children, mostly lower-to lower-middle-class whites, came on average to the Society for help. They were referred by dozens of social agencies throughout the community: parents, the social worker, Children's Court, the schools, private charitable organizations, medical authorities, and the like. They represented every behaviour and personality problem imaginable: enuresis, stealing, lying, extreme sex curiosity, sex perversions, sadism toward animals or younger children, extreme withdrawal or

aggressiveness, incest, stammering, eating dirt and worms, and numerous other comparable problems. (2007: 62–3)

It is unlikely that a modern person-centred practitioner working with a child or young person would use such descriptive and often judgemental language, but it does offer the reader some insight into the complexity of the young lives Rogers found himself working with. In 1939, Rogers wrote his first of many books, *The Clinical Treatment of the Problem Child*, from which it was clear that he was forming the basis of the 'Core Conditions' which were to be so influential later. Rogers had begun to challenge the psychological orthodoxy and theories, which he had previously understood. Brian Thorne (1992) puts it this way:

> Instead, what was required was a method of responding to the children and their parents which actually worked and proved effective in meeting their needs. In such a pressurised situation Rogers soon discovered that even some of the most elegant theories he had previously embraced failed to stand up to the test of reality. (pp. 8–9)

In developing his approach, Carl Rogers was progressively to devote much of his time to working with adults and the wider political implications of his new theories. However, in 1969, he did publish *Freedom to Learn: A View of What Education Might Become* and in 1983, *Freedom to Learn for the 80's*; books which emphasised the role of the facilitator and the 'relationship' in education and which still influence learning and pedagogy today.

To the present time, there have been few attempts to apply person-centred theory, and specifically the work of Carl Rogers to work with young people. Richard Bryant-Jefferies' (2004) book *Counselling Young People: Person-Centred Dialogues* remains an exception and explores in some depth the dialogues between young person, counsellor and supervisor and is worth a read for any practitioner working in this way. This paucity of relevant texts belies the influence of the Rogerian approach, for it is unlikely that on reading a book on counselling children and young people, the reader would not be able to discern his influence both in terms of theory and practice.

THE GROWTH IN COUNSELLING CHILDREN AND YOUNG PEOPLE

TO THE COUNSELLOR

A significant growth in the need for and delivery of therapeutic work with children and young people has increased employment opportunities, whether these be as part of an organisation or where counsellors offer their services to organisations as individuals.

TO THE HELPER

As the mental health and psychological needs of children and young people have become more pronounced and acknowledged, it is likely that non-counsellors working within educational and helping professions will have been called upon to offer informal support as an aspect or dimension of their work.

Counselling with children and young people has been one of the growth areas in the profession, as evidenced by the substantial rise in numbers joining 'Counselling Children and Young People', a division of The British Association for Counselling and Psychotherapy. There has also been an increase in the numbers of courses offered by colleges and universities in counselling specifically relating to work with children and adolescents.

In recent years, we have seen a growth in the ways in which adults have become involved in young people's lives. Schools have continued to evolve sophisticated pastoral systems and the introduction of mentors into schools has been celebrated as an initiative to support young people. Education social workers, attendance officers, careers advice workers, educational psychologists, teaching assistants and behaviour support workers have become part of a growing professional children's workforce, which aims to support the school in achieving its primary aim, that is, school achievement. Outside schools, social care workers continue to intervene in the lives of parents and children where a need has been seen, or more likely, where abuse or neglect of one kind or another has been identified. We are also seeing an expansion of mental health services for young people and Child and Adolescent Mental Health Services (CAMHS).

Any additional support that can be offered to young people is to be welcomed, especially at a time when organisations such as Young Minds, The Samaritans, The Mental Health Foundation and MIND are in agreement that mental health problems among the young are increasing. More specifically, the incidence of eating disorders, self-harm and suicide has been seen to be on the increase, with all the pain and heartache these bring to the young person, their families and friends.

Each of the professionals highlighted above has their own professional responsibilities and orientations. Schools have a responsibility to ensure that pupils are benefiting from the Every Child Matters agenda and, in particular, are in school, safe and learning. Where a child's behaviour is causing concern and affecting the rights of peers to learn, interventions are necessary, while in some schools, exclusion remains an option. Social workers are charged with ensuring that children are safe and this remains their stated priority. Child and Adolescent Mental Health Services workers are involved, along with psychiatrists, in the diagnosis of mental illness and offering either talk therapies or drugs, or indeed a combination of both. These professional responsibilities and an increasing emphasis on outcomes, sometimes prevent the kind of support young people, in my experience, value the most.

WHY WORKING WITH CHILDREN AND YOUNG PEOPLE IS DIFFERENT

Counselling and supporting children and young people using the person-centred approach is particularly rewarding because the emphasis is on the relationship and the focus is on the young person and what they need, as defined by themselves. In some ways, professionals working with young people from other orientations have an easier task, since the process is set out and reinforced by training and procedures. Counsellors and therapists using a wide variety of approaches have clear models to work with and sometimes the dialogue is clearly set out. Counsellors working in a solution-focused way or who use cognitive-behavioural approaches are such examples. Techniques and strategies are there to be used at appropriate times. These 'advantages' have been identified by Dave Mearns (1994) who writes:

> Most other approaches to counselling and therapy are much more exciting for the counsellor and perhaps also for the client with the practitioner playing a dashing role exhibiting mastery of sophisticated skills of analysis, interpretation and near mystical insight into the client's condition and the requirements for change. (p. ix)

It could be argued that counselling and supporting young people, i.e. using counselling skills and approaches, is different to working with adults because we are working with potential, with futures, with transition, with growth and becoming. However, the person-centred counsellor would argue that these ideas apply to all people, regardless of age or circumstance.

Jean Campion (1991) has explored why working with children might be different. She agrees with the assertion that person-centred counselling is 'basically the same regardless of the age of the client' (p. 1) but argues that working with children presents important challenges. She sees a 'good knowledge of the state of childhood' (p. 2) as being a necessary prerequisite for this kind of work. She also sees young people as having a greater tendency to 'take their personal circumstances for granted, and even to blame themselves when they find themselves in situations which are not their fault'. (p. 2) She also asks us to bear in mind that children are not normally 'independent beings' (p. 3) and therefore often still dependent upon parental care.

WITH CHILDREN AND YOUNG PEOPLE IN MIND

The person-centred approach to counselling and helping is especially powerful in that it begins to address some of the most basic and fundamental needs of the child or young person. They have a need to connect on a very human level in a way which suggests belief in their potential and acceptance of them, for who they are; not how we would like them to be. The power of the approach is there to be experienced. When adult and child or young person connect, as two human beings, the results can be quite memorable.

For me, the great rewards of working with children and young people in a person-centred way are fundamental. Despite all the important and valued interventions into the lives of young people in difficulty made by parents, family and professionals, it is, in my experience, very rare that a young person coming to counselling has ever experienced the kind of warmth, openness, acceptance and empathy which are characteristic of the person-centred way of working. It would not be unusual in such circumstances for the young person to say to a counsellor something like: 'This is the first time I have really been listened to and understood. I feel that you are here for me and you are not going to tell me what to do or what is best for me.' I am not suggesting here that professionals cannot be warm and caring but rather that often, pressures to achieve behavioural change predominate.

A number of brief case studies may illustrate some of the key points discussed above. These case studies and those throughout the book are drawn from my own experience of working with young people. The people identified and their stories of course do not exist in their own right but are rather an amalgam of young people's experiences and their interactions with counsellors and professionals working in a variety of settings. These contexts – schools, youth centres, social care and health – are not in themselves significant because the skills, attitudes and processes remain the same, regardless of the setting in which the work takes place.

Case study: Dean

Dean, aged 19 years, had been attending a youth counselling agency for just under two years. Much of the work had centred around relationship issues; Dean had a fairly sanitised relationship with his mother and very little contact with his father. He saw himself as overweight and defined himself as ugly. Whilst he had kept some friends since his schooldays, he saw them infrequently and felt they had little in common now. He could not remember ever being in what he would say was a 'relationship' and feelings about himself were so low that it was unlikely that he would risk this fragile sense of self by seeking intimacy. Dean was not in work or full-time education.

Dean had been hospitalised on a number of occasions having attempted suicide and self-injury had become a way of life. Glass and rope had left their marks on his arms but Dean's centre of attention was his abdomen which he cut regularly and which had become quite scarred and disfigured; this was the part of his body that he hated most. Dean had felt unhappy for as long as he could remember and sessions with the counsellor often involved sharing his sense of hopelessness and despair.

As the work continued, Dean started to bring in some art work, mainly drawings, and sessions often revolved around these. Each week, Dean would end the session with the same words:

'I don't think you are going to like me anymore.' The counsellor reflected back: 'You think I might reject you in some way?'

It took Dean six more weeks of checking out the strength of his relationship with his counsellor before he revealed how, when he was younger, he had been 'touched' by his father and that he had subsequently played a 'game' with his younger cousin which involved the removal of clothes. Dean had read articles in magazines about how the abused becomes the abuser and he was now convinced that this was happening

(Continued)

(Continued)

to him. It had taken Dean many years to share his own abuse and his shame that he might too become a perpetrator. Nearly two years passed before Dean felt able to share his experiences and fears with his counsellor, building up the courage to reveal his torment. Dean told his counsellor that this was the first time he had told anybody about any of this: 'I didn't think anybody would listen. I thought they would be disgusted with me and tell me to go away and die.' The counsellor replied: 'I'm glad that you have built the courage to share these very personal things with me. It could not have been easy. If anything, I feel a little closer to you at this moment.'

Dean had gone though the whole of his schooling and had been involved with a range of psychiatric services but was only able to reveal his feelings at this time. The counsellor, working in a person-centred way, had created the kind of relationship where Dean could feel accepted and understood to the point where he could trust his counsellor with his innermost fears and anxieties.

TO THE HELPER

If you met Dean in your non-specialist professional capacity, there is a great deal that you could offer him in terms of warm, empathic listening. In Dean's case, it is significant that, had he had an opportunity for this kind of help earlier in his life, appropriate support could have been offered to him, possibly at a time when he most needed it. However, as a professional using counselling skills, it is always important to be aware of the limits to your training and experience and know when to refer a child or young person for more specialised counselling. If you work within an agency or organisational setting, there will most likely be guidance on when and how to refer on.

WITH CHILDREN AND YOUNG PEOPLE IN MIND

Dean is 19 years of age and, unlike a younger child, he has the right to choose where he gets support from. Indeed, he may reject more formal counselling and this remains his choice.

Case study: Amrita

Amrita was in year 8 (ages 12–13) at secondary school when she was referred by her Head of House, to a school mentor. She had begun life in secondary school just where she had left off in her small junior school, that is, near the top of her

(Continued)

(Continued)

class. SATs and early testing predicted significant success at GCSE level and beyond. More recently, Amrita's performance in class had declined. Her normal 100% attendance was punctuated by occasional unexplained absence and, unthinkable before, homework tasks were not handed in on time, and sometimes not at all.

Concerned for her well-being, the school made every effort to re-motivate her, offering rewards and encouragement for any signs that she was returning to her 'successful self'. It was whilst working with her mentor that she talked about the pressure on her to succeed, to maintain a momentum that would take her through to the end of her school life. She told her mentor:

> People are not listening to me. I don't know what's wrong. If I did, I would put it right but I don't. The school is trying to help. They do care, but they are stressing me out. It's not what I need just now. I just need space and somebody to listen to me without trying to make things better. This is how I feel just now.

The mentor replied: 'It sounds as though people are trying to help you but it's only making matters worse. Right now, you just want someone to listen and understand your confusion.'

These two brief case studies illustrate how sometimes we let young people down, either because we do not recognise their pain and provide the space, opportunity and conditions for listening or where, in their enthusiasm and desire to help, the adults in a child's life fail to really listen. Well-intentioned interventions miss the mark because they represent the adult's solutions to the child's difficulties. In other words, help comes from the professional and not the child's 'frame of reference', a concept we will return to later in this book.

CRITICISMS OF THE PERSON-CENTRED APPROACH

This book has been written out of a passion for the person-centred approach and its potential for working with children and young people. However, this way of working is not without its critics. Some of these 'criticisms and rebuttals' are explored in detail in Thorne (1992). The person-centred approach is sometimes seen as lacking a strong and robust theoretical basis. It has been described as being naive and over-optimistic in outlook, highly subjective and as not having the backing of evidence and research. In addition, the approach is regarded as being too slow in achieving desired outcomes.

Any visit to a quality bookshop will reveal a vast array of books relating to counselling psychology, philosophy and psychotherapy. Certainly, books relating to the person-centred approach will appear to be outnumbered by psychodynamic texts and the writings of key theorists, from Sigmund Freud onwards. Similarly, books adopting cognitive approaches abound, with many of these spilling over into popular psychology shelves because of their emphasis on thinking and its effects on behaviours and the belief that these can be changed. Cognitive-behavioural approaches lend themselves to self-help books, which sell so well as people seek to find solutions to problems such as anxiety, depression and relationship difficulties.

There has of course been a significant increase in the numbers of books relating to person-centred theory and many of its basic ideas have been extended and refined. However, a reliance on philosophy and theory in the person-centred approach fails to understand what Rogers believed to be the essence of his approach. Tudor et al. (2004: 4) argue that they: 'do not want to reify and concretise person-centred theory precisely because this would be antithetical to its philosophy.'

Rogers himself always emphasised the predominance of experience over theory. In *On Becoming a Person* (1967), he wrote:

> Experience is, for me, the highest authority. The touchstone of validity is my own experience. No other person's ideas, and none of my own ideas are as authoritative as my experience. It is to experience that I must return again and again ... (p. 23)

In *Client-centred Therapy* (1951), he argued that: 'It is the writer's conviction that theory, to be profitable, must follow experience, not precede it.' Rogers saw the dangers of adherence to theory as leading to 'a closed and dogmatic approach to experience'.

The assertion that the approach being advocated here is simplistic, optimistic and naive has been challenged by Thorne (1992) who again cites Rogers' conviction, despite some doubts, in the positive and trustworthy nature of the person. Certainly, my own experience of working with young people has shown me that despite behaviours to the contrary, young people, regardless of their circumstances, have a deep inner desire to move forward in constructive, directional ways. This relates to Rogers' commitment to the idea that the human organism has an underlying 'actualising tendency'. We will return to this concept in the next chapter.

The idea that the person-centred approach is subjective, for me represents one of its fundamental qualities. Young people, like adults, construct meaning from experience. It follows therefore that we all experience the world and our relationships in different ways. Person-centred ideas are philosophically 'existential' and it is in this we are most interested, since objective reality, should it actually exist, does not determine our behaviour, rather it is our perception of events and people that gives us our reality. 'Existential' here refers to the philosophical position that life has no essential meaning, therefore sense can only be found within a personal view of the world.

Person-centred counselling has traditionally been 'open-ended' with endings determined by the counsellor and client together. This means that sometimes the work is long-term, sometimes taking years. Apart from those readers who are fortunate enough to work in the third sector, it is unlikely that you will be able to work with complete freedom and without some form of organisational expectations, and in recent years we have seen the introduction of more time-limited approaches to working in a person-centred way. Again, my own experience of working with children and young people suggests that the work does not have to be long-term and that a small number of sessions can be powerful and valued by the young person.

EXERCISES

1. Share with another person what draws you to working with children and young people.
2. Why are you interested in the person-centred approach?
3. Think of a time when you were unhappy or concerned. Were you able to share these feelings with another person? Why did you choose this person? What was the experience like? As you think back, what emotions are you experiencing now?
4. Can you think of any family member, friend or colleague who appears to have the kind of warm, empathic relationships with young people advocated by those who use the person-centred approach, but who does not occupy a formal therapeutic role?

2
THE PERSON-CENTRED APPROACH:
Theoretical Framework

INTRODUCING THIS CHAPTER

In this chapter, I have tried to contextualise the person-centred approach in some kind of theoretical way. We will look briefly at key philosophical ideas which underpin the approach and which give it its distinct character and quality. I also include a personal perspective of the approach, especially in light of my work with children and young people. The chapter also looks beyond Carl Rogers to examine the influences of other theorists and practitioners who have helped shape or extend the person-centred approach. The chapter begins with a discussion of the place of theory in an approach which largely focuses on people and relationships as opposed to prescribed ideas and assumptions.

TO THE COUNSELLOR

If you have trained as a counsellor, the ideas introduced in this chapter may well be familiar. However, as a counsellor, I have always found it important to re-examine the basic principles of the person-centred approach, especially at a time when there are so many theoretical influences which seem tempting. It is hard to see how other approaches and theoretical orientations can work without some understanding of the person-centred approach, if indeed they necessitate the establishment of a therapeutic relationship. This for me remains a prerequisite.

(Continued)

(Continued)

A return to the basic ideas of the person-centred approach can sometimes increase faith and belief in those ideas. To see them re-stated can help maintain confidence in the approach. Where we return to the original writings of Carl Rogers, we sense the power of the approach, put so eloquently by its finest exponent.

TO THE HELPER

You may already be a good listener and the kind of person who can strike up warm helping relationships with children and young people. Some awareness of theory may offer new insights and understandings, which will improve your work and enhance the quality of the helping relationships you try so hard to establish.

THE USE OF THEORY

The *Oxford English Dictionary* describes 'theory' as a 'system of ideas' explaining something. This chapter seeks to look at person-centred theory and, in particular, how it might relate to children and young people. Janet Tolan (2007) argues that to work with another person therapeutically, we need a set of assumptions and hypotheses. She writes:

> Person-centred theory is simple, elegant and universal. Just as an appreciation of atoms gives rise to an understanding of the whole of the physical world, so can an appreciation of person-centred theory give rise to an understanding of the complexity and richness of human experiencing. (2007: 1)

Rogers himself was quite wary about theory, identifying a danger that it might lead to the categorisation of people. Indeed, as Tudor et al. (2004: 4) suggest, any attempt to 'reify or concretise person-centred theory ... would be antithetical to its philosophy'.

WITH CHILDREN AND YOUNG PEOPLE IN MIND

Professionals who work with young people are often aware of how quickly judgements are made and of the tendency to 'identify' a child's problem – the danger being that we somehow manoeuvre the child to fit with our assumptions and understandings. In this way, we are less likely to listen to the young person and enter into her world as she experiences it, and more likely to guide and advise or at the very least see things from a perspective, other than hers.

The paradox here is that in attempting to make sense of Rogers' work and ideas, especially those where he eschewed formal theory in favour of experience, we need to understand these ideas and place them into some kind of context. Returning to Tolan (2007), she tends to see this issue more pragmatically:

> Without theory, how can we have any confidence in our way of working? Unless we have a hypothesis about what is happening and why, we will tend to fall into our own insecurities when the going gets tough. Theory is the map that guides us through territory which is alien and which can feel dangerous. It helps us to stick to the path, however rocky, instead of panicking and running into the woods. (2007: 1)

Tolan's words somehow echo many of the fears and concerns that adults working therapeutically with young people express in supervision – feelings which sometimes lead to self-doubt, uncertainty and anxiety.

SOME IMPORTANT IDEAS

TO THE HELPER

Where you are primarily using counselling skills and helping as an aspect of your work, philosophical ideas underpinning the person-centred approach may not seem overly relevant. However, an understanding of these origins and influences will help to place your work into some kind of context, whilst forming the basis for understanding person-centred approaches and practice.

The Humanistic approach, which is characterised by a constructive and hopeful view of human beings, draws many of its ideas from two very influential viewpoints found within the history of ideas. Firstly, 'existentialism' as a philosophy owes its development to key figures such as Søren Kierkegaard, Fredrich Nietzsche, Martin Heidegger and Jean-Paul Sartre. This way of looking at things focuses on the subjective and unique experience of the individual. It is opposed to 'rationalist' and 'empiricist' ideas which suggest that the universe is intelligible to the person who wishes to observe and study it. It is not concerned with psychological constructs and theories about personality. 'Being' cannot be understood objectively, but only understood by the individual through a process of reflection. Counsellors who work existentially are concerned with the immediate moment as experienced by the client. They are interested in 'existence' and how people change throughout their lives. They are not interested in establishing a diagnosis or looking at the causes of certain behaviours.

Secondly, existentialism adopts a philosophical method called 'phenomenology' which is literally the study of 'phenomena' and which is to a large extent the invention of Edmund Husserl. In contrast to behaviourism, it seeks understanding through enquiry into the subjective world of the client; that is, consciousness as experienced from the first-person perspective. For the counsellor or helper, this means working with the client's experience and rejecting any call to establish causation. As a way of working, it rejects the idea of the 'unconscious' and believes that we can learn about our client's world, not through a process of observation, but by looking at how the client perceives their own world.

TO THE COUNSELLOR

In essence, the person-centred counsellor is not concerned with trying to find out why the client feels or behaves in a certain way. Instead, they seek to work with the client's experience and to enter into their subjective world, without judgement.

WITH CHILDREN AND YOUNG PEOPLE IN MIND

Often, it is not easy when working with a young person, for sometimes our instincts are to act in a parental role; to protect and guide. Sometimes our young clients tell us things which are hard to relate to and which may seem fanciful, odd, distorted and possibly destructive. However, as adults working with children and young people, it is necessary to understand that this is how the child sees their world and this should be respected, in the belief that the child will find his own way, if we provide the right conditions for growth within a relationship which is authentic and real.

THE PERSON-CENTRED APPROACH WITH CHILDREN AND YOUNG PEOPLE: A PERSONAL PERSPECTIVE

Please permit me to indulge in some personal reminiscing. As I write, I am able to recall with some vivid colour, a very special moment in my own counselling training. For weeks, we had been learning theory and integrating this newfound wisdom into our practice. Often, this took the form of part-sessions, where course colleagues would each take turns at being the client and counsellor. It is most likely that many of you reading this will be able to relate to the approach. This 'goldfish' approach also required other members of the group to observe and offer feedback as to what they had seen, what they liked and what they might have done differently themselves. It became clear to me at the time that even where people took on roles, very soon aspects and dimensions of themselves became apparent that caused me to question whether role-play was ever just that: the playing of roles.

On this particular occasion, my 'client' was talking about his early years at home with his parents. From my perspective, the role-play was going well and I was assured of positive feedback from my client about their experiences of the session and the kind of comments from the observers I so dearly wanted to confirm my competence as a counsellor. In fact, I was finding the whole experience quite stressful, as I determinedly tried to display the right kind of body language and listening skills that would gain approval. Looking back, I am not sure how much I was actually hearing my client; perhaps I was listening more to his words, which I knew had to be reflected back with some accuracy. I began to struggle, with my own preoccupations getting in the way of me actually staying with my client. Panic-stricken, I lunged at making my client see that I was, indeed, understanding. I was wide of the mark and further attempts only served to show how disconnected we were as two people.

At this point, I had to say to my client that I had not heard what he had been talking about and that I was lost. This was a seminal moment for me and re-engagement with my colleague was intensely liberating. Of course, I knew the theory about the importance of the relationship, the need to be myself and not play a role. Somehow now it all made sense and I felt a burden to perform lifted.

For me, working with children and young people is truly about the meeting together of two people. The counsellor or helper's greatest asset is himself or herself, as a person. Children and young people already have many relationships with parents and professionals, but the person-centred approach emphasises the therapeutic nature of human understanding. The person-centred approach offers just this, the person, not the role. There is something quite valuing and respectful in the adult offering of themselves and not merely a professional face, however accomplished.

As adults, we often attempt to guide behaviour in children and young people, and in non-therapeutic contexts, this is wholly right. When we offer therapeutic help however, the person-centred approach asks that we avoid initiating direction and we avoid quantifying, assessing or judging what the young person brings. This can be very difficult, involving shedding many years of our own socialisation and conditioning. However, again, when we show deep acceptance of the child or young person as a person, we show profound respect for them as an individual.

When we are young people, we sometimes believe we know everything; when we are adults, we *know* we know everything. We may be more accomplished at mathematical calculations than the young child, we know more history and are more aware of how the natural world works. In some cases, although not always, we can draw and paint with greater accuracy and realism. The one thing we can never know better is the young client's world, as they see it. Empathy, the ability to enter the child's world and see it as they do, is probably the most difficult of all to achieve. I see empathy as when the child or young person has the trust to take us, metaphorically, by the hand and show us their world. As we walk alongside, we are more likely to see what they see – not what we think we see, want to see or what we want our young client to see.

The person-centred approach with children and young people requires a tremendous suspension of normal beliefs about young people – that is, that they cannot decide what is best for them. However, if we provide the right kind of environment and non-judgemental relationship and we are ourselves, I believe, confirmed by experience, that young people will find their own way forward and their own solutions to problems. In many ways, young people already know what is right for them and the person-centred therapeutic relationship offers the child or young person an opportunity to further experience this internally or express it in words. Sometimes we have to understand that there may not be immediate opportunities for structural change in aspects of young people's lives, but there can be personal growth. Adults and peers shape children and young people, almost from the moment of birth and these judgements, both overt and hidden, will often determine how the young person sees themselves in relationship to others.

The person-centred counselling room or helping relationship may be the only time when these judgements and self-perceptions can be challenged by the child or young person. Where they are, the young client is freer to become who they want to become: more resilient, more fulfilled, more confident and more inclined to be all that they possibly can be.

The concepts, which we now explore, are easily expressed in both writing and the spoken word, but their profound nature is often obscured. They have the power to change the lives of both adult and child. Words like self-actualisation, empathy, unconditional positive regard and congruence are easy to say, but harder to 'be'. They represent some of the most complex and sophisticated skills and qualities; possibly forming the essence of being human.

WITH CHILDREN AND YOUNG PEOPLE IN MIND

Whist many of the ideas and concepts presented here were developed in relation to work with adults, I have found them equally valuable in working with younger clients, of whatever age. Their impact may be even more evident with children and young people because the approach, which emphasises respect, acceptance, realness and empathy, stands in contrast to young people's sense of having little control or autonomy over their lives, and where they are constantly guided and indeed controlled by the adults around them, at home and at school. The person-centred approach offers them something very different and is most often received with appreciation.

THE ACTUALISING TENDENCY

Carl Rogers believed that humans are driven by an underlying 'actualising tendency'. This represented a positive view of human nature. Such ideas were in contrast to the psychoanalytic model which focused on unconscious drives and instincts, often sexual in nature, and the behaviourist schools of psychology which saw people acting upon learned behaviours. The actualising tendency was thought to be inherent in all living organisms. Rogers believed that people were motivated to become all that they were capable of becoming. In his writings, he drew on a number of sources, including Abraham Maslow (1968) who like Rogers was a key figure in the establishment of the Humanistic approach. Maslow first used the term 'the Third Force' to emphasise the departure from previous schools of psychology. He developed the idea of a 'hierarchy of needs', a basic concept which influenced Rogers' thinking. This was a theory which related to human motivation and self-actualisation. It suggested that we are motivated by needs which are there at birth and which have evolved over many thousands of years. Maslow's Hierarchy of Needs states that we have a range of needs, each of which must be satisfied. The most basic of these needs is of course survival. Only when these physical needs have been met does a person become concerned with 'higher order' needs, which are concerned with a sense of belonging, esteem and, ultimately, self-actualisation.

To explain the concept of the actualising tendency, Rogers often drew examples from the natural world. In *Carl Rogers on Personal Power* (1978), he described in sentimental detail the survival of seaweed pounded by waves on the shore, only to survive and thrive. He continued:

> It seemed incredible that it was able to take this incessant pounding hour after hour, day and night, week after week, perhaps year after year, and all the time nourishing itself, in short, maintaining and enhancing itself in this process which, in our shorthand, we call growth. Here in this palmlike seaweed was the tenacity of life, the forward thrust of life, the ability to push into an incredibly hostile environment and not only to hold its own but to adapt, develop, become itself. (1978: 237–8)

In our work with young people, we find similar resilience in the face of adversity.

Case study: Daleer

Daleer (aged 13) described his home as very unhappy and without love. Here he is alone, exposed, at best, to coldness between his parents and, at worst, to outbursts of anger, which sometimes spill over into the physical. He described his mother as having a 'mental health problem', but for which he has no name. He just knew that she wasn't 'right'. His father works long hours managing a newly formed business which remains fragile. Of central importance in Daleer's life had been his grandmother who died only a few months ago. However, nobody had spoken about this loss at home. Daleer was also close to his older sister but she recently married and has moved away from the family home.

   As if all of this was not enough to bear, Daleer was knocked over by a car whilst being chased by bullies after school. Whilst his injuries were not serious, he was kept off school for a month. When he returned to school, things had moved on and friendship groups had changed and he found himself isolated.

(Continued)

(Continued)

Daleer has been seeing a counsellor at school for around four weeks. His story had saddened his counsellor Julie, who wondered how he was coping when just about everything in his life had gone wrong. Somehow he remained strong and sometimes even cheerful with an eye to the future. Julie wondered whether she would have the same resilience to bounce back from such adversity.

WITH CHILDREN AND YOUNG PEOPLE IN MIND

The person-centred counsellor believes that all young people have a tendency towards self-actualisation. It is the role of the counsellor to believe and trust in this process and by creating the right therapeutic conditions, they facilitate this growth and help the young person find their own solutions to their problems.

THE ORGANISMIC VALUING PROCESS

Rogers told us that generally organisms know what is good for them and this is referred to as the 'organismic valuing process'. A neat description of this concept can be found in Merry (1995):

> Although the term itself is rather ungainly, the idea is quite simple. As infants, we start out in the world knowing what is good and not good for us. The yardstick we use to judge when to value something either positively or negatively is whether or not it contributes to maintaining or enhancing our development. This valuing process operates quite spontaneously; we do not put much thought into it. For example, when we are hungry we positively value being fed, and when we are no longer hungry we negatively value being fed. Positively valued experiences include being comfortable, being able to play and being able to express our curiosity about the world that surrounds us. (pp. 23–4)

In this sense, the organism in its drive towards being complete chooses how to respond to influences from the environment and other people. The person is also able to obtain feedback from experiences and learn from these. Mearns and Thorne (1988) explain it this way:

> The human organism, it is argued, can essentially be relied upon to provide the individual with trustworthy messages, and this is discernable in the physiological processes of the entire body and through the process of growth by which an individual's potentialities and capacities are brought to realisation. (p. 8)

The adult supporting the young person has to have confidence and belief in this process, recognising it when it shows itself, however briefly, in the counselling room or other setting.

A baby is driven by his actualising tendency and trusts in his organismic valuing process in a way that determines his thoughts, feelings and behaviour. The young child defines himself through his interactions with others and this becomes his self-concept. However, as the child develops, significant others, most notably the parents, show value in the child which is conditional. These influences continue as the baby grows into the child and the adolescent into the adult. Almost inevitably, the child introjects these influences, often critical and judgemental, and the young person acquires 'conditions of worth'. In its need to retain the love, respect and approval of parents and other important people in its life, the child learns to comply with these conditions of worth in order to shape and maintain his self-concept. This may be seen as acceptance 'only if'. In this way, the self-concept becomes based upon these standards of value rather than the natural organismic valuing process described above. We desire our parents' love and affection so much that we are prepared to behave in externally validated ways. Let us look briefly at a few examples.

Case study: Sarah

Sarah is a quiet eight-year-old child. Her mother and father often tell her how proud they are of her because she is not like the 'naughty' children who live and play near her home. Sarah tries hard to be well behaved and quiet all of the time.

Case study: Mohammed

Mohammed aged 11 years lost his mother through an illness around 18 months ago and is desperately sad. Dad has been struggling to come to terms with the loss of his wife. Mohammed's loss is never spoken about at home. Dad says that Mohammed has been a 'courageous' young man and he is pleased with how he is getting on with his life. Mohammed has to put a 'brave face' on his grief.

Case study: Tina

Tina is a very angry 12-year-old. She has every reason to be angry. Just over a year ago, she told her mother that her older brother had been touching her in 'private places' for about two years. Mum dismissed these complaints out of hand. Things are OK at home as long as she doesn't say anything. Tina learned early on that her mother becomes angry and defensive when she mentions what happened to her. Tina hasn't mentioned anything at school because she is afraid that they will tell her mum and she will be taken into care.

Case study: Dawn

Dawn is 10 years old and doing well at school; teachers have said that she is 'gifted and talented'. From an early age, she has had to 'perform'. She remembers when as a toddler, the whole family sat round watching her name all the plastic animals in a box. She can remember their delight when she could even name an 'aardvark'. Dawn has to work hard at school; anything less than top of the class would be regarded as 'failure'.

In these examples, each child has learned to behave in an acceptable way to avoid certain unwanted behaviours. They do this to win their parent's love and approval or avoid this affection being taken away from them. Each complies with conditions of worth and their self-image is adversely affected.

From the concept of organismic valuing, Rogers conceived of the idea of 'positive regard'. Where love, approval and affection are 'on condition', Rogers used the phrase 'conditional positive regard'. It follows that a young person may develop a 'conditional positive self-regard' which is where the child comes to like himself and develop a stronger sense of self-worth and esteem by submitting to the expectations and standards set by society and significant others.

The 'real self', which is defined by the actualising tendency and organismic valuing, often stands in contrast to the 'ideal self', i.e. that which develops in response to the positive regard of others. It is a state, which by definition, is not real and therefore cannot be achieved. This discrepancy between self and experience is referred to by Rogers as 'incongruence' and is well described by Boeree (2006) in his discussion of Carl Rogers' theory of personality:

> This gap between the real self and the ideal self, the 'I am' and the 'I should' is called incongruity. The more incongruity, the more the suffering. In fact incongruity is essentially what Rogers means by neurosis. Being out of synch with your own self. (Internet article)

Brian Thorne (1992) explains further:

> This incongruence leads to a psychological vulnerability which will often render the person anxious and confused whenever an experience is perceived, or in some way anticipated, as being incongruent with the structure of the self and the current self-concept. The outcome of psychological vulnerability of this kind is a defensive response to experiences that in some way threaten the person's concept of self. The defensive behaviour can take a number of forms but, for Rogers, the responses of distortion or denial are perhaps the most common. (p. 31)

We shall return to this subject in a later chapter when we look at why young people become unhappy.

THE CORE CONDITIONS

The work of the professional working with children and young people in a person-centred way is to provide a special kind of relationship which enables the young person to identify within herself the capacity to use that relationship for change and growth. Carl Rogers identified and described six 'conditions' which he felt were both necessary and sufficient for therapeutic growth. By this he meant that each had to be present within the helping relationship and that they alone would bring about change and growth, i.e. that they were 'sufficient'.

The significance of these principles set out by Rogers cannot be underestimated as Wyatt (2001) points out:

> It has been suggested by many writers that Rogers' theoretical statement of 1957 'The Necessary and Sufficient Conditions of Therapeutic Personality Change' was the most critical event in the development of client-centred therapy – and perhaps for psychotherapy as a whole. (p. ii)

Rogers described the six conditions as:

1 Two people are in psychological contact.
2 The first person, the client, is in a state of incongruence, being vulnerable or anxious.
3 The second person, the therapist, is congruent or integrated in the relationship.
4 The therapist demonstrates unconditional positive regard (UPR) for the client.
5 The therapist demonstrates an empathic understanding of the client's internal frame of reference and endeavours to communicate this to the client.
6 The communication to the client of the therapist's empathic understanding and unconditional positive regard (UPR) is to a minimal degree achieved.

With regard to these, Tudor et al. (2004) suggest that Rogers did not place a great deal of significance on 'psychological contact' saying that he was not describing a close relationship or even 'the client and counsellor recognising each other as human beings' or, necessarily, the relationship as having an 'emotional or affective content'. In this sense, psychological contact occurs when two people are 'simultaneously aware of each other'.

Whatever Carl Rogers meant, it is clear to those working with children and young people how important it is for the adult to connect with the young person as a prerequisite to working together. This perspective on working with young people is emphasised by Bryant-Jefferies (2004) who drew upon research by Everall and Paulson (2002). This research identified issues for young people where the counsellor took on an authoritarian role, emphasising power differentials characteristic of the young person's normal experiences of talking with adults. Bryant-Jefferies expands upon this point:

The fact that the young people saw the counselling relationship as 'special' and the therapist as 'a special friend', offers valuable insight into the inner world of the young clients. They indicated how important this was, and what a contrast it was to their usual experience of being in a relationship with adults.

He concludes from this that: 'For the effective counselling of young people there needs to be an adaptation in style, a readiness and willingness by the counsellor to be open, to really want to be psychologically alongside the young person' (Bryant-Jeffries, 2004: 7).

Rogers highlighted three 'core conditions' which he felt were especially important in the therapeutic relationship. It is not intended that these be explored in depth at this point since we shall return to look in more detail at these important personal qualities or attributes of the counsellor later in this book. However, it seems important for balance to introduce them at this time.

The first of the core conditions is referred to as 'congruence'. This suggests that the adult needs to be real, genuine, open, integrated and authentic with the young person before them. Rogers (1967) writes:

> It is found that personal change is facilitated when the psychotherapist is what he is, when in the relationship with his client he is genuine and without 'front' or facade, openly being and feeling the attitudes which at that moment are flowing within him. We have coined the term 'congruence' to try to describe this condition. By this we mean that the feelings the therapist is experiencing are available to him, available to his awareness, and he is able to live these feelings, be them and able to communicate them if appropriate. (p. 61)

Here, Rogers was stating the importance of being yourself and not putting on a false front. Anyone working with children and young people will know how perceptive they are and how easily they can detect falseness or an adult in an apparent 'caring' role.

The second condition is known as 'unconditional positive regard' (UPR). This refers to the acceptance of the client or what Rogers referred to as 'prizing'. He also mentions a non-possessive warmth. For Rogers, UPR:

> involves an acceptance of and a caring for the client as a 'separate' person, with permission for him to have his own feelings and experiences, and to find his own meanings in them. To the degree that the therapist can provide this safety-creating climate of unconditional positive regard, significant learning is likely to take place. (1967: 283–4)

An adult supporting a child or young person in a person-centred way may find such unconditional acceptance difficult, for we bring with us a set of values and beliefs which have become part of us over many years. To suspend judgement and accept the young person as they are is a truly wonderful ability and so powerfully received by the young person who is used to coercion, encouragement to conform, labelling, criticism and advice.

The third facilitative dimension of the therapeutic relationship is 'empathic understanding'. Rogers saw this as seeing the world 'from the inside'. In 1967, he described empathy as an attempt to: 'see the client's private world as if it were your own, but without ever losing the 'as if' quality – this is empathy, and this seems essential to therapy'. He continues: 'To sense the client's anger, fear, or confusion, as if it were your own, yet without your own anger, fear, or confusion getting bound up in it, is the condition we are endeavouring to describe' (1967: 284).

All of us at times are exposed to caring friends and family who offer us sympathy and concern. When we experience real empathy, we know the difference. The young person also feels this difference but may be unable to express what it is. This most powerful aspect of the therapeutic relationship is crucial to work with young people and along with congruence and UPR distinguishes it from the child's normal experience of helping.

THE FULLY FUNCTIONING PERSON

In *On Becoming a Person* (1967), Rogers explored the concept of 'The Fully Functioning Person' which was described as an attempt to look at the person who would emerge from therapy if the 'therapy were maximally successful'. The characteristic qualities of the process towards actualisation were described as:

- An increasing openness to experience. He writes:

  This phrase has come to have more and more meaning for me. It is the polar opposite of defensiveness. Defensiveness I have described in the past as being the organism's response to experiences which are perceived or anticipated as threatening, as incongruent with the individual's existing picture of himself in relationship to the world. (Rogers, 1967: 115)

- Increasingly existential living which is described as an 'increasing tendency to live fully in each moment'; and, finally,
- An increasing trust in his organism which meant people:

  who are able to trust their total organismic reaction to a new situation because they discover to an ever-increasing degree that if they are open to their experience, doing what 'feels right' proves to be a competent and trustworthy guide to behaviour which is truly satisfying. (1967: 189)

OTHER INFLUENTIAL THEORISTS

Up until this point, this book has adopted a rather purist position, largely building ideas around the life and work of Carl Rogers. However, this is not the intention and I would like to close this chapter with a very brief look at related theorists and practitioners who have contributed to the humanistic and existential approach and which may have real relevance to those adults who want to understand their work with children and young people in more depth. Only brief reference can be made here and the reader is encouraged to follow up with their own research, where interest dictates.

Martin Buber (1878–1965) was an influential Jewish thinker whose most famous work *I and Thou* was first published in German in 1923 and focused on what constituted an authentic relationship. He described the 'I–It' relationship as that which is akin to how we view objects and people as roles. This may be understood in this way:

> Rather than truly making ourselves completely available to [people] understanding them, sharing totally with them, really talking with them, we observe them or keep part of ourselves outside the moment of the relationship. We do so either to protect our vulnerabilities or to get them to respond in some preconceived way. (Jewish Virtual Library, 2008)

Conversely, the 'I–Thou' relationship enables us to: 'place ourselves completely into a relationship, to truly understand and "be there" with another person, without masks, pretences, even without words' (Jewish Virtual Library, 2008).

The comparisons with Rogers are not hard to see and the relevance to the adult working with children and young people is marked.

Victor Frankl (1905–1997) was born and educated in Vienna. He survived a number of concentration camp experiences, including Auschwitz. Amongst his most important writings is *Man's Search for Meaning* (first published in German in 1946 and later in translation in 1959). It was through these harrowing experiences that Frankl realised the importance of finding 'meaning' in life which he saw as the essence of being human. Those who have worked with young people's sense of hopelessness and meaninglessness might like to read more of Frankl's work.

I have to admit that one of my favourite writers has to be Haim Ginott (1922–1973). His work as a clinical psychologist, parent educator and writer has had a profound influence on how we think about relationships between adults and children. His books include *Between Parent and Child* (1965), *Between Parent and Teenager* (1969) and *Teacher and Child* (1972) and stressed the importance of empathy, listening and respect for children's feelings. These books were of course also about setting boundaries, but their respect for young people has something to say about working with young people in a supportive or therapeutic role. Ginott's ideas have since been developed by his students Adele Faber and Elaine Mazlish (1980) and John Gottman (1997).

Rollo May (1909–1994) is regarded as one of the best known and respected existential psychologists. He introduced a number of new existential concepts but is particularly noted for his identification of a number of 'stages' of development, although not in a strict Freudian sense. These were: innocence, rebellion, decision, ordinary and the creative. May was very much concerned with the problems of 'being' in contrast with 'problem-solving'.

Fritz Perls (1893–1970) is an important figure in the history of psychology and is known as the father of Gestalt therapy. 'Gestalt' is a term used to describe the 'whole' which cannot be understood by the examination of the parts which make up this whole. Perls believed that people separate from thoughts and emotions that cause discomfort. This results in a fragmented personality. The aim of therapy is to help people form a meaningful configuration of awareness, thereby helping them to develop a healthy gestalt or wholeness. I believe this resonates with our attempts to work with the 'whole child' rather than with aspects of their experience.

William Glasser's most noted books include *Reality Therapy* (1965), *Schools Without Failure* (1969) and *The Quality School* (1990). In contrast to psychodynamic approaches, Glasser focused more on personal choice and personal responsibility. He is particularly noted for his 'control theory' later known as 'choice theory' which states that many of our behaviours are chosen and that we are driven by basic needs, such as survival, love, belonging, power, freedom and fun. Whilst these are all of great significance to those practitioners trying to make sense of and work with young people, undoubtedly the need for love and belonging are perhaps the strongest. Many of Glasser's ideas were extended into educational settings. He concluded that many behaviour problems in the classroom experienced by teachers are where young people are attempting to fulfil their need for power. The experience of young people at home and in school is that of feeling powerless. Glasser helps us to understand why young people behave in ways that may cause distress in others.

The reader may also like to consider the contributions made by psychologists such as Eric Fromm (1900–1980) and Clark Moustakas (b. 1923) who considered questions such as what it means to be 'human'.

In recent years, we have seen considerable development in the world of the person-centred approach and indeed we have seen significant collaboration internationally by those who want to challenge, extend and evolve the approach. This is evidenced by the establishment of The World Association for Person-centred and Experiential Psychotherapy and Counselling and its influential journal *Person-centred and Experiential Psychotherapies*. Key modern writers in the field of the person-centred approach include Michael Behr, working in Germany, Peter Schmid and Margaret Warner. Other writers and practitioners in the field include Mick Cooper, Sheila Haugh, Suzanne Keys and Brian Levitt. A full list of contemporary contributors to developments in the person-centred approach can be found on the PCCS Books website (see useful organisations).

Having immersed ourselves in ideas, this book now turns its attention to more practical issues surrounding supporting and counselling children and young people.

EXERCISES

1. Think back to your childhood. What were some of your 'conditions of worth'? Share these with another person in your group.
2. How real or congruent are you able to be? Does this change with the nature of your relationships? What does it feel like to be incongruent?
3. What does it feel like to be judged by another person who is listening to you? How might you feel? Role-play this with another group member.
4. Talk about a time when you have felt really empathic. How did this affect how you related to the other person. What was happening to you?

3
HISTORICAL, NATIONAL, ETHICAL AND LEGAL ISSUES IN WORKING WITH CHILDREN AND YOUNG PEOPLE

INTRODUCING THIS CHAPTER

The theory and practice of counselling children and young people comes to us via a rich and impressive history. Although this book is very much about the person-centred approach, a brief outline of that legacy in this chapter may help to place person-centred theory into some kind of chronological and theoretical context.

In this chapter, we also look at how counselling for children and young people has developed and why there is an ever-increasing need for this kind of support today.

We will also look at a number of key ethical and boundary issues, which have particular significance for working with children and young people.

WITH CHILDREN AND YOUNG PEOPLE IN MIND

Some of the key concepts and orientations described briefly below currently have significant effects on practice with children and young people. Adlerian ideas have offered explanations for children's behaviour; attachment theory has become even more influential in recent years as professionals attempt to understand why children

(Continued)

(Continued)

and young people appear to have difficulties with adjustment. Rational Emotive Behaviour Therapy has been applied in schools and other settings because the approach offers structure and understanding to the non-specialist. The emergence of creative and expressive therapies, which are particularly useful when working with children and young people, have developed over the last decade or more and are given the time and space they deserve later in this book.

THE PERSON-CENTRED APPROACH IN CONTEXT

As far back as 1880, Sigmund Freud (1856-1939) was telling us of the significance of the unconscious and defence mechanisms whilst his daughter devoted much of her time to the analysis of children and improving this way of working with children. Freud was very close to his daughter Anna (1895-1982) who was devoted to him and carried on his work after his death. Whereas Sigmund focused almost exclusively on adult clients, Anna was more interested in working with children in practical ways and is regarded by many as the founder of psychoanalysis.

Melanie Klein (1882-1960), another of the early pioneers, developed 'object relations theory' as a result of her observations of and clinical work with children.

Donald Winnicott (1896–1971) is often remembered for his concept of the 'good enough mother' and an understanding of the psychic space between a mother and infant. The task of the therapist, he argued, was to create a 'holding environment' in which work could take place.

Alfred Adler (1870-1937) influenced a number of his contemporaries and future theorists, such as Rollo May, Victor Frankl, Abraham Maslow and Eric Fromm and has therefore assured his place in the development of person-centred theory. Adler is ranked alongside Freud and Carl Jung in importance in the psychoanalytic movement, and is best known for his 'individual psychology' and ideas such as the 'inferiority complex'.

Margaret Lowenfeld (1890–1973) was a paediatrician who is rightfully credited with significant developments in the fields of child psychology and psychotherapy. Recognising that children were not always able to express their feelings verbally and articulately, she developed a kind of symbolic play therapy often involving sand to represent the child's world and toys and figures which enabled the child to express themselves and their world. We shall return to Lowenfeld's work later in this book.

Although Erik Erikson (1902–1994) concerned himself with the full life cycle, his work has much influenced our understanding of childhood and his writings have been used by others to promote the healthy emotional development of young people. He is particularly remembered for his eight-stage psycho-development theory.

John Bowlby (1907–1990) was an English psychiatrist who developed attachment theory. These are ideas that still have a profound effect on work today with children and young people. Whereas Freud was concerned with a child's inner conflicts, Bowlby stressed the importance of the early years between parent and child, particularly the mother–child relationship. He is largely associated with three areas of study: attachment, separation and loss, each of which became widely read theories.

In addition to Fritz Perls and William Glasser who were briefly introduced in Chapter 1, three other names are important to mention because much of their work has been applied directly to working with children and adolescents. The first of these is Albert Ellis (1913–2007) who called his work Rational Emotive Behaviour Therapy. Whereas psychodynamic theorists focus on the exploration of childhood, Ellis preferred to concentrate on the present, the here-and-now. He argued that people's behaviour is most often due to mistaken cognitions and faulty thinking. Whilst they may be in the awareness of the unhappy person, they nevertheless cause that person to behave in unwanted and dysfunctional ways. Rational Emotive Behaviour Therapy challenges clients to challenge these irrational ways of thinking, which often involve people either over- or under-reacting to normal life events. In this way, people are encouraged to live more fulfilling lives. This approach has spawned a generation of self-help texts, and many of the books used in schools and organisations working with young people with 'behaviour problems', including anger, have been influenced by Ellis' ideas. These are easy to understand and use by teachers and non-specialists.

Non-directive play therapy was largely developed by Virginia Axline (1911–1988), the author of the well-read, *Dibs: In Search of Self* (1964) – a book often on the essential reading list of many counselling courses – and Violet Oaklander whose main works include *Windows to Our Children: A Gestalt Therapy Approach to Children and Adolescents* (1989) and *Hidden Treasure: A Map to the Child's Inner Self* (2006). Their humanistic approach to working with children and young people remains highly influential today. Again, Axline and Oaklander's work will be explored more fully in future chapters.

THE DEVELOPMENT OF COUNSELLING WITH CHILDREN AND YOUNG PEOPLE

The 1970s saw the beginnings of the evolution of counselling for children and adolescents. A number of names are worth mentioning in this growing movement, and include: Anne Jones who wrote *School Counselling in Practice* (1970) later to become *Counselling Adolescents in School* (1977); Alick Holden whose book had a similar title, *Counselling in Secondary Schools* (1971); Ken Williams who wrote *The School Counsellor* in 1973; Douglas Hamblin whose works include *The Teacher and Counselling* (1974); Patricia Milner whose writings include *Counselling in Education* (1974); and Ellen Noonan, author of *Counselling Young People* (1983). When we also include in this non-exhaustive list, the seminal work of C.H. Patterson, who wrote about school counselling as far back as 1962, we can see that counselling first found a home in the new comprehensive schools which were emerging at this time. These developments paralleled the growth in the concept of pastoral care, not in a theological sense but in the context of schooling.

At the same time, courses began in key universities keen to develop this new specialism, most notably at the Universities of Reading and Keele. Unfortunately, educational cutbacks during the 1970s saw a decline in the number of school counsellor posts, and teachers who had re-trained in counselling were re-absorbed into traditional pastoral and teaching posts. These new therapeutic approaches to working with young people had not of course always been welcomed and many teachers saw the role of the school counsellor as a threat to sound discipline, or to the aspects of teaching which they had most enjoyed. It is important to mention that whilst there was this decline in provision, the influence of Carl Rogers and the person-centred approach had left its mark. This was to allow the person–centred approach to re-surface whenever any renaissance occurred.

Encouragingly, as I write, a re-emergence of interest in the counselling of children has been growing quite substantially, supported by The British Association for Counselling and Psychotherapy (BACP) and its specialist division, Counselling Children and Young People (CCYP). Counselling for children and young people has also been growing specifically in terms of skills in related professions such as health and social work, whilst most cities and many towns will have a counselling service for young people. Dudley in the West Midlands became recognised as one of the first local authorities in the country to establish a centralised team of peripatetic school counsellors, and other authorities have found different ways of funding similar services, sometimes in association with voluntary agencies. Many schools have included part-time counsellors amongst their staff, and colleges and universities include counselling as part of their student services.

Parallel to this, and equally welcomed, has been a growing interest within government in the psychological and mental health needs of children and young people. Whilst the government advisory document *Promoting Mental Health in Early Years and School Settings* (DfES, 2001) passed largely unnoticed by many schools, a number of initiatives have stressed the importance of the emotional health and well-being of young people. The Department of Health National Healthy Schools Programme, a good summative outline of which can be found in *National Healthy School Status* (Department of Health, 2005), stressed not only healthy eating, personal and social education and physical activity as important in promoting health in children and young people, but it also made explicit a concern for emotional health and well-being. Developments in the personal, social and health education curriculum also encouraged the exploration of issues relating to mental health and emotional well-being. More recently, an interest in the emotional dimension to schooling and emotional literacy in the UK in the form of Social Emotional Aspects of Learning (part of the Government's National Strategies Programme) has found its way into both primary and secondary schools across the country, whilst 2008 saw the beginning of the Government's Targeted Mental Health in Schools project. The Labour Government's wide-reaching policy document *Every Child Matters* (2004) has had a growing influence on work with children across many agencies, bringing together organisations as diverse as social care, health and youth justice.

At the same time, significant non-governmental organisations and influential charities have all played their part in promoting the idea of emotional support for young people – organisations such as The Mental Health Foundation, The Samaritans and Young Minds, as well as major counselling organisations. This is why this book has been written with a sense of optimism that might not have been felt a decade ago.

TO THE HELPER

The listening role of the teacher, the nurse, the youth worker has always been an important part of these kinds of work. However, roles such as school mentor and non-teaching pastoral care workers in schools have increased opportunities for non-counsellors to work closely with children and young people, utilising counselling skills and potentially adopting a person-centred approach to their relationships.

THE GROWING NEED FOR COUNSELLING FOR CHILDREN AND YOUNG PEOPLE

The National Office for Statistics (2004) in its most recent survey into the mental health of young people found that one in 10 children aged between five and 16 had a diagnosed mental disorder and the most significant problems within these figures were anxiety and depression. Of course, person–centred counsellors view with some scepticism the labelling of children and young people, and those who work within the approach are confident in its focus on the person, rather than the 'disorder'. This issue is explored in more detail in Chapter 5. However, these figures do appear to mirror the growing demand for counselling with children and young people found in schools, voluntary agencies, social work and health settings.

While working with children and young people emphasises the 'personal' and the 'relationship', we need to be aware that the young people who come for counselling live within a social, political and cultural context. A number of factors will impact upon the lives of the child or young person who seeks out counselling or support. The influences which impinge on the lives of children and young people include: loss, especially through bereavement; divorce or separation of parents; domestic violence; bullying; all forms of abuse including physical, sexual, emotional abuse or neglect; the experience of prison; and the effects of poverty and deprivation. Children and young people may be seen to be at increased risk where they are refugees or asylum seekers with memories of traumatic events and with a need to establish new identities, gay and lesbian young people experiencing homophobia and the negative judgements of others, and children who are in care or who are carers to adults themselves. Also at risk are young people from minority communities, who may experience prejudice and racism from the host community, and of course those with parents who have mental health problems themselves.

Whilst children and young people have always needed support in time of difficulty, there has never been a time when there has been a greater need for the availability of counsellors, trained and willing to work with young clients. This not only applies to settings such as schools and in social work but with students at colleges and universities where being away from home, life on campus and academic pressure can either cause problems to begin or exacerbate those already present.

All work with children and young people should take place within clear ethical and legal boundaries. Some of these are now explored below.

WORKING WITH BOUNDARIES

Case study: Jayne

Jayne (aged 10 years) comes from a family where money is tight. All the children at her junior school wear uniform but it is clear from her clothes that her parents have little to spend on her and her sister and three brothers. Her personal hygiene has caused concern and her teacher visited the home to see if the school could offer any help. The teacher found very cramped living conditions in poor quality housing. However, it is clear to all who come into contact with Jayne's parents and siblings that this is a loving family and mum and dad are doing the best they can, under the circumstances.

Jayne is isolated at school and tends to play on her own. Despite the efforts of mum and dad, things do get a little stressful at home and with many older siblings, Jayne sometimes feels left out.

Her school decided to make provision for a learning assistant, Hilary, to work with her on a one-to-one basis at a designated time each week. The learning assistant was doing a counselling course and was delighted when it was suggested that she seemed the best person to support Jayne.

Hilary and Jayne met each week and Jayne would talk freely about home and school. Eventually, Jayne asked if she could have more time with Hilary but this was difficult because of Hilary's other classroom and support commitments. Increasingly, Jayne would seek out Hilary at break-time and lunch-time, and keen to give more support, Hilary would find the time to listen to Jayne. After some weeks, Hilary realised that Jayne was asking for more time than she could reasonably give. With her concerns rising, she raised the matter with her course tutor who talked to her about the importance of 'boundaries'. It was suggested to Hilary that her problem had arisen because whilst she had established an agreement with Jayne, she had allowed these to blur in terms of when and where she gave time to her young client.

This case study raises a number of questions. Firstly, what are boundaries in counselling? Secondly, do the same principles apply when working with children and young people and, finally, how are boundaries viewed within a person-centred context?

TO THE HELPER

It is possible for the person-centred approach to inform all your work with a young person. This then becomes your way of relating to the children and young people you work with. However, if as part of a role, you decide to offer some specific time for listening and helping, then this needs to be defined and mutually understood. You cannot make yourself available to a particular child or young person all of the time.

TO THE COUNSELLOR

It is your professional responsibility as a counsellor to set and maintain clear boundaries which are understood by your young client. For ethical reasons, professional practice as a counsellor can only really take place when these have been established. Boundaries are also there to make certain that you are able to function well within your job role. They offer clarity and surety and ensure that you retain a sense of self and separateness.

Boundaries are a way of ensuring that counselling takes place in a mutually understood and safe environment. In a sense, they are the ground rules which 'contain' the relationship and enable the client to make best use of the time available to her. Boundaries define when client and counsellor meet and how long sessions will last, where the work takes place, how sessions can be cancelled if needed and a clarity about the purpose of the session and what can be brought to it.

Boundaries also ensure that both client and counsellor maintain their separateness. Allowing for intimacy, it is also important for the counsellor and client to know where they begin and end as separate people. A good summary of the importance of boundaries can be found in Marian Davies' *Boundaries in Counselling and Psychotherapy* (2007). Drawing on the cited work of Webb (1997), boundaries may be seen as:

> 'Drawing a line' or using a 'limit line' that may be between, for example, aspects of the self (internal, psychological or intrapersonal), self and others (interpersonal), types of relationships (counsellor, friend, parent etc), and types of behaviour (what is appropriate behaviour in a particular context). (pp. 175–88)

WITH CHILDREN AND YOUNG PEOPLE IN MIND

Boundary setting is possibly even more important when working with young clients, especially very young children. They often crave friendship or parenting, but as helpers and counsellors, our role remains professional and different.

DUAL ROLES

Another boundary issue facing adults working in settings such as schools and youth centres, is that concerning a duality of role. Conflicts arise from the child or young person not being able to relate to the adult in different contexts, for example as teacher and counsellor. There are also related identity problems for the adult because, often, different roles require a different kind of relating. Where the adult helper has adopted a person-centred approach to a helping relationship, this is less of an issue. Where a more formal counselling contract has been established, dual roles are best avoided. The BACP *Ethical Framework for Good Practice in Counselling and Psychotherapy* (BACP, 2007a) sees dual relationships as 'seldom neutral' and practitioners are asked to consider the implications of entering into such roles. A similar discussion on duality of roles can be found in the British Psychological Society's *Code of Ethics and Conduct* (2006).

TO THE HELPER

You will probably be in a helping role as part of some other professional responsibility such as nursing, teaching or social work. Where this is the case and you adopt a person-centred approach, this is wholly appropriate. Indeed, working in this way will often enhance your effectiveness.

CONFIDENTIALITY

Perhaps the most important boundary issue when working with children and young people is that which is concerned with confidentiality and its limits. It is not the concern of this book to explore in any great detail the complex area of the law relating to confidentiality and the reader is directed to more specialist texts such as Daniels and Jenkins (2000) and Jenkins (2007).

It is impossible to underestimate the importance of confidentiality in the listening relationship. We only have to look into our own experiences of sharing very personal and sensitive information and feelings with another person to realise how more free we feel to express what is happening for us if we know that this will not be shared beyond the person we are talking to and in whom we have invested so much trust.

I believe this is doubly so with children and young people, who in life are afforded very little confidentiality. Information flows freely between parents and teachers and where agencies have been called upon to offer support, children's lives are shared between social workers, health professionals, youth offending workers and the like. In schools, it is rare for a confidentiality policy to exist or be active, and sensitive information is sometimes shared beyond the concept of 'need to know'. Despite a clear rationale, initiatives such as The Common Assessment Framework, which is a holistic process which seeks to identify a child's additional needs which are not being met by universal services, and the responsibility to share information across agencies as identified in Every Child Matters and the subsequent Children's Act, could be seen as detracting from the young person's right to talk about matters with a person they have chosen to share with.

Much of what children share with adults does not necessarily need to be passed on to others. There are of course major limits to confidentiality and these often apply to working with adults as well. This is especially the case where a person is likely to cause serious harm to themselves or others. It is important to note that counsellors are sometimes required to provide reports for courts and are sometimes even required to give evidence. An excellent book of guidance in these matters is: *Therapists in Court: Providing Evidence and Supporting Witnesses* (Bond and Sandhu, 2005).

TO THE COUNSELLOR

Where you work within a statutory setting, your responsibilities regarding confidentiality may be well defined and the organisation will have expectations as to when information should be passed on. Where you work in a voluntary setting, you may feel a greater tension between protecting your young client's right to confidentiality and the need to share critical information with other professionals.

WITH CHILDREN AND YOUNG PEOPLE IN MIND

Whilst younger children accept that some information will be shared between adults, older children and young adults often have different expectations and will expect a higher level of confidentiality. Striking the right balance between professional responsibility and the young person's right to privacy will have a deep and lasting effect on the therapeutic relationship you work hard to build.

CHILD PROTECTION

When working with children and young people, it is important to be fully acquainted with the child protection policies of the organisation in which a counsellor is working. Local Safeguarding Children Boards (LSCBs) were established in England under the Children's Act 2004. These replaced local Area Child Protection Committees. The work of these LSCBs is to promote the idea that we are all responsible for safeguarding the well-being of children and young people. Where any form of abuse is suspected or disclosed, including physical, sexual, emotional abuse or neglect, counsellors and adults working with young people have a responsibility to refer matters to social services, who are the investigating agency. Sometimes the police may become involved at an early stage. Wherever possible, the counsellor will discuss the referral with the young person first, although there may be occasions when this may not be the best course of action. Of course, once information has been passed on, the counsellor can continue to support the young person. Responsibility does not end with referral; indeed, this is probably the time of greatest need. In some cases, the continuance of counselling may be difficult, especially where it could lead to legal complications.

Not all referrals result in a case being opened, but where there remains sufficient cause for concern, a meeting will be called and later a decision will be made by key professionals as to whether the child should be placed on the 'child protection register' and further 'core group' meetings called to look at how best to protect the child from further harm.

For more information on child protection and safeguarding, the reader might like to access the Every Child Matters website at www.everychildmatters.gov.uk For those working in schools, guidance on child protection matters can be found in the BACP's (2009) *Good Practice Guidelines for Counsellors in Schools* and an information sheet on child protection in further education is also available from the BACP (2007b).

SELF-DISCLOSURE

As adults, I believe that we often have a need to share of ourselves with others. We are social beings and therefore often seek to define ourselves in relationship to others. When working with young people, there can be a tension between this need within ourselves and the expectation that we will do our best for the young person. Self-disclosure should not be confused with genuineness or congruence. A more detailed discussion of this theoretical dilemma can be found in Truax (1971). Some professionals working with young people might argue that we remain distant from the young person if we are unwilling to share information about ourselves. However, most of the literature guards against its use except in certain circumstances and only for the benefit of the client. Self-disclosure can take the focus away from the young person and in some cases may place additional stress or responsibility upon the young person. Where the adult may have convinced themselves that self-disclosure will help the young person, it should be remembered that the helper and child's experiences are different and experienced very personally. Judith Harrington in a paper delivered in Birmingham in the United States (2001) identified a number of 'temptations' for the counsellor to self-disclose, for example 'it worked for me, it could work for you'. She also made a distinction between authenticity in the relationship and self-disclosure. Authenticity is more about the 'use of self' rather than the temptation to 'tell'.

TOUCH IN COUNSELLING

Finally, sometimes in working with children and young people, the dilemma of 'touch' emerges. Discussion around contact between counsellor and client is different today than it would have been years ago, especially in relation to young people. Child protection concerns have made it far more difficult for contact to take place between adult and child. This not only affects counsellors, but, today, teachers and social workers are less likely to hug or put their arms around a young person in need. In some respects, there is something sad about this. Zur and Nordmarken (2009: 1) draw upon evidence to show that: 'Touch is one of the most essential elements of human development, a profound method of communication, a critical component of the health and growth of infants, and a healing force'.

An excellent summary of the arguments for and against touch in counselling can be found in Tolan (2003). Arguments against using touch include:

- Touch is unnecessary in the emotional 'holding' environment of the counselling relationship.
- Clients might find being touched intrusive, frightening or abusive.
- Being touched may be associated with negative experiences for the client.
- The counsellor may be meeting her own needs, rather than the client's.
- Touch can provide temporary comfort, blocking the client's most acute feelings.
- Touch can be misinterpreted, leaving the counsellor open to challenge or worse.

In favour of touch in counselling, Tolan argues that it can:

- harness the natural healing powers
- enable a client to feel sufficiently safe to explore difficult feelings
- anchor the therapeutic relationship in the here-and-now
- convey acceptability and encourage more congruent responses, especially where human contact has been denied.

The cautions outlined above are especially pertinent and to some extent amplified when working with children and young people, and, where touch is misinterpreted, the adult leaves themselves open to professional criticism or possibly legal action.

WITH CHILDREN AND YOUNG PEOPLE IN MIND

In terms of societal expectations, it is likely that touch is more acceptable with younger children and where child–adult relationships are less formal.

THE *ETHICAL FRAMEWORK*

The counsellor or adult attempting to work therapeutically with children and young people is advised to adhere to a code. In the UK, the British Association for Counselling and Psychotherapy publishes its well-respected *Ethical Framework for Good Practice in Counselling and Psychotherapy* (2007a). This has evolved over the years from a more prescriptive approach to one that sets out a range of values, principles and counsellor qualities which should underpin all therapeutic work. Values include, amongst others, respect for rights and dignity, the integrity of the practitioner–client relationship, a commitment to quality professional knowledge and the alleviation of personal distress and suffering. The counsellor or therapist is also expected to work towards increasing their own personal effectiveness and appreciate the variety of human experience and culture (BACP, 2007a: 2).

Ethical principles include:

- Fidelity: honouring the trust placed in the practitioner.
- Autonomy: respecting the client's right to be self-governing.
- Beneficence: a commitment to promoting the client's well-being.
- Non-maleficence: avoiding harm to the client.
- Justice: fair and impartial treatment.
- Self-respect: a commitment to fostering the practitioner's self-knowledge and care for self (BACP, 2007a: 2–3).

Personal moral qualities include: empathy; sincerity; integrity; resilience; respect; humility; competence; fairness; wisdom; and courage (2007a: 4)

The *Ethical Framework* also sets out principles and procedures in relation to dealing with complaints.

TO THE HELPER

Whilst the *Ethical Framework* has been designed primarily with professional counsellors in mind, I believe it has much to offer the non-counsellor as well.

BOUNDARIES: CHALLENGING THE ORTHODOXY

This chapter has highlighted the importance of establishing clear boundaries from the outset and the counsellor's responsibility to maintain these. However, I would like to return the reader to the first chapter of this book which attempted to establish that working with children and young people is different from working with adults. The image of a client sitting with a counsellor for the 'therapeutic hour', with two chairs at an angle to each other, is very much an adult model. Some of the best counsellors I have known who have worked with children and young people, have shown a willingness to be prepared to bend traditional boundaries. Of course, many children and young people can sit and share their thoughts and feelings with an adult in the way indicated above, but many others cannot. I have known counsellors to work on cushions or even work with a young person walking across school playing fields, because that is where the client felt most at ease. I have seen counsellors bring refreshments into the room and allow breaks whilst others have engaged the reluctant young client with a small collaborative activity such as a board game, aimed at establishing the relationship and enabling the child to feel at ease. As long as the counsellor continues to work ethically and with a professional code of ethics in mind, I believe the counsellor can work with a degree of freedom, in a way which establishes a therapeutic relationship with a child or young person.

It could also be argued that the person-centred approach expects us to work in ways different to those characteristic of typically contained professional–client relationships. An interesting article by Sarah Luczaj (2007) asks the question: how actively useful are boundaries in the therapeutic relationship? She suggests that in the psychodynamic way of working, boundaries may indeed be necessary, but what of the person-centred and humanistic approaches? She writes:

> There seems to be a contradiction in the upholding of strict boundaries, due to the fact that person-centred therapy is a kind of relationship which transcends and frees us from the confined terms in which we usually function. It can seem very strange from the client's side, to experience being received in such a way and then have it switched off for the rest of the week, and from the therapist's side too, as if such a way of being were only possible in small doses. (Internet article)

Whilst accepting that there are boundaries which are absolutes, such as the prohibition on sexual activity between counsellor and client, Luczaj maintains that it is the counsellor who needs to decide on the nature of boundaries; finding a balance in which they feel the integrity of the conditions of empathy, realness and acceptance remain central.

WITH CHILDREN AND YOUNG PEOPLE IN MIND

As with much of the work with young people, there are many issues, both practical and ethical for the adult helper or counsellor to decide on. For some young people, strict boundaries may be essential in the establishment of a safe and predictable environment in which to experience trust and in which to begin talking about the things most on their minds. For others, boundaries need to be flexible so as not to replicate previous overly defined adult–child relationships and where the growing relationship needs to be relatively free of structure, whilst maintaining the important distinction between counselling and friendship.

EXERCISES

1. What boundaries have you established in your own relationships? What purpose do they serve?
2. Talk about a time when you have shared something in confidence. What did assurances about confidentiality mean to you?
3. When has a young person shared something confidential with you?
4. What are the limitations to confidentiality in your own organisation or work setting?
5. With another person, role-play a situation where one person is sharing something of concern, only to be interrupted with the listener's self-disclosure. How did it feel for talker and listener?
6. What are you like with 'touch'? Are you generally a 'tactile' person?

4
MEASURING OUTCOMES

INTRODUCING THIS CHAPTER

This chapter takes a person-centred look at effectiveness, progress and outcomes in counselling. It asks the question whether such measurements are possible, meaningful or indeed desirable.

TO THE COUNSELLOR

Counsellors working within organisations are increasingly expected to demonstrate that their work is making a difference. Sometimes these pressures are made explicit, but often the counsellor feels under implied pressure from referrers and managers to achieve noticeable and measurable change.

I have found through my work with supervisees that these perceived pressures are a significant cause of stress in the counsellor and ultimately they can affect the nature of the work and the quality of the therapeutic relationship.

TO THE HELPER

You may already be under pressure to achieve more tangible results in your work with children and young people. Expectations about more pragmatic and functional interventions make it harder to justify more person-centred approaches to employers and stakeholders.

THEORETICAL AND PRACTICAL DIFFICULTIES

We begin this chapter with a short case study.

Case study: Claire

Claire is 12. She was recently referred by her GP to a voluntary counselling service after the sudden and tragic death of her friend Donna. The two girls had been out playing with a ball with another of their friends, Charlotte. On this occasion, Charlotte threw the ball which was chased by Claire and Donna. They playfully fought for the ball and soon Claire was able to wrestle the ball from Donna and run across a road to escape with her prize. Donna pursued Claire without checking that the road was clear. Within a few seconds, Claire heard a loud braking noise, and a thud. Donna was pronounced dead on arrival at the hospital. Claire almost immediately blamed herself for the accident and saw herself as the cause of her best friend's death. After this, Claire appeared to become depressed and neglected her other friendships and became quite withdrawn, only leaving her house to go to school or go shopping with her mother. Claire's change, from being a girl full of life and energy to a child isolated and perpetually sad, was the reason why her mother had initially taken her to the family doctor, who subsequently made the referral for counselling.

Claire's tragic story raises the question about how we measure progress, effectiveness or outcomes in counselling or indeed whether this is possible or even desirable. Claire's mother may feel that if and when Claire starts to re-engage with friends, this would indeed be a sign that things have improved. However, how do we know if regardless of the counselling that 'time would heal' or indeed whether Claire actually feels any better or whether her sadness and feelings of responsibility and guilt remain, hidden only by her desire to meet her mother's expectations about 'getting over it'?

The problems faced by young people are unique, individual and experienced by that child alone. There are of course similarities of experience but nevertheless the child's experience is exclusive to that young person. Claire's grief is experienced by her, in her own way. Humphrey and Zimpfer (1996) write:

> The process of grief is an individual journey. Although losses appear to have similar qualities, and there are universal dimensions of grief, each individual has unique issues to cope with and resolve. No two people grieve in the same manner or on the same timetable. Each individual is influenced by various perspectives at different times during the process. Who comes for counselling, when, and with what issues is always idiosyncratic. (p. 41)

Claire's story is about loss and grief, but the same principles apply with every child and with each problem they face.

WITH CHILDREN AND YOUNG PEOPLE IN MIND

When working with children and young people, referrers are likely to expect to see behavioural change. This is often the case with younger children. With teenagers and young adults, there may be a tendency to measure progress against educational, vocational outcomes as well as behavioural change.

THE EFFECTIVENESS OF COUNSELLING

My experience as a counsellor working with children and young people and as a supervisor of counsellors working with this age group has indeed raised a number of dilemmas or questions for me. What constitutes effective counselling; how do we know that what we are doing is making a difference? For some organisations, indicators are easy to find. A school which arranges counselling for a child may look for behavioural changes, such as a reduction in the number of fixed-term exclusions, and improved attendance may be 'evidence' that counselling is 'working'. Such outward signs may not give us any further insight as to what is happening for that young person. It is also my experience that counselling sometimes enables a child to touch upon feelings, previously hidden or suppressed, and whilst this may be a necessary part of the therapeutic process, outward behaviours may indeed appear to deteriorate before they get better. It could also be argued that counselling can offer support through a crisis; that the young person may be held through a difficult period in their lives. The fact that the child does not appear to be 'improving' may obscure the understanding that without counselling, the young person may have deteriorated further, had they been unable to find the right kind of support. The idea of the young person 'getting better' as determined by overt and measurable behaviours raises the question as to who the counselling is for. Sometimes a young person may be referred for counselling because the adult perceives the 'problem', but this may not be an issue for the child.

We live in a society that increasingly sets targets and seeks to measure outcomes. Ideas which had their origins in the world of business and commerce have now found their way into the human services. Schools have for some time been measured against externally set criteria, and failure to meet these standards causes schools to be criticised and, at worst, a school might find itself in 'special measures' which indicates a significant level of concern, and therefore 'at risk', ultimately, of closure.

The issue of outcomes in the caring professions is addressed by Hazzard (1995):

This debate has been intruded upon by a political and economic ideology of commoditization which perceives clinical relationships in terms of commerce and production. The expression of this ideology expects justification for the employment of professional counsellors through the measurement of outcomes that might be seen as analogous to the results of more concrete interventions like surgery or drug treatment. (p. 118)

These concerns should not of course fail to recognise that an organisation's existence might be dependent upon how efficient its services can be proven to be. For example, voluntary agencies working with young people are frequently asked to produce figures to show the number of clients they are working with and some indicator of how effective interventions have been before charitable trusts and statutory bodies are prepared to offer monies. This is because they themselves will be accountable for the grants and contracts they offer. It is also important to note that effective monitoring of services may lead to improved services.

In 1994, John McLeod began to open up discussion about research into the question of whether counselling 'works'. He wrote:

A significant amount of energy and effort has been devoted to researching the outcomes of counselling and psychotherapy. Does counselling work? This is the big question, the bottom line for therapists and therapy researchers. Some of this research has been motivated by a desire to demonstrate the effectiveness of one brand of therapy as compared to other approaches. Outcome research has also been motivated by a need to be able to legitimise counselling and psychotherapy in the eyes of resource providers such as government departments and health insurance companies. (1994: 121)

Studies into the effectiveness of counselling received a setback due to the work of Eysenck (1952). This work has been summarised by McLeod (1993) in his *An Introduction to Counselling*. Essentially, Eysenck's research found that, regardless of the orientation – he looked at psychodynamic and eclectic approaches – outcomes were no better than those that might have been expected had a client not had therapy. This was referred to as 'spontaneous recovery'. By this, he meant that people who did not experience therapy were often just as likely to 'get better' than those undergoing psychotherapy. This may be due to problems going away naturally over a period of time or because the client had personally developed new and effective ways of coping.

Hazzard (1995) notes that Eysenck's work has long since been challenged on methodological grounds. However, as McLeod (1994) suggests, this research may not only have stimulated interest in the idea of 'spontaneous recovery' but also initiated a series of research studies designed to study the effectiveness of therapy.

McLeod also identified a series of common assessment tools used in research to measure outcomes. Many of these are shared with other services whose primary work involves the support and development of people. They include:

- standardised 'self-test' tests or inventories
- client satisfaction questionnaires

- rating of target symptoms
- behavioural measures
- structured interviews
- ratings by significant others
- ratings by therapists
- cost–benefit analyses which relate to criteria established by the individual or organisations paying for the counselling.

More recently, we have seen a growing body of research and evidence into the effectiveness of counselling. Bondi (2006), in a number of controlled trials in health care settings, suggested that counselling is an effective intervention, both clinically and economically, in a way which makes talking therapies broadly comparable to the use of anti-depressant medication. Rowland et al. (2000) also showed that patients who were counselled were significantly more likely to have recovered than non-counselled patients. These are just a few of the research papers which have indicated the desirability of counselling either instead of, or in association with, drug treatments.

It is of course necessary not to confuse the counselling profession's attempt to prove the value of counselling and the practitioner working in a youth, educational or social care setting who simply wants to know whether what they are doing is making a difference.

Counsellors working with young people often prefer to use forms of client satisfaction questionnaires which are made available to clients at the end or soon after the counselling has ended. More recently, organisations providing counselling have started to use The Clinical Outcomes in Routine Evaluation (CORE), which is the UK's most widely used system for monitoring the quality of counselling services and was developed for managers and practitioners who needed some system to respond to the demands made by funders, commissioners and service providers to produce evidence of quality and effectiveness. There also exists a YP-CORE for professionals working with young people, which is probably of most interest to you, the reader.

As with counselling in general, there is a growing body of evidence as to the effectiveness of counselling with children and young people. For example, the University of Strathclyde (www.strath.ac.uk) has carried out a significant amount of work in this area, especially relating to counselling young people in the school setting – see Pattison et al. (2007) and Cooper (2006).

This book is primarily concerned with working with children and young people using a person-centred approach. Thorne (1992) records how Carl Rogers extensively researched his emerging 'client-centred' therapies:

> Rogers' research activities during the 1940s, 1950s and 1960s were prolific and the client-centred hypotheses were strengthened and elaborated by the completion and publication of numerous studies undertaken under his general guidance and inspiration. This body of research constituted the most intensive investigation of psychotherapy attempted anywhere in the world up to that time and showed that the delicate and elusive movement of therapeutic processes could be studied and measured purposefully. (pp. 60–1)

However, Robert Elliott (2007) describes how during the 1960s, Rogers moved away from the world of academia and scientific research, a development he believes was a major mistake and the reason why person-centred counselling encountered future problems relating to its credibility.

This lack of scientific enquiry meant that the person-centred approach was placing itself at a disadvantage compared to other therapeutic traditions. Person-centred practitioners 'woke up to the fact that they were being systematically and progressively excluded from training and health-care venues throughout the world and needed to do something' (Elliott, 2007: 327).

Elliott goes on to say that as a result of the above concerns, there has been a marked increase in the amount of research in person-centred therapies which have on the whole been favourable in their assessments of the efficacy of the approach. He does however draw attention to the fact that much of this research has been of a quantitative and positivistic nature, which emphasises the value of data and definitive knowledge as opposed to research of a more qualitative nature (Elliott, 2007: 327–8)

Examples of research into the effectiveness of the person-centred approach include Gibbard and Hanley (2008) which indicated that the person-centred approach to counselling was found to be effective with clients with common mental health problems, such as anxiety and depression, and may also be a positive intervention for people experiencing more severe problems of a longer duration.

The value of the person-centred approach in working with younger clients is also evidenced by the work of Freire et al. (2007) and Cooper (2007).

This returns us to some of the principles of the person-centred approach already explored in this book, and to some of the complexities highlighted in the case study of Claire; that is, how do we measure outcomes and identify progress as a child struggles to deal with the death of her friend? As Elliott puts it: 'Is it acceptable for political purposes to make use of research whose principles are antithetical to person-centred therapy, in order to fend off unfair attacks?' (2007: 328).

Elliott concludes that it is possible to research the person-centred approach scientifically. Drawing from the work of Mearns and McLeod (1984) and Barrineau and Bozarth (1989), he sets out some basic principles of what might be regarded as a more human kind of research which includes focusing on the client's understandings, without judgement. In this, the person-centred researcher attempts to be authentic and establish a more equal relationship with the client, where she is treated as a co-researcher and the researcher is seen as a fellow human being.

WITH CHILDREN AND YOUNG PEOPLE IN MIND

The discussion above suggests that any attempt at assessing the effectiveness of the person-centred approach needs to remain true to and consistent with the main principles of the approach. This means that when we are working with vulnerable children and young people, the core conditions are foremost in our minds.

A paper, 'Person-centred International' based upon the work of Bozarth and presented at The Association for the Development of the Person-centred approach in Las Vegas, May 1997, confidently argues for the effectiveness of the approach and suggests which elements are key to its usefulness to clients. Reviewing research into psychotherapeutic outcomes, the following ideas emerge in demonstrating effectiveness:

- Effective psychotherapy is primarily predicated upon: (1) the relationship between the therapist and client; and (2) the inner and external resources of the client.
- The type of therapy and technique is largely irrelevant in terms of successful outcome.
- The training, credentials and experience of therapists are irrelevant to successful therapy.
- Clients who receive psychotherapy improve more than clients who do not receive psychotherapy.
- There is little evidence to support the position that there are specific treatments for particular disabilities.
- The most consistent of the relationship variables related to effectiveness are the conditions of empathy, genuineness and unconditional positive regard.

It is not hard to see how such ideas appear to support the importance of Rogers' ideas in the development of counselling and psychotherapy. Bozarth emphasises the importance of the core conditions. He writes: 'The person who has, in my view, come closest to identifying the critical elements of psychotherapeutic effectiveness is Carl Rogers (1957)' (Bozarth, 1997: 1). He goes on to suggest that the core conditions were less about the development of 'client-centred' therapy and more about the 'necessary and sufficient' attitudes for helping relationships. This returns us to the point made in Chapter 1, that the person-centred approach is not just for use by counsellors and therapists, but anybody who is able to professionally establish a helping relationship with another person, in whatever setting.

Interestingly, this issue is explored from another perspective in a paper titled 'Evaluating Therapeutic Effectiveness in Counselling and Psychotherapy' (Mulhauser, 2006). Here, the argument is put forward that claims made by those in favour of the person-centred approach are undermining their own position:

> Some proponents of person-centred theory suggest that it is unsurprising that different therapeutic orientations do not differ in terms of aggregate effectiveness. They suggest that only individual therapists who manifest the 'core conditions' of person-centred theory will be effective, and that anyone from any orientation could do a good job in offering the core conditions. (Internet resource)

It is further argued that this position is not backed up by evidence remaining an 'item of faith':

> Moreover, if it *were* true, it would imply an interesting conclusion which person-centred proponents would presumably find unpalatable: namely, that counsellors who successfully manifest the core conditions are no more likely to be found in the ranks of the person-centred tradition than within any other therapeutic tradition. In other words, it would imply that person-centred counsellors are no more likely to be person-centred than any other type of counsellor. (Internet resource)

There still exists considerable debate as to whether Rogers' core conditions are indeed not only necessary but also sufficient to bring out therapeutic change. Many person-centred counsellors still subscribe to this position which emphasises the importance of the 'relationship' in counselling rather than the deployment of a number of techniques. Others have taken the approach further, introducing a number of other key skills which are felt to facilitate the therapeutic process; these include skills such as those associated with challenging the client, confrontation and immediacy. These additional concepts will be explored in more detail later in this book.

Returning to the counselling resource paper mentioned above, I am drawn to what feels like a common-sense conclusion when it comes to attempts to evaluate therapeutic effectiveness:

> For some, scientific research is irrelevant anyway, and even if the particular benefits of a given approach became empirically evident, they would still prefer to maintain the purity of their own particular therapeutic orientation and their own ways of dealing with individual clients. (One psychologist wrote that 'one can no more argue someone out of a counselling model by advancing empirical evidence than one could argue them out of a religious belief'). (Internet resource)

In many ways, working in a person-centred way does require 'faith' in the process. I feel that it is important too that we do not dismiss the importance of subjective experience.

WITH CHILDREN AND YOUNG PEOPLE IN MIND

Those who have already worked with young people in this way will often know when a trusting, open, real and empathic relationship has been established with a young person. They may also sense that what they are doing is making a difference and is valued by that child. It is my belief that we sometimes 'know', without being able to provide evidence, and it is important to protect from measurement, that which cannot be quantified – only experienced. Of course, others may disagree or challenge this belief.

EXERCISES

1. What for you constitutes 'success' with a young client?
2. How does your organisation measure 'progress' when working with a young person?
3. Do you experience any pressures externally or internally to make progress with the young person you are working with? Where do these pressures come from? Do these influences have an effect on the way you work with a young person? Share examples with a colleague.

5
WHY YOUNG PEOPLE BECOME UNHAPPY:
The Person-centred Approach in Context

INTRODUCING THIS CHAPTER

This chapter begins with some discussion around the ideas of happiness and unhappiness from a number of theoretical positions. We will look at how these differing perspectives determine the kind of language we use when talking about children and young people.

We will then look at the interplay between key concepts such as 'conditions of worth', 'congruence', 'incongruence' and 'locus of control', to develop some understanding of 'unhappiness' in children and young people from a person-centred perspective. A number of case studies are included by way of illustration.

PERSPECTIVES ON SADNESS

In 2007, UNICEF rated the UK at the bottom of a league table of well-being. In particular, British children and young people were identified as being amongst the unhappiest in the world. In February 2008, the BBC reported that an NOP survey of 8000 teenagers, and another conducted by Newsround, found that many young people in the UK are depressed or anxious. The BBC (2008) also noted the words of Marjorie Wallace, the chief executive of SANE: 'We know that one in ten young people have a mental disorder of some kind and it is concerning that over a quarter of young people in this survey say they often feel depressed'.

Richard Garner (2008) reiterated these concerns in an article in the *Independent* where he expressed concern that young people were increasingly depressed and anxious. Stress and family breakdown in addition to academic targets and general pressures to achieve at school were cited as causes of this malaise.

WITH CHILDREN AND YOUNG PEOPLE IN MIND

These concerns are echoed by my own experiences of working with children and young people and the issue of there being a great unmet need for support, particularly when problems first begin to emerge.

How we view unhappiness in young people will determine the kind of care and support we offer. Some discussion of different explanations of unhappiness is necessary to place person–centred ways of working in context. Only then can we be clear about what is special about this way of working.

TO THE COUNSELLOR

Depending upon your work setting, you may receive referrals from a variety of professionals using different kinds of language to highlight what they consider to be reasons for referral. Sometimes person-centred counsellors prefer not to have this information prior to meeting the child or young person. Whether you choose to read a doctor's diagnosis or a school's explanation or justification for referral, it is important to remember that you are working with the young client and not another person's interpretation of a child's difficulties.

There are a number of different ways in which professionals view emotional problems in young people. Mental health professionals sometimes classify problems into categories, for example neurotic disorders such as depression, anxiety, obsessive-compulsive disorders or phobias. This perspective on happiness tends to result in a focus on 'the problem', which might be treated through drugs or a variety of forms of 'talking therapies'. In schools, young people's problems are often defined in terms of associated behaviours and are therefore responded to in this way. Young people who have been diagnosed with ADHD are often offered drugs which alter behaviour whilst their 'difficult' behaviour is managed in the classroom and playground.

Children and young people who are habitually bullied or who are lonely or isolated are sometimes withdrawn for lessons in 'social skills'. More recently, when confronted by young people who are unhappy, professionals have adopted a 'solution focused' approach where the 'problem' is seen as less important than the solution. Writers such as O'Connell (1998), Davis and Osborn (2000), Rhodes and Ajmal (1995) and Selekman (1993) have been keen to advance this approach.

Rachel Freeth (2007) suggests that the predominant view of unhappiness found in the NHS and Western societies is the 'medical model' with its emphasis on assessment, diagnosis and treatment.

WITH CHILDREN AND YOUNG PEOPLE IN MIND

Counsellors and helpers working with unhappy children and young people often report that, once work has begun, the client or helpee wants to talk and explore problems and issues, other than those identified as being of critical importance by the referrer.

Case study: Ravi

Ravi was referred to Child and Adolescent Mental Health Services (CAMHS) by his school who noted with concern behaviours which appeared to be affecting his ability to function effectively in school. A meeting with his mother (his mother and father had separated after a prolonged attempt to stabilise the marriage) highlighted a number of 'habits' which dominated his life on a daily basis. These involved an over-concern with order and neatness. Ravi's bedroom was uncharacteristically neat for a boy of his age and he seemed reluctant to sleep inside the bed through a fear of disturbing or dirtying his sheets. Everything in his room had its place and appeared to be located for show rather than actual use. Ravi's mother was also anxious about his unusual eating habits, which were very predictable and routine-like. In particular, his mother was most concerned about Ravi's preoccupation with counting and prediction. Ravi was not doing well at school and his mind seemed 'hijacked' by these thoughts and behaviours which also resulted in his isolation at school.

After a number of consultations, Ravi was diagnosed with Obsessive Compulsive Disorder (OCD) and was given a course of anti-depressants that coincided with his attendance at a series of sessions with a cognitive-behavioural therapist who focused on the way Ravi was thinking and how this affected his unwanted behaviour.

In this particular example, Ravi's unhappiness was seen as a consequence of his obsessions and ritualised behaviours. After diagnosis by a mental health professional, a course of treatment was prescribed with the intention of bringing relief to both Ravi and his mother.

In her article, Rachel Freeth (2007) carefully examines the relationship between the medical model and more therapeutic approaches. The medical model is seen as relying upon biological explanations, that is the 'disease model', which sees problems in terms of pathology, which therefore requiring 'fixing'. The medical model attempts to try to find out what has gone wrong and identify ways to treat the problem, most commonly through drug therapy. Where there are linked physiological causes, courses of psychological therapy, based upon changing irrational and distorted thinking and their consequent behaviours, are offered.

Freeth outlines a number of criticisms of such a medical approach. This way of working is seen as potentially reductionist, denying the complexities of human existence, and overly concerned with the eradication of disorders. The medical model is also subject to concerns about the nature of mental illness and whether such problems have a biological basis.

Freeth also sets out three further discussions that are particularly relevant to a book about working with children and young people in a person-centred way. The first identifies issues around power and expertise. An approach which focuses on the ability of the professional to decide on the causes of unhappiness in young people and which identifies a potential cure runs counter to the humanistic model. The person-centred approach also gives emphasis to the importance of the relationship in helping, whereas a medical approach implies a more mechanistic, predetermined and less personal approach based around procedures and methods. Finally, Freeth asks us to consider the nature and purpose of therapy. Is it only about making people feel better or is it a facilitative process concerned with growth and development?

The idea of the 'expert' identifying and naming a client's problems is seen by Mearns (1994) as in conflict with the person-centred approach, with its primary focus on the relationship between client and counsellor. Authority and control are rejected as interfering with this relationship and the focus on the client, which is seen as central to person-centred philosophy. He refers to Rogers' disapproval of diagnosis as an element in therapeutic work, which turns the therapist into an expert and therefore responsible for determining the future direction of the work. This, he suggests, should lie firmly with the client. Mearns and Thorne (1988) refer to the mistrust of experts felt by many person-centred practitioners:

> In some ways, it is fair to state that the person-centred counsellor must learn to wear her expertise as an invisible garment if she is to become an effective counsellor. Experts are expected to dispense their expertise, to recommend what should be done, to offer authoritative guidance or even to issue orders. (p. 6)

To defer to the role of expert would be to deny one of the key principles of the approach, namely that the client can be trusted to find their own way, as long as the right therapeutic conditions are offered, particularly those concerned with acceptance and non-judgementalism.

> **TO THE HELPER**
>
> Where your helping responsibility constitutes part of a more generic support role with children and young people, you may feel less pressure to be an 'expert' by both child and young person and those with parental or management expectations.

Children and young people are already labelled and 'diagnosed' by many of the adults they come into contact with. At school, they may be referred to as having 'emotional and behavioural problems' whilst mental health professionals are keen to attach a name to the unhappiness they see. Young people may be seen as abused, looked after, delinquent, disaffected or aggressive. When the young person arrives in counselling, it can take some time before the counsellor is able to work with the young person and not the problem, and identified issues may have taken precedence over what is really at the heart of the young person's unhappiness. So how does person-centred theory see unhappiness? To answer this question, we must re-visit some of the basic concepts already introduced in this book and develop them more comprehensively in order that a concept of 'disturbance' can be understood.

CONDITIONS OF WORTH RE-VISITED

Much of who we are is determined by our early experiences, particularly our relationships with our parents or key carers. No parent sets out to lay the foundations for unhappiness. Merry (1995) in his *Invitation to Person-centred Psychology* makes this point:

> Parents, when asked what they want from life for their children, often reply that, above all, they want their children to be happy. Happiness seems to be one of the most desirable things in life, but all too often, achieving it turns out to be elusive. (p. 56)

Merry describes how we entered the world without 'values or belief systems': 'We were spontaneous – when we felt hungry, we expressed it in the best way we could, and when that hunger was satisfied we were content. When we were in some other state of discomfort, we communicated it openly' (1995: 62). Merry suggests, therefore, that we were being *fully congruent*; that is, we expressed our needs and desires without editing. However, as we increasingly interact with those who are significant to us, we learn that our feelings are conditional. Merry offers us an example:

> A child is playing in the garden and falls off the swing. The child is hurt, shaken, scared and a little shocked and, inevitably, starts to cry. Mother hears the cries and

runs to respond to them, also a little afraid that the child may be badly hurt. The mother is happy to see that there is no real damage, and with a sense of relief, she tries to comfort the child. She says 'It's OK, it doesn't hurt, you're not hurt, be a big boy now, don't cry.' Whilst she does reassure and comfort the child, she scolds him for making such a fuss, 'Come on now, stop making such a noise or I'll take you indoors and take the swing away'. (1995: 62)

Merry suggests that whilst the mother did demonstrate caring, she initiated within the child a 'condition of worth', which probably takes the form of: 'It's not OK to show hurt feelings; being grown up means to choke back a spontaneous expression of feeling'.

By the time we as helpers and counsellors meet with the young people we want to help, they are already striving for acceptance. They have learned to avoid certain feelings, thoughts and behaviours, which will bring disapproval. In this way, their sense of worth, in effect their value, is determined by attempts to avoid the negative judgement of others, which lead to further loss of self-worth and even more unpleasant feelings, particularly those which they have already striven to avoid. The attempt to avoid these unpleasant experiences affects the choices the young person makes and behaviours peculiar to one situation are transferred to others.

The problem with conditions of worth which were most often developed and established in childhood, is that they often remain out of our awareness but continue to adversely affect how we relate to others and how we think and feel.

Whereas psychologists and therapists working from a psychodynamic perspective, often have a negative view on the influence of childhood on the adult, person-centred theorists and practitioners have a more optimistic view of change, believing that the self-concept can change and that we can learn to be more true to ourselves.

Tudor et al. (2004) record Rogers' view that:

No conditions of worth would develop if the infant always felt prized. Although some behaviour would have to be prohibited, for safety's sake and out of consideration for others, the attitude of valuing and the practice of acknowledging the child's feelings as well as those of the adult would result in the child feeling as if he had a genuine choice about his behaviour. (p. 102)

It is the provision of acceptance that forms one of the key components of the person-centred approach and which attempts to address these conditions of worth therapeutically, thereby facilitating change.

INCONGRUITY, DISTURBANCE AND UNHAPPINESS

The person-centred practitioner believes that the young person in front of them has the capacity within them to self-actualise. However, where there are many conditions of worth, they may be separated from their *organismic self*. Mearns and Thorne (1988) remind us of the meaning of this concept:

> The human organism, it is argued, can essentially be relied upon to provide the individual with trustworthy messages, and this is discernible in the physiological processes of the entire body and through the process of growth by which a person's potentialities and capacities are brought to realisation. Left to itself, the organismic self knows what it needs for its enhancement both from its environment and other people. (p. 8)

However, where the young person's need for approval overwhelms or takes 'precedence' over the organismic self, the result, Mearns and Thorne tell us, is 'confusion'. Where this happens, they say, the young person may develop a self-concept which is estranged from his 'organismic experiencing'.

Merry (1995) sees this division as a struggle between our two 'selves', that is, the organismic self and the conditioned self.

The self-concept may be seen as our view of ourselves. For example, a young person might see themselves as confident or shy, happy or sad. Where her behaviour matches her self-concept; that is, where what she describes herself as matches her behaviour, then we can say that the girl is behaving *congruently* with her *self-concept*. However, where she sees herself in a particular way but behaves differently, then she has reached a state of *incongruence*.

Case study: Preeti

Preeti (aged 13) had some very long talks with her youth worker Mandy, who had approached Preeti because it appeared that she was not joining in with activities, but instead, would prefer to sit outside the group, looking in. Preeti told Mandy all about her home life and how, because she had so many brothers and sisters, it was impossible to find a peaceful spot at home, never mind do her homework without interruption. The second youngest of five, Preeti told Mandy that being in a busy home had given her lots of confidence and that's why she had so many friends at school and on club nights.

In this example, Preeti describes herself as feeling confident in a crowd but in reality avoids eye contact, says very little and experiences discomfort. Therefore, we might say that there is *incongruity* between Preeti's self-concept and her observed behaviour.

Many children and young people seek our support when they are in a state of incongruence. Prochaska and Norcross (1994) elaborate on this concept of incongruence and its consequences. Incongruence is seen as the estrangement between self and experience. Due to conditions of worth, organismic experiences exist which are threatening to the self which means that the person cannot live as a 'unified whole':

> Instead, we allow ourselves to become only part of who we really are. Our inherent tendencies for full actualisation do not die, however, and we become like a house

divided against itself. Sometimes our behaviour is directed by the self we like to believe we are, and at other times behaviour can be driven by those aspects of our organism that we have tried to disown. Psychopathology reflects a divided personality, with the tensions, defences and inadequate functioning that accompany a lack of wholeness. (Prochaska and Norcross, 1994)

WITH CHILDREN AND YOUNG PEOPLE IN MIND

Where a child or young person has lived with judgement and criticism, however subtle, he is less likely to trust his organismic self and the quest for approval and liking results in a denial of self. The young person will build a repertoire of judgements, which guide his thoughts, feelings and behaviour. The child has learned how to behave, what to feel, what to say and has also built a picture of himself as being the kind of person who must always behave in a certain way, for example; he should be brave, friendly, tough or likeable. The result of this disturbance – the word not used in its common way – is commonly unhappiness.

Another related concept found within person-centred theory that relates to incongruence is that of *locus of control*. Where we are able to rely on our own internal valuing process, we are said to have an 'internal' locus of control. Where we are conditioned to rely upon the judgements of others, we are said to have an 'external' locus of control.

In *Client-centred Therapy*, Carl Rogers (1951) explores the concept of locus of control in detail:

As the therapy progresses, the client comes to realise that he is trying to live by what others think, that he is not being his real self, and he is less and less satisfied with this situation. But if he is to relinquish these introspected values, what is to take their place? There ensues a period of confusion and uncertainty as to the values, a certain sense of insecurity in having no basis for judging what is right or wrong, good or bad.

Gradually this confusion is replaced by a dawning realisation that the evidence upon which he can base a value judgement is supplied by his own senses, his own experience. Short and long term satisfactions can be recognised, not by what others say, but by examining one's own experience. The individual discovers that he has within himself the capacity for weighing the experiential evidence and deciding upon those things which make for the long-run enhancement of self. (pp. 149–50)

It is likely that where there is an internal locus of control, the young person is likely to be more resilient and consequently less likely to experience unhappy feelings, particularly those concerned with anxiety and depression, the two most important reasons why children and young people seek counselling support.

DEFENCES

All people, both children and adults, are threatened by incongruency. It is perhaps a natural reaction to want to prevent, at all costs, any feelings that might cause distress or anxiety.

Case study: Rohima

Rohima (aged 14) spends much of her time in class avoiding work of any kind. Indeed, it is not uncommon to see Rohima at her desk with her textbook and exercise book closed. Initially, when challenged, she attempts to reassure her teachers that she is about to start work as soon as she can find her pencil, which on discovery needs sharpening. Her books contain very little work and lessons are often recorded by a title and date and very little else. With so-called 'softer' teachers, she will spend time with her book up on the desk in an attempt to hide the fact that she is applying her make-up or checking her mobile phone for messages from friends. Growing frustration in her teachers is often met with accusations that the lesson is boring and that the teacher cannot teach or control the class. The reality is that Rohima's learning needs have never really been addressed and now that she is in Year 9, she has fallen so far behind that deep down she finds work impossible and believes that however hard she tries, she will achieve low levels in her SATs and that any success in her GCSEs is beyond possibility.

Rohima will use any defences to avoid feelings of failure or a poor self-regard. She blames the work for being uninteresting and her teachers for not being able to teach, and concentrates on her make-up, believing that her looks are her only asset and thus they make her feel worthy.

Biermann-Ratjen (1998) refers to this defensive process as the 'self-defending tendency'. The young people we work with will attempt to maintain some kind of consistency and compatibility between their experience and their self-concept and therefore in line with their conditions of worth. Young people may feel compelled to over-work at home and school in order to maintain the belief that they are only loveable when they achieve academic success. A child may project uncomfortable feelings and only see them in another person, for to recognise them within themselves may violate their conditions of worth. A child who has learned that the expression of anger is unacceptable may develop psychosomatic symptoms such as stomach aches or headaches rather than express feelings which will encourage disapproval. Rohima denies that she has problems with her work rather than accept the need for help, which may conflict with her view of herself as able but just more interested in other things.

Psychologists have identified a large range of 'defence mechanisms', however Rogers distilled these essentially into two types, that is, denial and perceptual distortion, or a combination of both.

Defences are a necessary part of all of us and as adults, working with young people, it is not our responsibility to challenge them. Even where we see them in operation and observe their negative and sometimes destructive effects, we understand that they are necessary for the preservation of a positive self-regard. Defences in young people sometimes have undesirable consequences affecting relationships, causing deep sadness and anxiety or other kinds of distress. This is particularly the case where events in the young person's life become so acute that defences are threatened, and appear to be unable to hold back the flow of feelings, which present a direct threat to the child's sense of worth and being. Our role as counsellors is not to interfere with the fine balance that serves to maintain self-worth, but is to facilitate the progressive integration between self and experience. Rogers believed that this would occur because of the therapeutic relationships we establish with children and young people and, most importantly, through the provision of the core conditions, discussed elsewhere and covered comprehensively later in this book.

EXERCISES

1. Share with a partner a time when you have felt really unhappy in your life.
2. Describe a happy time.
3. Are young people unhappier today than they were in the past?
4. When working with young people, what phrases or terms do you use? Do some of these suggest conditional acceptance or judgement?
5. What kinds of things cause you to feel anxious? How do these relate to the concepts of incongruence or disturbance?
6. With a partner, role-play a conversation in which one person talks about a situation in their lives with real emotional content but at the same time their body language and expressions suggest that there is a discrepancy between what they are saying and what they actually feel.

6
THE IMPORTANCE OF THE RELATIONSHIP

INTRODUCING THIS CHAPTER

The pre-eminence of the 'relationship' over technique within the person-centred approach with children and young people is explored in some detail through a number of case studies.

The voices of young people are heard as they are asked to consider the kind of relationships with adults they find most helpful.

The voluntary nature of counselling is shown to be crucial to the establishment of such relationships, whilst concepts such as 'trust' and 'love' are considered.

TO THE COUNSELLOR

Often, you will be asked to establish a therapeutic relationship with a child or young person from the first time of meeting. Sometimes, you will have to overcome a young client's perceptions of your role as being in authority or as a giver of advice and guidance. In this sense, there is often some un-doing to be achieved.

TO THE HELPER

Whether you have been working with a child or young person for some time or whether they are new to you, it is important to be clear about what you are trying to offer and ultimately achieve. There may be aspects of your role which conflict with a person-centred approach and these will need to be identified and understood if a helpful relationship is to be established and nurtured.

WHAT IS IMPORTANT TO YOUNG PEOPLE IN A HELPING RELATIONSHIP?

Young people are part of an intricate array of complex interpersonal relationships involving parents or carers, siblings, grandparents, friends, teachers and other adults. Bearing in mind that most adults have problems negotiating such relationships, it's not surprising that, as well as being supportive, for a young person, relationships can bring both joy and distress, comfort and conflict. Establishing and maintaining a relationship is a key task of the counsellor or helper working with children and young people and, as we shall see, that which is most valued by young people in any therapeutic encounter.

During the process of writing this book, I asked just under 100 young people aged between 12 and 13 years to reflect upon helping relationships. I was particularly interested in gaining some insight into the nature of helping relationships formed with an adult.

A significant number of children said that they would choose to speak with their parents, which is heartening:

> I would talk to my mum and dad because they listen to what I say.

> If I did have a problem then I would tell a member of my family because I trust them more than anyone else.

A number of young people said that they would prefer to share a problem with a friend rather than an adult:

> If I had a problem I would talk to one of my best friends because I know they would take it seriously and help me sort the problem out.

In a linked way, some students referred to an already established relationship being necessary before they would talk about difficulties in their lives:

> It would have to be a familiar face – someone you know well and not a stranger.

> I would need to know them for a while.

> Teachers you are close to and who know you properly.

It is clear from this that young people value existing relationships more than talking with an unknown adult. This observation stresses the importance of establishing a warm empathic relationship with a young person as a prerequisite of successful counselling and helping.

Confidentiality was also key to young people's assessment of a good helping relationship:

> I would have to know that the teacher will not go away and talk about it.

> I would like to talk with someone who can keep secrets.

> The conversation would have to be confidential.

> They will not say anything to anyone else.

> An adult who doesn't gossip.

In terms of marrying up young people's understanding of a good relationship, we find a concern for acceptance and an absence of judgement or criticism:

> They would have to respect me and not tell me I am wrong to do this or that.

> Somebody who would not laugh at me.

This idea of not being taken seriously was a barrier to a significant number of the young people who responded.

The idea of empathy was expressed by these children with key words such as:

- understand me
- know me
- caring
- know what I am feeling.

Congruence was implied in statements such as:

> Somebody who really wants to help me and is not just saying they do.

> I would talk to someone who doesn't lie.

As many readers might have expected, the children interviewed felt a relationship needed to include advice, guidance and practical help:

> Someone who knows what to do.

> Somebody who will be able to do something about my problem and sort it out.

> Experience is like they have dealt with this problem before and it got better.

> Someone who is good at giving advice and can make you happy again and cheer me up.

The potential discrepancy between the young person's expectations of the helping relationship and what the counsellor is able to offer is something which has to be addressed by the counsellor in supervision and through training.

Time and space were seen as crucial to a successful helping relationship:

> Someone who has time for you and a private place to talk

as was being able to trust the adult. This was felt very strongly by the young people.

Interestingly, some children used words like brave, confident and 'not shy' to describe the helper they would be prepared to share with. This implies that the relationship in some way needs to be managed and the young person 'held' during the time the adult and child spend together.

Other expectations about the helping relationship included qualities in the helper such as:

- can listen
- thoughtful
- considerate
- kind
- take my problem seriously
- calm
- helpful

- reliable
- supportive
- nice
- treats me as a grown up
- gentle
- friendly

Readers might also like to note that some of the young people interviewed felt that the counsellor had to be a happy person too!

WHY THE RELATIONSHIP IS SO CRUCIAL

Case study: Scott

Scott (aged 12) was referred to a school mentor because of his isolation in school. He rarely took part in any activities, always sat alone in class and rarely spoke. He wasn't being bullied; rather, he just went unnoticed by teachers and pupils alike. His mentor James met with him on a number of occasions but there was rarely any eye contact and certainly very little was said bar a few communications involving the nod of a head. James tried everything, asking Scott how things were in school, whether he had any friends, what subjects he liked, who he lived with at home.

James realised that he had yet to establish any real contact with Scott. At the start of their next session together, James brought out a well-known game which involved building a tower of wooden bricks and each player then taking turns to remove a brick without the tower collapsing. They played at least three games during that 45 minutes with James ensuring that Scott won two games. On each victory, Scott laughed as James caused the bricks to come crashing down. James felt guilty, feeling a little bit of a fraud; his role was to integrate Scott with other pupils but here he was only playing a game.

Case study: Leon

Leon (aged 16) was quite a handful at the youth centre, often showing aggression towards other teenagers. Where he was not invited to participate, he would set out to cause disruption, thus ensuring that others could not have fun either. Emma was tasked with talking with him and finding out why he was so angry. She took him into an office and spoke to Leon who sat slumped in his chair with his jacket drawn across his mouth so that anything he did say would be unintelligible anyway.

(Continued)

(Continued)

It was quite a pleasant evening and Emma asked Leon if he would walk with her around the playing fields, which were situated between the centre and nearby school. Leon asked to take a ball and as they walked, the youth worker and young person kicked the ball to each other. They spent a number of evenings like this until Leon began to talk about home, school and the relationships which were making him so upset.

In these two case examples, both the mentor and youth worker had established quite early on that no helping can happen where a relationship did not exist. Both Scott and Leon based their way of relating on previous relationships, which had caused them to feel inadequate and unhappy. How could James or Emma expect the two boys to behave in any different way? Both workers decided to move away from the problem and to concentrate on the relationship.

Often, adult and child come together for the first time as counsellor and client and it is not therefore surprising that sometimes things do not go well. There may already be a host of 'barriers' to the relationship based on difference. Such differences may take the form of gender, ethnicity, age, perceived role and expectations. It is also important to recognise the difference in size and height, which can be daunting for a younger child. It is not hard to see how a middle-class, middle-aged counsellor would need to work especially hard to establish a relationship with, say, a small girl aged 10 from a poorer part of the city. It is important also not to underestimate the importance of power differences in any therapeutic relationship with a young person.

Clearly, establishing a relationship with a young person in need is a central prerequisite of any kind of helping alliance.

Carl Rogers himself reflected a great deal on the nature of the therapeutic relationship and its centrality.

In a seminal article published in 1957, he set out his understanding of the relationship between therapist and client and the idea that the relationship is what really matters. The 'conditions for therapeutic change' permeate all his major and subsequent works. Person-centred therapy, he argues, is less about the skilful therapist doing things 'to' a client and more about the quality of the relationship and the psychological climate that can be established where the therapist offers warmth, acceptance, openness and understanding.

Wilkins (1999) draws attention to Wood's (1996) analysis of the person-centred approach. Wood writes:

The person-centred approach is not a psychology, psychotherapy, a philosophy, a school, a movement nor many other things frequently imagined. It is merely what the name suggests, an 'approach'. It is a psychological posture, a way of being, from which one confronts a situation. (1996: 161)

Wood therefore argues that the person–centred approach is a way of being within a relationship. Wilkins also notes Mearns' (1996) observation that in his early work, Rogers himself referred to what later became known as client-centred therapy as 'relationship therapy'.

Recalling his time as a student, Khan (1997: 1–2) recalls how his teacher gave so much emphasis to the importance of the relationship in therapy. Khan asked why so much attention should be paid to the relationship, to which his tutor responded: 'Because the relationship *is* the therapy'.

Khan struggled to make sense of this because of his analytical training: 'I was at the time deeply immersed in learning about analytic insights and how they are discovered and revealed to the client. I thought **that** *was* the therapy, and told him so.' Khan goes on to explain his 'conversion' recognising that his teacher was 'ahead of his time'.

The existential psychotherapist Irving Yalom who has worked with both individuals and groups has also emphasised the importance of the relationship over other curative factors in therapy. In his book *Existential Psychotherapy* (1980), he noted that: 'It is the relationship that heals – it is the single most important lesson the therapist must learn'.

In the summary to his best-selling work, *The Gift of Therapy* (2001), Yalom suggests that existential therapy is comprised of two elements, namely process and content. 'Content' is seen as what is actually spoken about in he session, whereas 'process' refers to the interpersonal relationship between the counsellor and client. He states:

> If my therapy sessions were observed, one might often look in vain for lengthy explicit discussions of death, freedom, meaning, or existential isolation. Such existential *content* may be only salient for some patients (but not all patients) at some stages (but not all stages) of therapy. In fact, the effective therapist should never try to force discussion of any content area: *therapy should not be theory-driven but relationship driven.* (Yalom, 2001: 5–6)

There has been a great deal of discussion over what makes therapy successful. Researchers at the Institute of Therapeutic Change in Chicago (1999) found that next to changing social and environmental circumstances, unrelated to therapy, the client–counsellor relationship is the largest contributor to change in clients, whereas clinical methodology, that is adherence to a specific theory or technique, accounts for only 15% of change.

Gina Langridge (2007) also questions the pre-eminence of one kind of therapy over another; she writes:

> There are a number of factors involved in counselling that stay the same across different orientations: one person seeking help from another, the boundaries of time and space, the fact of talking to a stranger, confidentiality, the chance to explore one's problems or one's life in general. It would make sense that it is one or more of these that is effective in therapy, since no one theory is shown to be the only effective one. (Internet resource)

Greg Mulhauser (2006) supports this position; in his review of the work of Hubble, Duncan and Miller. He states: 'For over four decades, the message from psychotherapy outcome research has been getting louder and clearer: the theories and techniques of professional therapy have very little to do with therapeutic success' (Internet resource). Emphasising the importance of the counselling relationship in therapy, he goes on to say:

> Their review of the research on the therapeutic relationship – perhaps the most frequently studied of the common factors – highlights the fact that it is not enough to focus on the therapist-provided contributions to the relationship (such as the 'necessary and sufficient' core conditions of the person-centred approach), but that attention should be paid to the *relationship itself*. No one questions the importance of core conditions like acceptance, accurate empathy and therapist genuineness; but it turns out that client perceptions of the relationship are consistently more correlated with outcome than those of objective raters. In other words, how clients experience the characteristics offered by therapists is more important than what those therapists are 'objectively' offering. (Internet resource)

There is no contradiction here in equating the person-centred approach with the core conditions. Also, in stating that no one therapeutic approach is necessarily dominant in terms of effectiveness, I am not reducing the value of the person-centred approach which I believe is the best way to connect with children and young people. It is also argued by Rogers and others that working with a child or young person is essentially about working *with* the child, and as Khan (1997) states:

> finding a category into which the client may be fitted adds nothing to the therapist's effectiveness. It doesn't make any difference whether you think your client is borderline or narcissistic or schizophrenic or mildly depressed. If you can be genuine, if you can communicate you are managing to grasp your clients' experiences, and if you can let them know of your unshakable regard for their worth as human beings – if you can do all that to a significant degree, then your clients will grow and change, whatever label is applied to them. (p. 49)

COUNSELLING IS A VOLUNTARY ACTIVITY

Young people are often 'sent' for counselling, often by parents or other adults who have a genuine concern for the child's well-being or because they are unable to cope with the young person's behaviour.

Sometimes the child, for whatever reason (and there could be many), may not want help or even see themselves as having a problem which needs help. For a real and lasting relationship to develop between a counsellor and child, there should be no coercion or pressure. This does not of course mean that when an adult feels that a child needs help, they should not be offered such support: rather, that the young person should feel they would benefit from working with a caring adult and that they also understand that their attendance is entirely voluntary.

Case study: John

John (aged 13) had been referred to a counselling agency by his mother who was concerned by his angry outbursts. Despite this being a person-centred agency, John's mother insisted that his anger was a direct consequence of his diagnosed ADHD.

John arrived at his first session and stated quite clearly that he felt that he did not have a problem but attending sessions was going to be far easier than falling out further with his mother.

Despite her person-centred training, his counsellor Salma felt a great deal of pressure to 'deliver' on the referral and found herself uncharacteristically working in ways she felt uncomfortable with. This took the form of identifying targets, albeit informal ones, and offering John suggestions as to what he might do when confronted with someone in a situation which caused him to lose his temper.

Salma took her different way of working to supervision. After this, she concluded that counselling should not be 'forced'. It should be voluntary and should not involve coercion or be designed to gain approval from another person.

At the start of the next session, Salma emphasised to John that attending counselling sessions was voluntary and really his choice. John was clearly taken aback and took Salma at her word and failed to attend the next scheduled session. The following week, he arrived and told Salma that he had thought about what she had said and now did want to come and work with her and that he had many things on his mind.

It appeared that when John knew he didn't have to attend for 'anger management', he chose to come himself under his own volition and with his autonomy and dignity intact. Salma knew that this therapeutic relationship was well on the way to becoming one based on trust and mutual understanding.

TRUST

Without doubt, a key component of a therapeutic relationship between an adult and young person is trust. Without it, time spent in a helping relationship becomes false and determined by role. Trust was identified by many of the young people who responded to the survey which opened this chapter.

Feltham and Dryden (1993: 200) define trust as: 'Confidence in another; willingness to be intimate and vulnerable with another. Trust is shown in relying on another, and believing that one will come to no harm from the other in doing so'.

Where a relationship has been established, trust is a belief by the two people involved that they can rely upon and understand each other. To understand the meaning of trust, it is sometimes useful to reflect on those people whom we never learned to trust or where trust was broken. If we do not feel safe or do not have confidence in the other person, we are less motivated to form a relationship with that person. If anything, we seek to avoid such people who we feel would misuse information about us or take advantage of our vulnerability. The converse is of course true: where we trust someone, we are more likely to want to share with them in open ways, sometimes risking our most sensitive secrets and feelings.

Young people growing up often learn difficult lessons about trust, sometimes sharing with a best friend, only later to fall out and find that their most intimate thoughts and feelings have become available to all. Psychologists have suggested that a trusting personality is established in childhood and in relation to our parents or caregivers. Where parenting is chaotic, critical and unsafe, young children are likely to develop the kinds of fears that may prevent them from trusting adults in the future. A trusting child has probably already experienced trust with important adults in their lives.

Sometimes children and young people trust easily, others are more guarded, especially where trust has been broken, as, for example, where a child has been abused or let down by significant people in their lives. The counsellor may have to work hard to build trust and this can take time. Young people in the survey noted above described reliability and being non-judgemental as important in any relationship with an adult and/or counsellor figure. Realness and empathic listening will establish trust over time. Sometimes the adult needs to be aware of the young person's previous encounters with others and offer the time and space and patience to allow trust to develop.

Counselling with young people often goes through a phase where the child needs to test out that trust. It may be that this happens many times during the relationship as the young person returns to the fundamental question: can I really trust this person?

LOVE AND THERAPY

At first sight, the reader might be a little concerned about the concept of love within a counselling relationship with a child or young person. Rogers (1967) felt that his approach to counselling was a therapy based upon 'love'. He wrote:

> One hypothesis is that the client moves from the experiencing of himself as an untrustworthy, unacceptable, and unlovable person to the realisation that he is accepted, respected, and loved, in his limited relationship with the therapist. 'Loved' has here its deepest and most general meaning – that of being deeply understood and deeply accepted. (1967: 159)

Khan helps us to understand what Rogers was saying:

> By 'love', Rogers meant what the Greeks called 'agape'. Greek philosophy distinguished between two kinds of love, eros and agape. Eros is characterised by the desire for something that will fulfil the lover. It includes the wish to possess the

beloved object or person. Agape, by contrast, is characterised by the desire to fulfil the beloved. It demands nothing in return and wants only the growth and fulfilment of the loved one. Agape is a strengthening love, a love that, by definition, does not burden or obligate the loved one. (Khan, 1997: 39)

In a sense, Khan has summarised key aspects of the person-centred approach. The theme of 'loving' has also been taken up by Mearns and Thorne (1988). They suggest that the person-centred approach involves the counsellor: 'Freeing their "loving" selves, with the first stage of being that of helping them to be able to "love" themselves, to achieve the self-acceptance which they hope to facilitate in their clients' (p. 19).

The child or young person we are working with has a deep need to be loved. For some children, this comes in abundance from parents and other adults in the child's life. For others, whose worth has been conditional, criticised or where love has been withheld, the counsellor can do much to create the kind of love which is growthful and facilitating, enabling the young person to believe in their value and do what they need to bring about change in their lives.

EXERCISES

1. Talk to another person about a close friendship you have had. How would this have been experienced by other people looking on? What would they have seen?

2. Think about your own work context. Are young people coerced into being helped? Are they given the right to choose for themselves? Has anybody ever insisted on giving you support when you really didn't want to be helped?

3. Share with a partner a relationship based upon trust. What made the other person trust you and what made them trustworthy? Can you think of a time when trust within a relationship has been broken? What were your feelings at the time? What about now?

PRACTICE

7
WORKING WITH FEELINGS AND EMOTIONS

INTRODUCING THIS CHAPTER

Feelings and emotions are what makes us human. We begin this chapter with an attempt to define and differentiate between the two. We will then go on to look at feelings and emotion in children and young people; at how they recognise and express what is happening deep inside them. Finally, we return to the role of the counsellor and helper, exploring ways in which it is possible to reflect children and feelings more accurately.

TO THE COUNSELLOR

The client's story and struggles will be infused with emotion and feeling. These represent the window through which we see into the child or young person's life, as they see it. Recognising and understanding what a child or young person is experiencing emotionally is essential for the counsellor trying hard to offer the core conditions of unconditional positive regard, congruence and empathy.

TO THE HELPER

There is always the temptation to want the child or young person we are working with to feel better. This can sometimes lead to our not accepting feelings and subtly trying to sway children away from unpleasant sensations. This may have more to do with ourselves than with the young person we are working with.

ELUSIVE DEFINITIONS

Before we continue with this chapter, some definitions are necessary. Defining emotion and its relationship to feeling is not an easy task. According to Reber and Reber (2001): 'Historically, this term has proven utterly refractory to definitional efforts: probably no other term in psychology shares its combination of non-definability and frequency of use' (p. 236).

Feltham and Dryden (1993) note that the two terms have been used synonymously, although they offer a distinction suggesting that feelings are experienced whilst emotions are exhibited.

Bayne et al. (1994) refer to the attempt by Nichols and Jenkinson (1991) to distinguish between the two words. Feelings are seen as being more complicated than emotions. Feeling is described as: 'the current physiological and psychological stance of the person and the general "atmosphere" of your body' (Bayne et al., 1994: 64–5).

Of course, etymology is a useful companion here. The word 'emotion' originates in the Latin word *emovere*, which means 'to move' or 'excite'. For some, feeling is seen as the subjective experience of the emotion.

It may be that the pursuit of definitions is an academic venture and of little concern to the adult helper or counsellor. What is clear is that there is a massive literature out there and it is unlikely that many disciplines of human knowledge do not in some way touch upon these two related concepts. What is also apparent is that humanistic and person-centred approaches focus more on a feelings dimension than do other approaches such as the cognitive-behavioural therapies. It is also important to note that working with children's feelings and emotions is a key issue in counselling, and hopefully this chapter will at least begin to explore some of the issues.

In attempting to define emotion and feeling, it is perhaps important to describe what these two words do not mean. David Geldard (1998) wants us to distinguish between thoughts and feelings; he writes:

> Feelings are quite different from thoughts. Thoughts mill about in our brains. They are at a 'head' level, whereas feelings are to do with emotions. Feelings are at a gut level, not a head level and they tie into our physiological sensations. (p. 73)

In attempting to understand feeling and emotion, Rogers in *Carl Rogers on Personal Power* (1978) writes: 'Inevitably, in a person-centred situation, there is increasing recognition of the importance of feelings, as well as reason, of emotions as well as intellect'. Rogers goes on to say that: 'A feeling is an emotionally tinged experience together with its personal meaning. Thus it includes the emotion but also the cognitive content of the meaning of that emotion in its experiential context' (pp. 49–50).

Rogers also wants us to work with the whole person. Reason, thinking and rationality are an attempt to separate or divorce the complete experience of being human. He concludes: 'The divorce of reason from feeling is one of the first myths to disappear in a person-centred approach. Individuals find themselves communicating with their whole beings, expressing their experiences, not some desiccated intellectual representation of them' (p. 50).

In his book *A Way of Being* (1980), Rogers continued to explore this theme:

> Most of us spent twenty or more years in educational institutions where the intellect was all. Anything that counted, anything of any importance, occurred above the neck – in absorbing and memorizing, in thought and expression. Yet in life, in therapy, in marriage, in parent–child and other intimate relationships, in encounter groups, in university faculty meetings, we were forced to learn that feelings were an equally important part of living. But, due largely to our education, we still tend to dichotomize these two aspects. (pp. 248–9)

Rogers' words still have relevance today, as schools continue to focus on the achievement of academic and intellectual goals and interventions which largely take the form of changing behaviour or thinking. This point is made by Tudor et al. (2004): 'Many of the structures of schools militate against intimacy, and emotional literacy, which is arguably more important than the 3R's, and is not even on the curriculum' (p. 180).

WITH CHILDREN AND YOUNG PEOPLE IN MIND

There have been some developments here as more recently schools have been asked to focus more on emotional development and well-being. At the time of writing, many more schools are becoming 'Healthy Schools', where to achieve this status some emphasis needs to be given to emotional health, whilst the Government's SEAL initiative (Social and Emotional Aspects of Learning) is beginning to influence primary and secondary schools throughout the country.

CHILDREN AND THE EXPRESSION OF EMOTION AND FEELINGS

It is an accepted belief that it is better for children and young people to express their feelings than hold them inside. When we stop and consider what we are actually asking young people to do, it is not surprising that they, like adults, will attempt to avoid those feelings which cause them anxiety or stress, or make them feel sad or despairing. In counselling, we often talk about the intellectualisation of feelings. That is, we talk about feelings without actually feeling, without experiencing any emotion. If young people are helped with the expression of feeling, they are more likely to be able to deal with the problems and choices they face in their lives. Suppression of feeling means that they continue to influence their relationships in often destructive ways.

These sentiments can be found in Rogers (1980):

> I have learned that in any significant or continuing relationship, persistent feelings had best be expressed. If they are expressed as feelings, owned by me, the result may be temporarily upsetting but ultimately far more rewarding than any attempt to deny or conceal them. (p. 44)

In trying to understand why children and young people find experiencing and expressing emotions difficult, we can draw from Rogers' (1967) own observations:

> In our daily lives there are a thousand and one reasons for not letting ourselves experience our attitudes fully, reasons from our past and from the present, reasons that reside within the social situation. It seems too dangerous, too potentially damaging, to experience them freely and fully. (p. 111)

A writer who has contributed much to our understanding of why young people find it difficult to feel and express emotions in therapy is Martha Straus (1999), who writes:

> Therapists often place high value on helping children identify their feelings and describe them with words – an emphasis derived directly from the treatment of adults. The capacity to attend to, understand, and talk about emotions is, of course, the essential focus of adult psychotherapy. In adult treatment, successful outcomes appear to be linked to this ability to focus on and understand emotional experience. But for kids, such skills may develop slowly, if at all. This fact alone is sufficient to distinguish child from adult therapy. (p. 17)

She argues that emotional development in children and young people follows an identifiable timeline. The first task is to be able to recognise and identify feelings. This, she argues, is directly connected to the development of an appropriate vocabulary and the more sophisticated use of feeling words. Straus also sees a problem for young people in the expression of feelings, that is, putting them into words. This developmental situation is further exacerbated by life experience:

> But their emotional experience is even more complicated because these kids typically have endured hard times that produce many concurrent and conflicting feelings. Abused kids provide a clear example of this; they may feel love, fear, rage and sadness, among other potent emotions – often all at once. (Straus, 1999: 18)

Straus also sees the link between emotional expression and development. She provides us with a number of examples, noting how very young children deny or distance themselves from feelings of sadness and often present a happy picture of their lives. She says that children often project negative feelings onto others, while denying their own:

> Even kids under seven can explain why a puppet is crying and think about what might make it feel better. If they have sufficient language skills, they will also be

able to figure out a response to a speculative question like, how will the puppet feel if –? Thus, a child's expression of feelings may be greater when her own pain or confusion isn't the central concern. (1999: 19)

A FEELINGS VOCABULARY

WITH CHILDREN AND YOUNG PEOPLE IN MIND

Younger children will have fewer words to describe how they are feeling. They may not even be aware of what is going on and are more likely to express themselves through behaviours. Some of these cause concern in the adults around them.

As stated earlier, person-centred counselling gives a greater emphasis to 'feelings' than a number of other approaches. Person-centred therapy was developed with adults in mind so it makes use of language, the main medium being words. It is also generally accepted that a client will communicate feelings without the use of words by the way they sit and the expression on their faces. The person-centred therapist is trained to look beyond the words to find hidden or additional meanings. Sometimes there is some discrepancy between what the person is saying and what is seen by the therapist. For example, a client may be saying that they are not angry with their partner who rarely helps with childcare when their voice and demeanour suggests otherwise. This point is made by Tolan (2003):

> When you simply repeat what the client has said, you are staying on the surface of what he has communicated. It is important to listen to (or note, if you are a deaf counsellor) his tone, his hesitations and garrulousness. If you are sighted and working face-to-face, you will have additional information from his facial expressions and posture. All of this conveys meaning beyond the surface meaning of the words alone. (pp. 23–4)

When sitting with a young person in a helping capacity, we find that some children and young people express themselves well and draw upon a wide range of feeling words to express how they feel. Others find it hard and simply don't have the means to understand what they are feeling, never mind the vocabulary to put these emotions into words. Emotional literacy seeks to help young people understand their own and other people's feelings and be able to express them clearly. Counsellors working with young people may not formally teach feeling words, but through their reflection of feelings, they help the young person by offering them words that seem to capture how they feel. In this way, the young client increases their capacity to talk about their inner world.

When young people cannot find the words to express how they feel, they either become frustrated or deny that they are feeling anything at all. Boys often find it harder to get in touch with their feelings or say what they feel. This issue has been explored by Kindlan and Thompson whose book, *Raising Cain* (2000), was concerned with the 'emotional miseducation' of boys and found that, emotionally, boys and girls are encouraged to develop in different ways.

Children and young people often use only a limited vocabulary. When asked what they feel, they will often use words like 'sad' or 'unhappy'. Sometimes, these words do not give expression to the degree to which a child has feeling. For example, a child my say they are sad when they are, in fact, despairing.

Of course, when working with young people, it is important to work within the child's frame of reference and the more sophisticated use of language is designed only to more accurately reflect what the child is feeling at that moment in time. Merry (1995) records how Carl Rogers saw reflection of feeling:

> I am trying to determine whether my understanding of the client's inner world is correct – whether I am seeing it as he or she is experiencing it at this moment. Each response of mine contains the unspoken question, 'is this the way it is for you? Am I catching just the colour and texture and flavour of the personal meaning you are experiencing right now? If not, I wish to bring my perception in line with yours'. (Rogers, 1986: 125–40)

EXERCISE

All words used to describe emotion or feeling have a degree or strength to them. For example, furious is a much stronger word than 'annoyed', which is also stronger than 'irritated'. Take a number of key emotions such as anger, sadness or fear, and firstly see how many words you can find that have a similar meaning. Can you then put them into some kind of order of degree of feeling?

The person-centred counsellor or helper is more likely to capture what a young person is feeling if they too have a developed vocabulary. There are literally thousands of 'feelings words' in the English language and the reader may find the list in the Appendix of this book useful.

EXERCISES

1. Look at the list of feeling words in the Appendix. How rich is your own language? Which words do you use most often?
2. On one day, try to be more aware of what you are feeling. Think of more accurate ways of expressing what you feel.

EMOTION-FOCUSED THERAPY

A humanistic way of working originating from the ideas of Carl Rogers is worth introducing at this point. Person-centred approaches place much importance on feelings and emotions. Emotion-focused therapy (EFT) regards emotions as the source of healing and encourages their exploration rather than their avoidance. The client is encouraged to resolve unpleasant emotions by not opposing but working *with* them. In this sense, unpleasant emotions are seen as the source of information, insight and understanding rather than things which need to be suppressed. Emotions are seen as partners in therapeutic change and through the experiencing and expression of emotion, they are made more comprehensible to the client. Further information about the rationale and processes behind EFT can be found in Rice et al. (1996) and Greenberg and Paivio (2003).

REFLECTION OF FEELING

The word 'reflection' in general usage implies the use of a mirror-like object, which throws back an image. In counselling, it has a specific meaning. It means giving back to the client his or her own material in a way which is accurate and faithful to what has originally been communicated. The aim is to offer the client a mirror image which they can recognise and which conveys personal meaning.

A distinction needs to be made here between the reflection of 'content' and the reflection of 'feelings'. The former is concerned with giving back to the client what has been said, whereas reflecting feelings is a skill that requires empathy and allows the counsellor to offer back to the client feelings which have been discerned in the client's words as well as behaviour.

Nelson-Jones (1993) describes reflection of feeling in the following expressive way: 'Reflecting feelings may be viewed as "feeling with" another's flow of emotions and experiencing and being able to communicate this back to the speaker' (p. 101). Nelson-Jones is quick to make a distinction between somebody talking 'about' feelings without offering what he refers to as 'an expressive emotional companionship'. He writes: 'Reflecting feelings can be seen as responding to your clients' music rather than just to their words' (p. 101).

It is important to be aware of the difference between thoughts and feelings. A young person may say: 'I feel that my only option is to leave home and get a job'. Here the client is expressing a thought rather than a feeling. Whereas a child who says, 'I get no freedom at home and just want to get away from my parents. I feel trapped and without any hope that things will get any better', is more likely to be expressing a range of feelings, especially where sadness, fear or other emotions can be detected in their eyes, hands and body.

As mentioned above, the reflection of feelings comes with empathy. It is not the same as offering pity or sympathy, which achieves little. Often, unhappy young people share their concerns with friends and relatives who are sympathetic and often encouraging and reassuring. This is not to suggest that in life we should avoid being sympathetic to other people in our lives; all of us need a little sympathy at times! However, as counsellors or adults working within the person-centred approach, reflection through empathic understanding is important because it involves viewing the world from the young person's frame of reference.

Reflection of feelings allows the young person to continue with their flow. In this sense, it facilitates communication rather than hindering it. In addition, young people are less likely to be defensive or protected when they are being offered back that which is their own. Reflection of feeling suggests no assessment and is non-judgemental.

WITH CHILDREN AND YOUNG PEOPLE IN MIND

Children and young people, like some adults, are sometimes able to tell their story with clarity, but without feeling very much. Often, their concerns, perspectives and even feelings have been rehearsed or have become ingrained, almost as though they were talking about another person. Reflection of feeling makes counselling a different kind of relationship and encourages the young person to consider their lives from a deeper perspective.

Nelson-Jones (1993) offers us advice on how we can become more skilled in reflecting feelings back to our young clients. We need to become more proficient in the following:

- observing face and body movements
- hearing vocal communication
- listening to words
- allowing the client the space to listen to their own experiencing
- tuning in to the flow of your emotional reactions
- sensing the meanings of your client's messages
- taking into account the client's degree of self-awareness
- responding in a way that focuses on feelings
- checking out the accuracy of your understanding. (pp. 101–2)

Perhaps the best way to explain reflection of feeling, is by way of a number of examples.

Oliver:	I know a lot of people at university keep their boyfriends and everything works out fine but I know that there are male students who are looking for girls. If she goes, I could lose her forever.
Counsellor:	You feel anxious about losing your girlfriend and terrified that the relationship might end.

Wasif:	Every day I get bullied at school. I tell the teachers but they blame me for stirring things up. They should do something about it.
Mentor:	You are fed up with being picked on at school and angry with your teachers for not acting and even placing the blame on you.
Dionne:	I know that if I tell you about what is happening at home, people will come and take me away and I'll end up with foster parents away from all my friends.
Social worker:	You're frightened about what will happen.

Of course, these examples are one-dimensional because we cannot see the young people's non-verbal cues, which convey so much of the meaning. When face-to-face with a child or young person, it is easier because we can draw upon our all of our senses. This enables us to become more attuned to what the young person is feeling. In all of the above examples, a different tone of voice or facial expression might convey a very different meaning to what is actually being said. Oliver may convey anger, Wasif, desperation and fear and Dionne may be testing out her social worker to see what might happen and may be feeling hopeful that, with some reassurance, she can tell without being put into care.

Before the close of this chapter, I would also like to make a final point. This applies to adults as well, but is particularly relevant to working with young people. Here, I am referring to the counsellor or helper being themselves and not a machine. By this, I mean that the reader should avoid a range of stereotyped responses such as 'what I'm sensing is' or 'I get the feeling that'. It is easy for young people to feel patronised or inferior, neither of which is conducive to a good therapeutic relationship.

EXERCISES

1. Choose a number of key emotions such as fear, happiness, sadness or anger and make a list of non-verbal information that might come with these feelings. For example, what may be seen in a young person's eyes or the way they hold themselves, what might their voice sound like, what is expressed through their face and so on?

2. In your work with young people or colleagues, listen to what is being said in conversation but also attune yourself to the feelings behind the words.

3. When working with a young person, try to be aware of your emotional reaction to what is being said.

4. What are you actually feeling here and now?

8
UNCONDITIONAL POSITIVE REGARD

INTRODUCING THIS CHAPTER

In the following three chapters, we will explore in further detail the 'core conditions' which Carl Rogers argued were necessary for therapeutic change and growth. We begin here with the concept of 'unconditional positive regard'.

This chapter starts with an attempt to capture the meaning of UPR and goes on to explore these ideas with regard to 'non-directivity'. That is, where the young person relies on their own 'organismic valuing process' and where the counsellor or helper is non-interventionist and largely reflective. A number of case studies help to explore the concept and its practice in relation to work specifically with children and young people.

Case study: Robert

In his fourth session with his counsellor, Robert, aged 16, described in some detail his home situation. He lived at home with his mother and his two sisters Anna and Lizzie who were 12 and 14 respectively. He said that he resented having to live in a house 'full of girls' and complained that he couldn't watch his programmes without having to get 'nasty' with them.

Attending college, he felt that it was not his responsibility to keep the house clean, especially because college work was more taxing than just GCSE courses. He said that he was prepared to cook, but mainly for himself, saying that mum could prepare meals for herself and the girls.

Robert held his mother responsible for dad 'walking out', accepting that his father had no option but to find another woman because of mum's nagging. For this reason, Robert was often unkind to his mother, sometimes even blaming her

(Continued)

(Continued)

for the break-up directly to her face. He regarded Anna and Lizzie as on mum's side and consequently saw this as a betrayal of dad and somehow contributing to the separation.

Robert said that he regarded his mates as more like his family than his mother and sisters and as soon as he could get a flat, he would leave home and live as he always wanted to. He said that being at home was 'rubbish'.

In the next session, Robert talked at some length about his girlfriend Kate whom he had met at college. He admitted flirting with other girls and sometimes kissing them, but only for fun. He didn't see a problem with this because 'that's what guys do'. However, he was quite categorical that Kate should not play around with other boys, otherwise she would get a reputation and he would have to 'dump' her.

Case study: Trudy

Trudy (aged 14) was always getting into trouble at school. Often falling out with friends, she was not averse to fighting those girls who had been her friend the day before. Trudy regarded herself as 'tough', and probably the girl that most other girls in the school feared. She had many 'friends' but her mentor felt that these girls stayed with her because it made them feel 'hard', and whilst with Trudy they felt protected.

Trudy described her fights with other girls with some sense of her own physical superiority and she appeared to have little compassion for the girls that she hurt.

Trudy could also be unpleasant to teachers, seeking out those whom she considered 'weak'. Those teachers who were less patient with her, were often singled out for 'revenge', and she boasted that if she wanted, she could destroy a lesson or even make a teacher cry. She was confident that she was the main reason why Mrs Arnold was off with depression. Trudy said that 'if she can't control the kids, she ought to do something else'.

EXERCISE

1. What were you feeling as you read these two case studies? What was happening for you?
2. What would it be like for you to work with Robert and Trudy?

I have to admit that when remembering and recording here these two clients, I experienced a range of feelings, many of which were not too positive. Words like selfishness, sexist, blaming, insensitive and lazy came to mind with Robert, whilst Trudy made me want to step away from her selfishness, cruelty and lack of concern or empathy for others. As counsellors and professionals working within the person-centred approach, we are encouraged to work without judgement. What does this mean and what would working with unconditional positive regard look like? Is this always possible?

TO THE COUNSELLOR

Acceptance of a young client lies exclusively with you and therefore there should be few restrictions on your ability to be entirely non-judgemental with your young client. However, where you are working in an organisational setting, the expectations of others will remain a factor. Colleagues who are not aware of the approach of the counsellor, may well see acceptance of certain behaviours in children and young people as collusion or not in the young client's best interests.

TO THE HELPFER

If you are working within a statutory organisation such as a school, there may be some pressure upon you to offer some moral or behavioural guidance to a young person. Indeed, this may already have been identified as a key aspect of your role. Your freedom to offer acceptance without conditions therefore needs to be explained to and negotiated with your line manager or senior professionals within the organisation.

WITH CHILDREN AND YOUNG PEOPLE IN MIND

Your ability to offer complete unconditional positive regard may be directly related to the age of the child and, as an adult, you may need to intervene where there are concerns about a younger child's safety or well-being.

WHAT IS UNCONDITIONAL POSITIVE REGARD?

In *Person to Person: The Problem of Being Human,* Rogers sets out his understanding of the concept:

I advance tentatively the hypothesis that the relationship will be more effective the more the positive regard is unconditional. By this, I mean that the counsellor prizes the client in a total, rather than conditional way. He does not accept certain feelings in the client and disapprove of others. He feels an unconditional positive regard for this person. This is an outgoing, positive feeling without reservations and without evaluations. It means not making judgements. I believe that when non-evaluative prizing is present in the encounter between the counsellor and his client, constructive change and development in the client is more likely to occur. (Rogers and Stevens, 1967: 94–5)

Further insight into Rogers' thinking can be found in *On Becoming a Person: A Therapist's View of Psychotherapy* (1967). He elaborates:

It involves an acceptance of and a caring for the client as a 'separate' person, with permission for him to have his own feelings and experiences, and to find his own meanings in them. To the degree that the therapist can provide this safety-creating climate of unconditional positive regard, significant learning is likely to take place. (pp. 283–4)

WITH CHILDREN AND YOUNG PEOPLE IN MIND

As adults working with young people, offering the kind of relationship here described by Rogers, is no easy task. We are used to advising our own children and sometimes even telling them off 'for their own good'. We bring to our relationships our own upbringing and values which may become more conservative with age. Our attitudes to childhood and adolescence are influenced by media images and contemporary concerns around the behaviour of young people. Being judgemental, one could argue, comes naturally and certainly more easily than offering the kind of attitudes and communications suggested by Rogers.

Mearns and Thorne (1988) describe unconditional positive regard as an 'attitude' of the counsellor. They offer with some clarity the following description:

Unconditional positive regard is the label given to the fundamental attitude of the person-centred counsellor towards her client. The counsellor who holds this attitude deeply values the humanity of her client and is not deflected in that valuing by any particular client behaviours. The attitude manifests itself in the counsellor's acceptance of and enduring warmth toward her client. (1988: 59)

Mearns and Thorne highlight the importance of 'consistency' in this attitude. We may find it easier to value the young person who appreciates the help we are offering and behaves in ways which we personally find more moral and acceptable. It may be more difficult, they suggest, to value a client who: 'is repeatedly self-defeating, sees himself as worthless, actively manipulates other people to their detriment, or masks his vulnerability with direct aggression towards the helper' (1988: 59).

WITH CHILDREN AND YOUNG PEOPLE IN MIND

If we are working from a person-centred perspective, we are still able to work as effectively with each individual child or young person who seeks our help as those following other approaches. It is also clear that as well as this attitude of unconditional positive regard existing equally between the young people we meet, it is important for this consistency to be apparent 'within' a therapeutic relationship. We cannot be selective as to what we approve or disapprove of and sometimes, therefore, we will be severely tested.

EXERCISE

What sort of attitudes, beliefs and behaviours in children and young people might you find difficult? Consider and discuss the following with a partner:

- a 14-year-old boy who admits he gets a 'kick' out of bullying others
- a young male client who feels that counselling is for girls only
- a client who says that you are not good at your job because 'nothing has changed'
- a boy who says that being gay goes against nature
- a girl who enjoys going up to town on a Friday night, getting drunk and having a fight
- a 13-year-old client who swears profusely when ordinary words will do
- an 8-year-old girl who doesn't want to sit next to a partially sighted boy in class
- a 13-year-old boy who says that there is no point in going to school because it's boring
- an 18-year-old young man who says that since his girlfriend left he just wants to kill himself
- a 16-year-old girl who says she wants to leave home and have a baby with her boyfriend.

WHY UNCONDITIONAL POSITIVE REGARD IS THERAPEUTIC

Bozarth and Wilkins (2001) stress the importance of the need for positive regard in human beings. Everybody has an innate desire to be valued, accepted and loved. So much so, that when these are missing from a person's life psychologically, they will do all they can to maintain their self-concept. We have already seen how a gap between the perceived self and actual experience can lead to a stage of incongruence. According to Bozarth and Wilkins:

> Client incongruence is necessary ... for constructive personality change to occur, indeed person-centred therapy is about increasing (or bringing about) harmony between the self and experience, the inner world and the outer such that they are in accord and situations evaluated and choices made in line with a personal valuing system rather than an introjected one. (2001: ix)

Unconditional positive regard is a necessary pre-condition for change because the young person feels acceptance, which is a counter to conditions of worth. In a sense, it makes it more likely that many of the negative judgements that have shaped the child or young person will move towards being fully functioning and therefore towards: *a desirable outcome of therapy.*

These ideas are also explored by Mearns and Thorne (1988):

> The client who has been reared under oppressive 'conditions of worth' will have learned that he has value only in so far as he behaves in accordance with the expectations of others. Unconditional positive regard on the part of the counsellor towards her client is important because it directly sabotages such conditions of worth: the counsellor values her client irrespective of the client's conforming to 'conditions'. (p. 61)

Quoting from Lietaer (1984), they refer to this process as 'counter-conditioning'. Mearns and Thorne propose that sabotaging conditions of worth 'breaks into the client's negative, self-defeating cycle'.

Case study: Maira

Maira (aged 10) was seen by her teachers as a 'difficult' child. All efforts to link her socially with other children at her junior school appeared to fail. When sat next to other children, she would walk away at the first opportunity and play on her own. When approached by other children, she would snap at them or use her arms and body to hide her work. Maira never smiled or showed any emotion; her face remained 'silent' and she spoke very little. Eventually, the other children gave up on her and left her alone. Her teachers became frustrated with her unsociable attitude which persisted despite all efforts to include her.

Maira had learned that she was not acceptable to others, that she was not as pretty or clever as they were. By withdrawing, she confirmed in her own mind that she wasn't lovable and deserved to be rejected.

In therapy, her counsellor Ian did everything he could to ensure that Maira felt accepted and valued. Ian ensured that he did not repeat, however subtly, the attitudes and judgements of others. Ian did not talk about why friends were important or

(Continued)

(Continued)

reinforce the message that 'if you don't speak others will ignore you'. By offering acceptance and positive regard, Ian hoped to counter some of the conditioning which had characterised Maira's short life. After some time, Maira became less defensive, realising that Ian could be trusted not to hurt her feelings.

EXERCISE

If you already work with young people, can you think of any young person who behaves in a self-destructive, self-defeating way?

DO I HAVE TO LIKE ALL THE YOUNG PEOPLE I WORK WITH?

Bozarth and Wilkins (2001) believe that unconditional positive regard is a necessary condition for constructive change. They also suggest that it is 'the' necessary and sufficient condition in the model advanced by Rogers.

They then pose an important question: 'the world is full of hostile, reprehensible, malefic individuals. How can they possibly be acceptable to anybody?' (p. xii). Quoting Masson (1992), they ask, what about the person who brutally rapes and kills a child? Why should any therapist have any unconditional regard for him? Their response is a considered and theoretically consistent one: 'There is no reason at all why any therapist *should* but the therapeutic endeavour will be pointless without it' (Bozarth and Wilkins, 2001: xii).

They argue that:

> Whilst therapists may be limited by their ability to offer unconditional positive regard, this in no way implies that person-centred therapy is similarly limited. Theory asserts that if (for example) a paedophile consistently experiences the six conditions, then therapeutic change *will* occur. Of course it may be that this is a big 'if'. But what is important is that it is realised that the limitation is in the practitioner, not the theory. (Bozarth and Wilkins, 2001: vii)

Of course, those of us who work with young people are unlikely to experience such extreme testing of Rogers' ideas, but nonetheless we will meet with young people who do challenge our belief in our ability to offer unconditional positive regard. It may be that more discussion of this concept is necessary.

Tudor et al. (2004) see unconditional positive regard as something that is 'experienced' by the counsellor, rather than merely demonstrated; it has to be felt and believed. They are therefore making a distinction between unconditional positive regard and 'liking' someone. They say that whilst it is possible to pretend affection for our clients, we cannot force it. For this reason, it is possible to see them as individuals with the capacity to grow and develop: 'From this perspective, unconditional positive regard can be seen as the operational evidence of a counsellor's trust in her client's capacity and tendency to actualise' (Tudor et al., 2004: 43).

This argument is taken up by Dave Mearns (1994). He also draws a line between 'liking' and an attitude of unconditional positive regard towards a client: 'Unfortunately, these two concepts do not have much in common between them' (1994: 3). He suggests that in ordinary life we are quite selective about whom we choose to like. Most often, this is down to shared ideas, beliefs and needs. It is unlikely that many of the young people we meet will fit this description and, as Mearns warns us, where these needs and perspectives on life are close to those of our young clients, we need to guard against the dangers of over-identification and over-involvement. He continues: 'Unconditional positive regard is unrelated to any similarity of values or complementarity of needs with the client. Unconditional positive regard is about the counsellor *valuing* the client in his or her totality' (1994: 4).

NON-DIRECTIVITY AND UNCONDITIONAL POSITIVE REGARD

Carl Rogers referred to his new way of working as non-directive, largely as a reaction to the analytical approaches which predominated at the time. This has raised questions about whether indeed the therapist can actually be non-directive, or as Suzanne Keys (2003) asks, whether such non-directivity means that the therapist is 'passive'. It would follow that an 'active' therapist would be a directive therapist.

Unless we are completely non-directive, we cannot say that we are offering unconditional positive regard because any lead taken by the counsellor, however subtle, implies choice and therefore judgement as to what is important and what is not.

Levitt (2005) in his detailed discussion of the concept of non-directivity sets out the problem thus:

> If the process is to be fully directed by the client, then the therapist must let go of trying to decide upon what should or should not be explored, how a process should be furthered, or what is useful or good. (p. 11)

To be able to offer unconditional positive regard, the counsellor would have to believe in the client's ability to find their own way. Levitt continues:

> From a non-directive stance, unconditional positive regard would mean that clients are inherently valuable and powerful (including their process), and that the therapist consciously renounces a need, interest or goal to actively change the client or their process, no matter how different, frightening or strange. The non-directive therapist does not need to change clients to value or understand them. Clients are embraced as they are. Further, and of the utmost importance from a non-directive perspective, the therapist trusts the client's 'process' and goals as inherently valuable. (2005: 11–12)

Questions are often raised as to whether complete non-directivity and therefore total unconditional positive regard is ever possible (Feltham and Dryden, 1993). It is possible that we get too hung up on such a purist debate.

Keys assists us with this problem by reference to Grant (1990) who develops the idea of 'principled non-directiveness', which is defined as a moral stance or an 'expression of respect'. In a commentary on Grant's work, Keys explains that: 'Instead of prescribing what should or should not happen in a therapeutic relationship he brings the concept back to the attitude and intention of the therapist' (Keys, 2003: 11). She continues: 'This "principled non-directiveness" comes from a respect for the client and a lack of therapist investment in a prescribed outcome. From it flows the active engagement of the therapist in whatever emerges from the idiosyncratic encounter' (2003: 11).

Keys also notes the contribution by Bozarth (1998) to the discussion. He writes: 'Any ethical activity or action that emerges from the attention to the internal world of the client is a viable and congruent activity in person-centred therapy' (Bozarth, 1998: 128)

WORKING UNCONDITIONALLY WITH CHILDREN AND YOUNG PEOPLE

As indicated earlier, working with young people with a non-judgemental attitude is not easy. Wilkins (2001) offers some clarity about the problem: 'It [UPR] cannot be effectively faked, and tolerance (the ability to endure or "allow") is quite different' (p. 42).

Wilkins also cautions us against a false kind of unconditional positive regard:

> While it is neither ethical nor appropriate for a therapist to condone anti-social or harmful behaviour or to collude in its perpetuation, there is a real risk that in attempting to hold the attitude 'I disapprove of what you do but I accept you', the therapist will fail to offer unconditional positive regard, and the client experience is then one of censure and perhaps rejection. (2001: 42)

He goes on to say that what is needed is: 'An ability to see and connect with the person behind the "repulsive" or "repugnant" behaviour or attitude' (p. 42). In this way, the adult working with the child or adolescent who displays 'unacceptable' behaviours does not have to collude with their young client. The behaviour is neither 'condoned or opposed'.

Mearns (1994) stresses the importance of personal development work for adults hoping to use this approach with young people, otherwise: 'Any "display" of unconditional positive regard on the part of the counsellor tends to be superficial and usually wilts under the challenge of well-developed client self-protective systems' (p. 4). He adds:

> For the person-centred counsellor, unconditional positive regard is about being rather than portraying. The consistent valuing of clients stems from the fact that the

counsellor has come to be less threatened by others and can prize rather than feel fearful about their differences. (1994: 4)

A useful insight into the experience of unconditional positive regard can be found in Stewart (1997). He lists some statements made by clients who have felt unconditional positive regard from their counsellor. They include:

- always seems very concerned about me
- always appreciates me
- thinks I'm a worthwhile person
- still likes me even if I criticise her
- I feel safe with her
- I feel free to be myself
- makes it OK to talk about anything
- seems to trust my feelings about myself
- would never knowingly hurt me.

DEMONSTRATING UNCONDITIONAL POSITIVE REGARD TO A YOUNG CLIENT: WHAT DOES THE COUNSELLOR OR HELPER ACTUALLY DO?

Perhaps the best answer to this question is: what does the counsellor or helper *not* do? They do not make judgements or point out the strengths and weaknesses of their client or, indeed, what they say. They avoid criticism or evaluation and steer away from taking control of sessions, or leading clients to a position or perspective where the adult thinks they ought to be. They also avoid trying to change the child or young person into someone they would prefer. It is also important to avoid giving weight and acceptance to those things which our young client brings, which some-how matches our own sense of right and wrong. Approval, although well meaning, does imply judgement on that which has not been approved.

What the counsellor or helper is asked to demonstrate is 'acceptance'. Acceptance communicates that the adult values the young person, unconditionally. Sutton and Stewart (2002) describe acceptance in this way:

Acceptance is a special kind of loving which moves out towards people as they are, and maintains their dignity and personal worth. It means accepting their strengths and weaknesses; their positive and negative attitudes; their favourable and unfavourable qualities; their constructive and destructive wishes, and their thoughts, feelings and behaviours. (p. 10)

Acceptance is conveyed through showing respect to the young person and an inter-est in what they say. It means conveying through posture, eye contact, gesture, as well as words, that what has been said has been received without judgement.

It is not surprising therefore that Geldard (1998) has come to the conclusion that UPR is not easy to achieve. He does however offer some further guidance. Firstly, we are asked to see the world though the eyes of the client. In this way, it may be possible to understand the client's motivations for his behaviour and therefore acceptance becomes easier. Geldard writes:

> The longer I've been a counsellor, the more convinced I have become that even the most terrible behaviour is often understandable if I first understand the world that the client lives in and has lived in. I try to take the view that inside every person, behind the facade that the world sees, there is somebody who has the potential to be a good, creative, loving person. I am rarely disappointed by this expectation. (1998: 8–9)

Geldard also refers to caring for the client in the same way as the adult cares about themself. Whilst this can be difficult, he sees this position as one worth striving for.

Finally, Geldard asks us to be clear about who *we* are and what values we hold. He writes:

> I have to explore them [values], to scrutinise them and to question them. I have needed to carefully consider different values from my own and to understand where my feelings about those different values come from. This is an ongoing process which will never be finished ... Through sorting out my own value system, understanding myself better, and consequently being less threatened by views diametrically opposed to mine, I am better able to take a non-judgemental attitude towards clients who have very different value systems from mine. (1998: 9)

WITH CHILDREN AND YOUNG PEOPLE IN MIND

Before the close of this chapter, I would like to offer one final observation. When I work within the person-centred approach and I recognise that I am not expected to guide, offer advice or direct the child or young person towards some goal, the personal experience is quite liberating. It is as though my responsibility for the child has been lifted from my shoulders, and the relationship between that young person and me can truly begin and grow.

EXERCISE

How accepting are you of young people. Do you change your attitude when working therapeutically with a young person? Why?

9
CONGRUENCE

INTRODUCING THIS CHAPTER

This chapter explores the idea of being congruent, especially with regard to working with children and young people. Being 'congruent' is defined, and case studies and opportunities for personal reflection aim to illustrate the concept in practice. The reader is encouraged to gain some sense of what 'being congruent' might look and feel like.

TO THE COUNSELLOR

You will meet your young clients through a professional role which will have already conjured up a variety of fantasies about your purpose and authority. It is not difficult to see why avoiding a formal or insincere facade, and meeting your young client as a real person, is such an important quality in the counsellor and so crucial to the therapeutic relationship you hope to create.

TO THE HELPER

When working with children and young people, it is important that there is some harmony between your attitudes, your body language, your behaviour and of course what you are feeling. In this way, you will appear more genuine and are more likely to be accepted as a person with a genuine desire to be of help. Your own congruence will encourage greater harmony between the young person's feelings, what they say and how they relate to you.

In both these ways, a more real relationship between you and your helpee is established.

WHAT DOES BEING 'CONGRUENT' MEAN?

A person may be said to be congruent when they are not trying to appear to be anything other than who they are. Generically, 'congruence' is a term characterised by the notion of 'a coming together', of harmony, agreement and similarity. In therapy, the concept is defined as a consistency between the inner and outer selves and is essential to any sincere relationship. Wyatt (2001) notes that congruence has at times also been referred to as genuineness, transparency, authenticity and realness.

A simple explanation of the idea of congruence can be found in Howe (1993): 'Clients express a preference for therapists who come across as "real" people. Such therapists are more than a "technique-in-action"; they have their own personality and sense of humour and a recognisable character' (pp. 22–3).

WITH CHILDREN AND YOUNG PEOPLE IN MIND

Children and young people have an acute awareness of when an adult is being genuine or acting out a role. Incongruity in the adult is unlikely to develop trust between child or young person and the adult who is offering support or counselling. The young person is likely to equally engage in such 'role-play' or fail to attend any future sessions. In either case, very little is likely to be achieved.

Case study: Debbie

Debbie (aged 11) is a young carer. Her father works full time and is often away from home. Her mother has been depressed for a number of years and has developed a fear of the outside world. This means that in the last four years, a great deal of responsibility has fallen upon Debbie. Because her mother sits for long periods of time, she has developed leg ulcers and when the doctor has called, mum refuses to open the door.

Debbie has a young sister who is six. Before school, Debbie gets her sister up and dressed and walks her to school which makes her late herself. She gets mum breakfast as well as grabbing some toast for herself. Often, she doesn't have time and goes without food until lunchtime.

After school, instead of going out with the friends who live on her road, she goes shopping, before cooking an evening meal. Debbie does most of the cleaning and washing at home which leaves her with very little free time. She feels isolated from her friends who have become tired of asking her out to play. Debbie is physically and emotionally tired and any sense of her own needs leaves her feeling guilty and ashamed.

(Continued)

(Continued)

Debbie began seeing a mentor at school.

Mentor: Sounds like you have lots of jobs to do at home and have very little time for yourself?

Debbie: Not really. I like helping my mum and I don't like the girls on my road anyway.

Mentor: You prefer helping at home rather than meeting up with other children?

Debbie: I really don't mind and it keeps me busy and out of trouble.

Janice, the mentor, noticed how Debbie averted her eyes and she didn't feel convinced by what Debbie was saying. Slumped in her chair, Debbie looked tired and worn out, as if she had given so much – there was only emptiness left.

Case study: Dennis

Dennis (aged 14) was in his sixth session with his counsellor William, who was a volunteer at a local agency in the town. Dennis had been referred by his mother who was concerned about his behaviour at school. He said that he really liked school and couldn't see what the problem was. Dennis said that he frequently messed around in lessons but said that most of his friends did too. He also told William that there was 'no point' in school and he was 'all sorted' for a job when he left in two years time. He said that he would sometimes pass on drugs to other pupils at the school and said that if he didn't, somebody would. Dennis said that he and his friends sometimes picked on the 'brainy kids' at the school, saying: 'They think they're better than me and they aren't. In a few years they might be in a nice job but I'll be earning more than them and have lots of girls'.

This was all affecting William quite badly. He felt that he hadn't achieved well at school and he believed that he had to get qualifications later on in his life. He felt that he had struggled to get where he was now and felt uncomfortable with Dennis' attitude. He made a concerted effort not to convey his feelings towards Dennis, but he felt frustration and sometimes anger. The discrepancy between what William was feeling and what he showed became intolerable and he found himself responding less and less to Dennis, waiting for the final session to arrive in a month's time. He was aware that his displeasure would be evident to Dennis.

Both Debbie and William, as young client and counsellor respectively, were not being congruent; what was felt within was not consistent with the way they were in sessions, in words and non-verbally. In the example of Debbie, it is unlikely she was aware of such incongruence, whilst William knew he was not being genuine.

Mearns and Thorne (1988) have attempted to place congruence in some kind of context in relation to the core conditions. Empathy is described as a 'process' and unconditional positive regard as an 'attitude', whilst congruence is defined as a 'state of being' of the counsellor in relation to the client.

Carl Rogers (1967) described congruence in the following way:

> If therapy is to occur, it seems necessary that the therapist be, in the relationship, a unified, or integrated, or congruent person. What I mean is that within the relationship he is exactly what he is − not a facade, or a role, or a pretence. I have used the term 'congruence' to refer to this accurate matching of experience with awareness. It is when the therapist is fully and accurately aware of what he is experiencing at this moment in the relationship. Unless this congruence is present to a considerable degree it is unlikely that significant learning can occur. (p. 282)

By way of example, Rogers felt that congruence is perhaps best exhibited in the small child:

> If he is experiencing hunger at the physiological and visceral level, then his awareness appears to match this experience. He is hungry and dissatisfied, and this is true of him at all levels. He is at this moment integrated or unified in being hungry. On the other hand, if he is satiated and content this too is a unified congruence. (1967: 339)

Rogers interestingly postulates that as adults we are drawn to the infant, because of this apparent genuineness. By contrast, he gives an example of incongruence in a man who becomes angry during a group discussion:

> His face flushes, his tone communicates anger, he shakes his finger at his opponent. Yet when a friend says, 'Well, let's not get angry about this', he replies, with evident sincerity and surprise, 'I'm not angry! I don't have any feelings about this at all'. (1967: 339–40)

Certainly, it is a very special experience to work with a child or young person being themselves. Sometimes this may only happen for fleeting moments. Rogers (1980) felt that such experiences were 'sparkling'. He wrote: 'It is so obvious when a person is not hiding behind a facade but speaking from deep within himself. When this happens, I leap to meet it. I want to encounter this real person' (1980: 16).

When a young person's tears match their words; when sadness is reflected in posture and expression; when happiness is seen in the child's eyes; when we feel that we are experiencing the real person, with no front or façade; when as the adult, we feel at one, real and not in some sort of role, then there is congruence − these are very special and rewarding experiences.

Lietaer (2001) suggests that there may be two sides to congruence, an inner one and an outer one. This point is expanded upon in the following way:

> The inner side refers to the degree to which the therapist has conscious access to, or is receptive to, all aspects of his own flow of experiencing. This side of the process will be called 'congruence'.

The outer side, on the other hand, refers to the communication – through verbal and non-verbal ways – by the therapist of 'himself'; his perceptions, attitudes and feelings. This aspect is called 'transparency'. (2001: 37)

Lietaer also suggests that it is possible for the congruent therapist to be minimally transparent, whilst a transparent therapist may be congruent or incongruent. Where she is the latter, it is possible that the therapist could be harming the client.

WHAT CONGRUENCE LOOKS AND FEELS LIKE

Stewart (1997) lists a number of comments that a client might express about a counsellor's genuineness:

- What she says never conflicts with what she feels.
- She is herself in our relationship.
- I don't think she hides anything from herself that she feels with me.
- She doesn't avoid anything that is important for our relationship.
- I feel I can trust her to be honest with me.
- She is secure in our relationship.
- She doesn't try to mislead me about her own thoughts or feelings.
- She is impatient with me at times.
- She is sometimes upset by what I say.
- She sometimes looks as worried as I feel.
- She treats me with obvious concern. (p. 88)

We might expect a young person to say things like:

- he's alright
- she's not like a teacher (or social worker, etc.)
- he's not afraid to say what he is feeling
- you can read what he's thinking and he tells you.

In a similar way, Mearns and Thorne (1988) offer us a number of reflective questions:

In response to my client, can I dare to:

- feel the feelings that are within me?
- hold my client when I feel he needs to be held?
- show my anger when this is strongly felt?
- admit my distraction when challenged about it?
- admit my confusion when that persists?
- voice my irritation when that grows?
- put words to my affection when that is there?

- shout when something is seething inside me?
- be spontaneous even though I don't know where that will lead?
- be forceful as well as gentle?
- be gentle as well as forceful?
- use my sensuous self in relation to my client?
- step out from my professional facade? (p. 75)

Mearns and Thorne (1988) suggest that congruence is a 'state of being' and not always perceived by the client. However, the counsellor's congruence may become apparent when the counsellor expresses a feeling or observation which may seem uncharacteristically 'honest' to the client. Mearns and Thorne (1988) offer a number of examples, including a counsellor telling their client that they do not understand or expressing frustration with their client. These and other examples illustrate that congruence may be experienced by the client when the counsellor responds in ways which are distinctive, different or direct. This idea of the counsellor's congruence not always being evident to the client is also explored by Brazier (1993b):

> Congruence can exist for a person even when it is not communicated to the other person in a dialogue. If I am aware that I am frightened and I do not make a deliberate attempt to hide this fact, then I am being congruent. I may not still actually tell you that I am frightened and you might not notice. Congruence does not, therefore, necessarily imply that the inner state of a person has been successfully communicated to another person. (Internet resource)

Being congruent requires a degree of self-awareness. Without it, there are dangers. It is also important to make it clear that being congruent does not give the counsellor 'permission' to say whatever they want to the client. This point is made by Bryant-Jefferies (2004):

> Being congruent does not mean that you have to keep saying what you are feeling. It does not give free licence to anything being said because you are experiencing it. This is a fundamental fact. Congruence is an attitude of being, a condition in which the counsellor can actually experience what is present for them, and to be able to appreciate within that experiencing what is present in response to being in relationship with the client, and what is simply their own stuff having little or no relevance to the session. (p. 68)

Wilkins (1999) takes this argument one step further by suggesting that inappropriate self-disclosure can be problematic where the focus of the client is taken from the child or young person, and shifted onto the counsellor. Wilkins refers to the views of Gaylin (1996) who goes so far as to suggest that self-disclosure under the guise of 'being congruent' can lead to the abuse of the client:

> I define abuse of the client as that moment when the therapist's feelings for the client, either positive or negative, take the focus off the client and onto the therapist and, consequently, the activities of the therapist become self rather than client serving. The pursuit of therapist genuineness and transparency should never be construed as a licence to use the client. (1996: 61)

This statement stresses the importance of counsellor self-awareness. Without such insight, the adult working with the child or young person may, under the guise of being congruent, knowingly or unknowingly, use time with the client for the expression of their own needs rather than their young client's.

THE IMPORTANCE OF BEING CONGRUENT

WITH CHILDREN AND YOUNG PEOPLE IN MIND

Congruence is an essential part of work with children and young people and of central importance to any therapeutic relationship, possibly even key among the core conditions. Even without resort to theory, it would be clear to anyone working with a child or young person that being an open, real human being is something most valued by young clients. It is hard to see how the core conditions of unconditional positive regard and empathy can exist where the adult is playing a role or presenting a false front.

Mearns and Thorne (1988) observe that the person–centred approach is: 'often characterised as mild and unchallenging, but nothing could be further from the truth: the challenge of the counsellor's congruence is vibrant with possibilities' (p. 87). They set out four ways in which congruence is important to the counselling relationship. Although writing with adult clients in mind, their reasoning is highly relevant to those adults who work therapeutically with children and young people.

Firstly, congruence is seen to enhance trust between the counsellor and the client who knows that the counsellor's response is open and honest. This can lead to more freedom in the relationship and the client becomes increasingly aware that the counsellor is not trying to manipulate him. As stated earlier in this book, building trust with a child or young person is a prerequisite for the establishment of a helpful and therapeutic relationship.

Secondly, Mearns and Thorne state that the counsellor's willingness and awareness to express weakness often expressed as statements relating to confusion, powerlessness and mistakes can build self-acceptance in the client.

WITH CHILDREN AND YOUNG PEOPLE IN MIND

Children and young people have become used to adult confidence and assertiveness. My own experience of working with children and young people suggests that when faced with the counsellor behaving in ways which are perceived as more real, this is valued and sometimes treasured by the young client who comes to see the relationship as a partnership in change.

Thirdly, congruence may be seen as helping the client to be congruent in the relationship. Mearns and Thorne quite rightly argue that 'modelling' is not a goal of the person–centred counsellor but nonetheless congruence in the counsellor is likely to 'facilitate' this in the client. Where a child or young person experiences the adult's realness and transparency, they are more likely to trust this aspect of themselves.

Finally, Mearns and Thorne refer to the counsellor responding as a 'vibrant and trustworthy human being'. They write:

> Congruence is significant because it enhances the quality of the response which the counsellor gives to the client. In being consistently congruent the counsellor is offering to the client a reflection of the effects which the client's behaviour has on another human being whose integrity can be trusted, and whose profession-alism has ensured that as far as possible that reflection is not discoloured by the counsellor's own need system. (1988: 87)

With children and young people, such a real way of relating enriches the relationship with an adult and differentiates it from the relationships they ordinarily share with adults in their lives.

BEING CONGRUENT

Mearns and Thorne (1988) offer us some advice as to the use of congruence by the professional. They reiterate the point made earlier that the counsellor or helper can-not simply express what they are feeling at any given moment simply because they are being 'congruent'. They suggest three principles for the use of congruence.

The first makes the point that congruence should be 'in response' to the client's experience and not an expression of what is happening for the counsellor. They write: 'The counsellor may have lots of feelings and sensations flowing within her but it is only those which are in response to her client which are appropriate for expression' (1988: 81). At this point, they make a clear distinction between being congruent and self-disclosure. When working with children and young people, it would never be appropriate for the adult to talk about their own lives, however much they connect with the young person's experience. It is important that for the time the adult and child work together, the focus remains on the child.

The second guideline for congruence offered by Mearns and Thorne is that the response to the client should be of 'relevance' to the client. However much linked a child or young person's experience is to the lives of others or relates to broader issues, it would not be helpful to respond to a young client talking about the death of a parent with examples of how other young people have coped with such loss. Neither would it be appropriate for the adult to talk about bereavement in general.

Finally, Mearns and Thorne insist that the counsellor's response should be to feelings which are 'persistent' or particularly 'striking'. The adult working with children and young people will experience a range of feelings when working in a person-centred way. Many of these will be fleeting responses to things that the child has expressed. If the adults were to respond each time they experience something with the client, it would affect the flow of the session and again take the focus away from the young client. However, where the adult experiences strong emotion, especially over a period of time, it may be appropriate to share this with the young client as long as the purpose is to be fully congruent and real.

In an historical overview of the development of the concept of congruence, Sheila Haugh (2001) highlights some advice offered by Rogers himself. These include the therapist using congruence when feelings are so strong that they interrupt the core conditions; when the therapist's feelings are so persistent that the therapist finds himself focusing on his own feelings, rather than the client's; and when there is a danger that the counsellor is not being 'real' in the relationship. It is difficult to see how an adult working therapeutically with a child or young person can be empathic and show unconditional positive regard without being congruent. Being congruent with a young client involves a certain amount of risk taking and therefore judgement. The adult needs to treat the young client with care and sensitivity and ultimately ensure that their own expression of feeling or emotion is both relevant and ultimately helpful to the client and the therapeutic relationship.

EXERCISES

1. When are you most congruent, real or truly 'yourself'? In which relationship? Why?
2. Think of a time when you have experienced somebody hiding behind a facade. What was happening for you at the time?
3. Being real is likely to encourage self-disclosure in a child or young person. Can you think of times when you have felt more congruent and this has encouraged a child to be more open and trusting?

10
EMPATHY

INTRODUCING THIS CHAPTER

In this chapter, 'empathy' is defined from a number of perspectives, and its therapeutic power discussed. The differences between being empathic and sympathetic when working with children and young people are explored through a variety of case studies. The chapter looks at how the adult can offer empathy without losing their separateness or own identity. The chapter closes by drawing some conclusions from our look at the core conditions.

TO THE COUNSELLOR

A number of observers of the person-centred approach to counselling see empathy as the most important of the core conditions. This quality and the ability to communicate it to your young client is also regarded as a prerequisite to a number of other counselling approaches.

TO THE HELPER

It is possible, because of the potentially multi-dimensional nature of your work, that you might find yourself being sympathetic towards the children and young people and the situations they find themselves in. Whilst sometimes a little sympathy is appropriate and a valued dimension to caring, empathy has the power to transform your relationship with young people and show that you really are alongside them.

WHAT IS EMPATHY?

The word 'empathy' has its origin in the Greek word 'empatheia' which means 'physical affection'. The concept was later developed in the German language as Einfühlung by Theodor Lipps in the 1880s, where 'ein' means 'a' or 'any' and 'füh-lung' means 'contact'.

At one level, we have an understanding as to the meaning of empathy but in a counselling context, the concept requires more complex thought to understand its deeper meaning.

WITH CHILDREN AND YOUNG PEOPLE IN MIND

It is clear to me that children and young people, like adults, have a vital and compelling need to be heard and have their feelings understood. Empathy signals to the young person that they are valued, loved and cared about. This returns human beings to their most basic needs for security, attachment and belonging.

Feltham and Dryden (1993) describe empathy as:

An attitude and skill of following, grasping and understanding as fully as possible the client's subjective experience as if from the perspective of the client himself. In addition, it is the communication to the client that the counsellor is experientially alongside him and that she is sensitively striving to understand what he is feeling or struggling to articulate. (p. 58)

Geldard (1998) offers us a more visual and personal interpretation of empathy. He writes:

When a client is talking, I imagine that he is walking along a path. Sometimes he meanders away from the path, goes into the woods, trips over, climbs over rocks, wanders through valleys, crosses streams and generally explores. Sometimes he goes right around in a circle and comes back to the same point again. As a counsellor, I am neither a follower nor a leader most of the time, although at times, I will follow and at times, I will lead. Most of the time, what I try to do is walk alongside the client – to go where he chooses to go, to explore those things he chooses to explore, and to be warm, open, friendly, concerned, caring, real and genuine. This way trust develops between the client and myself and I experience the world in almost the same way that he experiences it. I try to think and feel the way the client does so I can share with him what he is discovering about himself. I go on a journey with him, listening to everything he says, matching his every move, being right beside him. This is what is meant by empathy. (p. 8)

Whilst adherents to the person–centred approach may wish to debate Geldard's inclination towards 'leading' occasionally, without doubt, his description gives a real sense of what it means to be empathic with those we offer support or counselling to.

A more technical definition of empathy is offered by Thorne and Lambers (1998):

> Empathic understanding is an interpersonal process whose level depends on emotional amenability to the perceived feelings of another person, i.e. one assumes for the moment a person is capable of receiving the signals of the other person and that the other is capable of sending these signals. The closer the two persons are in their experience, the easier this process becomes. (p. 218)

Carl Rogers made great efforts to define this important concept. In 1980, he recalled one of his earliest attempts:

> The state of empathy, or being empathic, is to perceive the internal frame of reference of another with accuracy and with the emotional components and meanings which pertain thereto as if one were the person, but without ever losing the 'as if' condition. Thus it means to sense the hurt or pleasure of another as he senses it and to perceive the causes thereof as he perceives them, but without ever losing the recognition that it is as if I were hurt or pleased and so forth. If this 'as if' quality is lost, then the state is one of identification. (pp. 140–1)

A more illustrative description of empathy from Rogers can be found in this same work:

> An empathic way of being with another person has a number of facets. It means entering the private perceptual world of the other and becoming thoroughly at home in it. It involves being sensitive, moment by moment, to the changing felt meanings which flow in this other person, to the fear or rage or tenderness or confusion or whatever he or she is experiencing. It means temporarily living in the other's life, moving about in it delicately without making judgements; it means sensing meanings of which he or she is scarcely aware, but not trying to uncover totally unconscious feelings, since this would be too threatening. It includes communicating your sensings of the person's world as you look with fresh and unfrightened eyes at elements of which he or she is fearful. It means frequently checking with the person as to the accuracy of your sensings, and being guided by the responses you receive. You are a confident companion to the person in his or her inner world. (1980: 142)

WITH CHILDREN AND YOUNG PEOPLE IN MIND

For the adult working with a child or young person, the task is both clear and daunting: to somehow enter the child's world, feel and experience it as they do and communicate this to the young person, but without ever losing sight of themselves as a separate entity.

EMPATHY OR SYMPATHY

Case study: Nadine

Nadine (aged 12) had recently lost her mother after a sudden illness. She had been referred to the school-based nurse by the attendance officer who knew that she was having real difficulties coping with her loss. Each day, Nadine would find a way of getting out of lessons by saying she was ill or telling her teachers that the nurse wanted to see her.

Kathryn, the nurse, was a superb listener and, above all, she was prepared to see Nadine whenever she arrived at the door. Kathryn felt she had some affinity with Nadine because she too had lost her father at an early age. Nadine could feel Kathryn's concern. Her kind words, at times when she felt low and empty, were comforting and welcomed by Nadine, who felt that Kathryn really understood.

Kathryn was able to tell Nadine how sorry she was for her tragic loss. Often, she would say to Nadine that she admired her courage and strength. Kathryn said she could see how much Nadine was sad and reassured her that this was 'normal' and that she would need time to heal.

The first thing to recognise in this brief case study is the wonderful caring and sensitive work by Kathryn. Clearly, Nadine valued her support and felt that she had found someone she could turn to. All young people, like adults, need a little sympathy at times. However, it is possible that Kathryn could have offered Nadine something deeper and more profound – empathy. We need now to look at the difference between these two ways in which we might try to show a young person that we care about them.

Empathy can be seen as experiencing the world of a young person. Sympathy however can be seen as experiencing from a distance, the feelings of the child. Also associated with sympathy is 'pity' which the *Oxford Dictionary* (Hawkins and Allen, 1991: 1106) sees as 'sorrow and compassion aroused by another's condition'. In this way, showing a child or young person pity can be seen as 'feeling for' the young client, a perspective which implies some distance. As with the support offered by Kathryn to Nadine, it would be wrong to suggest that a young person may not sometimes need a little 'tea and sympathy' or feel an adult's concern expressed by pity. What is clear, however, is that sympathy and pity have no place in the person-centred approach to working with children and young people.

The following examples illustrate the differences between sympathy, pity and empathy.

Case study: Krystian

Krystian (aged 11) has recently arrived from Poland and finds himself in school with very little ability to speak or understand English. The school's policy is to 'immerse' children for whom English is a foreign language, believing that they will,

(Continued)

(Continued)

by necessity and with appropriate support, learn English more quickly this way than if the child attended some 'reception-type' facility where English is learned before attendance at a mainstream school. Here, Krystian is talking (English translation) with his specially assigned teaching assistant, Aniela:

Krystian:	Everything is so different here to my home town. There I knew everybody but now I don't have any children to talk to. I think they tried when I first came but I could not keep up and now I walk around the playground at break on my own. I look out for the big boys who I think are teasing me. It's difficult to tell because they have smiles on their faces, so they could just be trying to be friendly; I just don't know.
Sympathetic response by Aniela:	I feel for you Krystian. You are finding school difficult and you are not sure what people are saying about you.
Pity:	From what I know about you, Krystian, I know you are strong. It's going to be hard for you until you can speak more English, then I am sure that you will begin to make lots of friends.
Empathic response:	You think back to your life in Poland with some sadness. You want to make friends but now you feel isolated and alone. Not being able to understand the other children leaves you with a sense of confusion and uneasiness.

Case study: Niki

Niki (aged 7) is talking with a teaching assistant Rose, during the lunch-time. Rose had been sensing that Niki had become more clingy over recent days. She would also hang around in the classroom, offering to tidy up, when the other children had gone out to play. Rose sat down with Niki and sensitively asked if there was anything she wanted to talk about. Rose asked her if she was OK, because she seemed a little sad this week.

Niki:	My mum and dad had to put my rabbit Flossy to sleep. She was very sick and the man at the animal hospital said she needed to rest now. I've had Flossy since I was very little. I had to say goodbye to her and I was crying and so was mummy. Daddy drove her to the hospital so now I won't see her anymore. They said that she will go to a special place for rabbits but I just want her in her hutch again, so we can play.

(Continued)

(Continued)

Sympathetic response by Rose:	I'm so sorry to hear about Flossy. I'm sure it was for the best. You have been together for a long time and you are going to miss her.
Pity:	Oh, you poor little thing! What must you be going through? Why didn't you tell me on Monday?
Empathic response:	It sounds as if it was very hard for you seeing daddy take Flossy to the hospital, knowing that you were saying goodbye. It is as though there is a big space in your life, where Flossy used to be.
	She meant so much to you and although she needed to go to sleep, you miss her a lot and want her back home with you, just like it's always been.

EMPATHY IN ACTION: WHAT THE COUNSELLOR OR HELPER ACTUALLY DOES

Whilst the adult's own feelings are of great importance in listening to children and young people, feeling empathy for the young client is not enough; empathy needs to be visibly and audibly demonstrated in such a way that the young person *feels* understood.

Put in simple terms, empathy is offering back to the child that which has been expressed. However, empathy is more than just this; it is showing that the counsellor or helper has really understood. Tolan (2007) develops this point:

> At its richest, it involves a fearless exploration of another's world, a sensing of meanings unspoken, a compassionate naming of pain, suffering and humiliation, and of mischievousness and joy. The fullest empathy does not censor or discriminate. It sees the world as the other person sees it and is wholly accepting of that world. (p. 18)

Before we look at some examples, a number of principles about the use of empathy with children and young people need to be mentioned. Brodley (1993) identifies a number of these and some are worth highlighting here.

The first of these relates to 'tentativeness'. This is about *checking* that you have understood rather than asserting that you have understood in some kind of definitive way; Brodley writes:

> You may express this tentativeness simply by your intonation, or you might preface your empathic response with an introductory statement that communicates your tentativeness and your interest in your client's assessment of the accuracy of your understanding. Examples of such introductory statements are: 'Is this right?' or 'Are you saying?' or 'I think I understand. Is this what you mean?' (1993: 106)

Brodley also makes it clear that some introductions to empathic responses might suggest a degree of interpretation or that you are 'searching' for deeper meanings. These should be avoided.

Brodley also emphasises the need to stay within the client's *frame of reference*. This is described in the following way:

> As you are listening, try to grasp the client's viewpoint with the meanings and feelings that are the client's at that time. Try to absorb those things into yourself – without the reservations and interferences of scepticism or criticism – in order to reach a feeling of understanding. Put aside any doubts or critical feelings about the client's statements and try to understand the client's point of view and feelings. (1993: 107)

Other advice offered includes a preparedness to say that you havn't understood the client, and asking the client to express themselves differently, when you have been distracted or when you have been unable to make sense of what the client is saying. Some counsellors in training and in the early months of practice feel that to not understand implies not listening and are afraid to say. As well as avoiding probing questions, Brodley also asks us to offer the client time to reflect upon our empathic responses, to relax and allow the client to think and feel and decide where to go next.

In everyday conversations with children and young people and their problems, we often miss out the empathy. Feeling the need to show we care, we sometimes take control and fall into a guidance role, drawing upon our own life experience in order to offer advice and solutions. This makes us feel as though we are helping and that we have heard what the young person has told us. Although well intentioned, the absence of empathy or a declaration of sympathy means that we miss the opportunity to show that we understand at a deeper level.

It is recognised in person-centred theory and counselling practice in general that empathy operates on a number of levels; an insight recognised by Rogers himself. Whilst understanding that there has been resistance within the person-centred approach to divide up what might reasonably be thought of as intensely human responses into some sort of structure which implies evaluation, Vincent (2005) argues the case for such a description of this process. This takes the form of acknowledging that much counselling takes place in formal settings, which raises the issue of accountability. He also sees such monitoring as leading to the personal and professional development of counsellors. In setting out his 12-level analysis of empathetic responding, Vincent does recognise the dangers of such a hierarchy. These include undue emphasis on levels which may not sit comfortably with unconditional positive regard and where the person-centred approach gives status to feelings and 'gut stuff' over and above thoughts and 'head stuff'. He also suggests that the counsellor or helper striving to reach the highest level 'might be more to do with a therapist needing to prove their own cleverness than with demonstrating respect for and sensitivity to the client' (2005: 175). However, whilst such analysis of a counsellor or helper's empathy may not always be necessary, some understanding of the different degrees to which empathy can be expressed almost certainly is.

I believe that it is possible to identify three levels of empathic response:

- The first level concerns reflecting 'meaning' and an understanding of the content of what the child or young person might have said.
- The second level of response begins to take regard of and express relatively accessible feelings as they exist for the young person at that particular time and implies a greater degree of accuracy.
- The third level is sometimes referred to as 'advanced empathy' and suggests that the counsellor or helper is able to go beyond that which is evident or just below the surface, to a deeper level, with a tentative exploration of what has not been said, or which has been half expressed or not said at all but sensed by the adult.

The following brief example may serve to illustrate these differences.

Case study: Scott (aged 14)

Scott:	You dunno what it's like round our area. Lots of big kids with guns and knives and you know they will hurt you just for looking at them. If you say the wrong thing to someone, they come looking for you. It's all drugs, gangs and things – every way you look. Sometimes it's safer to stay indoors but then they come knocking and you have to go out otherwise they say your disrespecting them.
Level one response:	You live in an area where there are youths who use drugs, carry weapons and go around in gangs and you don't feel safe.
Level two response:	You live in an area where there are drugs, gangs and where young people carry weapons. You are frightened and want to stay away from trouble but it's not always easy to avoid joining in. Is that right?
Level three response:	Trouble is all around you. You worry a lot of the time about getting hurt and whilst you want to stay out of trouble yourself, you feel trapped and unable to escape from those you fear most. You don't feel in control of your life? Is that what it's like for you?

LEARNING TO BE EMPATHIC

The concept of empathy is not an exclusively person-centred one and the idea of empathy as being crucial to the establishment of a therapeutic alliance can be found in psychodynamic literature, as well as being a key theme in other approaches. This idea is touched upon by Tudor et al. (2004) who record that similar ideas can be found in the work of important psychologists such as Jacob Moreno (1890–1974), Karl Jaspers (1833–1965) and Heinz Kohut (1913–1981).

To an extent, we are all born with a degree of empathy. Even a very young child cries when another child cries in a way which seems to indicate that the child is experiencing similar distress. The development of empathy in children is considered by Kutner (2008), who writes: 'By the time a child is about four years old, he begins to associate his emotions with the feelings of others. While one child says that he has a stomachache, some four-year-olds may come over and comfort him' (Internet resource). Even where a child's response to the child in pain is aggressive, Kutner argues, this may still be a sign that she is feeling the pain of the other. As a child develops emotionally, her self-awareness grows, as does the ability to read and recognise the emotions of others. This forms the basis of the development of empathy.

The idea that empathy develops in infancy is also touched upon by Vaknin (2008), albeit from a psychodynamic perspective. He writes:

> It may be innate. Even toddlers seem to empathise with the pain – or happiness – of others (such as their caregivers). Empathy increases as the child forms a self-concept (identity). The more aware the infant is of his or her emotional states, the more he explores his limitations and capabilities – the more prone he is to projecting this new found knowledge [o]nto others. By attributing to people around him his new gained insights about himself, the child develops a moral sense and inhibits his anti-social impulses. The development of empathy is, therefore, a part of the process of socialisation. (Internet resource)

It is often suggested that young people diagnosed as having autism or Asperger Syndrome have difficulties with empathy because the disorder affects a young person's ability to read and respond to another person's emotional state. This position, however, is questioned by Attwood (1993):

> The initial impression of a person with autism is that they are indifferent to the emotions of others. Indeed, they do have difficulty interpreting emotional cues given in facial expression, gestures, posture or voice. Thus one can never be sure that the person with autism fully grasps the feeling, that the person's face or action may express.

> However, it is not true to say that they are totally indifferent, as the child with autism may become very distressed by the emotional behaviour of other people. The problem is that the child with autism may not know what the movements and vocalisations of another person mean, or how they are expected to respond. (p. 12)

There is an increasing sense that empathy can be taught, or at least its development can be facilitated, a point made by Feltham (1999): 'There is widespread agreement that it [empathy] is a natural trait but one which often becomes masked. With training and practice, this ability can be rediscovered' (p. 64). This forms an important principle for the emotional literacy movement who believe that such skills can be fostered in both children and adults and can become what is collectively known as 'emotional intelligence'. Whilst it is likely that children who grow up in homes characterised by listening and respect for feelings may find it easier to develop empathy, I believe that it is possible for children to develop this aspect of themselves. It therefore surely follows that the adult wanting to work with children and young people can equally develop this dimension to their way of relating to young people in difficulty.

THE 'AS IF' QUALITY

Empathy is an essential ingredient in any meaningful therapeutic relationship and involves sensing the client's experience from the young person's point of view. The counsellor or adult working with a child or young person seeks to know the young client's inner world. However, Rogers was quick to point out that the adult should not lose the 'as if' condition. Mearns and Thorne (1988) offer us additional understanding of this important idea:

> In empathising with the client the counsellor leaves aside her own frame of reference and, for the time being, adopts the frame of reference of her client. She can then appreciate how the client experiences the events in his world; indeed she can even sense how he feels about events as if these feelings were her own. (p. 40)

However, Mearns and Thorne also alert us to using empathy with some caution:

> The 'as-if' quality of empathy is a crucial aspect of the professionalism of the person-centred counsellor. She is able to work in this intense and feelingful way with her client, and yet not become overwhelmed by those feelings. This control by the counsellor is crucial for the client: it offers him the security of knowing that although he may feel desperate and lost in his world, the counsellor will be someone who remains reliable and coherent, as well as sensitive. (1988: 40)

Some writers have questioned whether it is indeed possible to really feel what another person is feeling. The question is also raised as to whether it is necessary for the adult to have experienced the same events and happenings in a child's life to gain some sense of how the child may be feeling and share some of those profound emotions.

Clearly, the adult working with a child or young person will not have shared the same story as their young client or helpee. However, whilst the situations may not be the same, the adult will have experienced the full range of emotions inherent in each of the circumstances faced by a child. The adult's parents may not have divorced when they were young but they may have experienced the loss and pain of losing a parent through bereavement or losing a best friend at school. The adult may not have experienced the dilemma of leaving school to find work or going to college but they may have had to make difficult decisions in their own life which has left them torn, unsure and fearful of making the wrong choice.

This ability to draw upon our own experiences in order to experience another person's grief, hate, love or isolation is an important part of our ability to empathise, but herein lies a danger. There is a fine line between seeing the world through the child's eyes, accompanying them on their journey through a range of complex feelings and emotions and seeing their world though our own eyes, from our own perspective, simply because the child's experiences trigger similar emotions and feelings of our own. Every adult has experienced childhood and transition into adulthood. The danger is that we believe that we are walking alongside when actually we are re-living experience in a parallel sense.

Also problematic would be where the adult becomes so entangled in the thoughts and feelings of the child that they no longer maintain the 'as if' quality and become consumed by the child's or young person's experience to the extent that they are no longer able to maintain their sense of self. The boundaries between the young person's and the adult's life become indistinguishable as a result of over-identification, so that the adult becomes over-involved and, at best, ineffective. Concerns such as these emphasise the importance of supervision in the helping professions, a topic we will explore later in this book.

THE POWER OF EMPATHY

In the person-centred way of working, there is no room for analysis, for this would contradict many of the beliefs surrounding the counsellor's conviction that given the right conditions, the client will find their own way. Also, it should be emphasised that empathy is about the counsellor's attempt at forming an accurate understanding of the client's experiences. Tudor et al. (2004) emphasise the importance of 'accuracy' and argue against empathy being seen merely as a technique which can be taught in the training room:

> In this, 'accurate' means that the therapist sees things as the client sees them, not as the therapist would see them if she were in the client's place, nor how she thinks the client should see them. It is essentially an attitude, a stance of willingness and openness towards another person, rather than the technique of reflective listening with which it is sometimes confused and equated. (2004: 43)

In a similar vein, Mearns and Thorne (1988) talk about the 'permeating' nature of empathy in the helping relationship. They explain further: 'Sometimes these particularly intense empathic experiences lead us to forget that in person-centred counselling empathy is going on most of the time and not just at profound moments' (p. 40).

The distancing from an analytical stance and the positions that see empathy as an attitude rather than technique, as well as the ongoing nature of empathy in counselling, are all key concepts in helping us to understand how empathy works and how it helps facilitate client growth.

Rogers (1980) felt that too little attention had been paid to what he regarded as: 'a special way of being with another person which has been called empathic' (p. 137). He came to see empathy as possibly the most important factor in successful therapy. He writes:

> Over the years, however, the research evidence has kept piling up, and it points strongly to the conclusion that a high degree of empathy in a relationship is possibly *the* most potent factor in bringing about change and learning. (1980: 139)

In what he described as a 'fresh look at empathy', Rogers envisioned a move away from the role of 'expert' in therapy towards approaches which: 'look at ways of being with people that locate power in the person, not the expert' (p. 140).

In an important discussion on the nature of empathy, Rogers goes on to describe a number of findings. These are summarised as follows:

- The ideal therapist is, first of all, empathic.
- Empathy is correlated with self-exploration and process movement.
- Empathy early in the relationship predicts later success.
- In successful empathy, the client comes to perceive more empathy.
- Empathic understanding is provided freely by the therapist, not drawn from him or her.
- The more experienced the therapist is, the more likely he or she is to be empathic.
- Empathy is a special quality in a relationship and therapists offer more of it than even helpful friends.
- Experienced therapists often fall short of being empathic.
- Clients are better judges of the degree of empathy that exists than are therapists.
- Brilliance and diagnostic perceptiveness are unrelated to empathy.
- An empathic way of being can be learned from empathic persons. (Rogers, 1980: 146–50)

Rogers was in no doubt that empathy in a counselling or helping relationship is related to progress and positive outcomes. So why is empathy so potentially powerful? Haugh and Merry (2001) eloquently point us in the right direction:

> To some extent, each of us inhabits a world with a population of one, while at the same time, we move through, deal with and experience a world populated by millions. Distress is created when our experience of the populated world somehow doesn't match our own internal world. 'In extremis' this mismatch leaves us feeling isolated, vulnerable, anxious and defensive. If our isolation, vulnerability, anxiety and defensiveness are misunderstood by others, we are likely to retreat further into the relative safety of our private worlds and create even more distance between ourselves and others. (p. vii)

Haugh and Merry go on to say that attempts to help and support, however well-meaning, may actually make matters worse. They also suggest that people with problems may find temporary comfort in being assessed or labelled in some way, but in the long term such diagnoses may have no long-term benefit or worse still may lead to unfortunate or damaging consequences. Empathy, in contrast however, often leads to more permanent and meaningful outcomes:

> Being understood for who we are, no matter in what unusual idiom we speak, or how unacceptable our ideas, rather than for how closely we fit pre-existing diagnostic categories, works to dissolve alienation in a more profound and persistent way. That our experience, however bizarre, can be understood by another person means that we are not as excluded from social life as much as perhaps we feared. (Haugh and Merry, 2001: vii)

WITH CHILDREN AND YOUNG PEOPLE IN MIND

Very few children and young people who seek our help have experienced the empathy of an adult. Empathy keeps the focus firmly lodged in the child's frame of reference and allows us to enter freely into the young person's often complicated, fragile, confusing and sometimes traumatic world. Empathy shows respect for, and validates, not only the child's world, but the young person themselves.

Mearns and Thorne (1988) highlight what they consider to be some of the key reasons why empathy is linked with positive outcomes in therapy. The first is that empathy communicates the counsellor's understanding which might lead to increases in client self-esteem. The second relates to the point made above, that is that the power of empathy may lie in its difference; that is, that people don't often experience empathy which, as Mearns and Thorne suggest, may lead to a client believing that for once 'someone is really trying to understand me'. The third perspective offered by Mearns and Thorne is that empathy, by focusing on the client's feelings, may help the client to a deeper understanding of them. Deeper understanding, they argue, is likely to lead to the client taking more personal responsibility for their feelings.

The final position on the effectiveness of empathy set out by Mearns and Thorne is that when the counsellor demonstrates that he understands the client's expressed thoughts and feelings, this is more likely to lead to increased levels of awareness in the client.

Perhaps most importantly, they argue that displaying empathy is more likely to 'dissolve alienation': 'for it is almost impossible to maintain an alienated position in the face of someone who is showing you profound understanding at a very personal level' (1988: 46).

IN CONCLUSION

These last three chapters have examined the key concepts which Rogers regarded as essential in any therapeutic relationship. In a sense, to examine each independently is perhaps to emphasise their independence as opposed to their inter-dependency. These three concepts of unconditional positive regard, congruence and empathy have been developed more recently by Mearns and Cooper (2005). In their important work on 'relational depth', they suggest that these core conditions have often been seen as separate concepts. Drawing upon the work of Bohart et al. (2002), they record how there is:

> empirical evidence which suggests that a high degree of correlation is often found among the three 'core' conditions of empathy, unconditional positive regard, and congruence … In other words, while many person-centred therapists have been

trained to conceptualise these three conditions as discrete variables, in reality it may be more appropriate to think of them as facets of a single variable: relational depth. More specifically as Bohart and colleagues suggest, we might think of empathy, congruence and unconditional positive regard as analogous to the hue, brightness and saturation of a colour. 'While in principle any given color can be dissected into these three qualities, the impact of that particular color depends on all three' (2002: 102). (Mearns and Cooper, 2005: 36–7)

Whether the core conditions are seen as separate qualities or just one with separate dimensions, what is without doubt is their importance to the counselling relationship. When children are offered all three, healing is more likely, relationships are established, barriers are overcome and hope is found.

EXERCISES

1. With a partner, talk about yourself for around 10 minutes but from the perspective of someone who knows you well.
2. Sit with another person. Ask them to think about something of emotional significance, but not to speak. Stay with them. Try to get a sense of what they might be feeling.
3. When has somebody shown you real empathy? What was it like? How did it make you feel?
4. Reflect upon a time when another person's story has evoked strong emotions within you.
5. Think of a time when you have offered sympathy, say, for example, in an attempt to comfort somebody suffering a bereavement. What did you say and how was it received?
6. In *On Becoming a Person*, Carl Rogers (1967) held out the following challenge. You might like to give it a try!

   The next time you get into an argument with your partner, or your friend, or with a small group of friends, just stop the discussion for a moment and for an experiment, institute this rule. 'Each person can speak up for himself only after he has first restated the ideas and feelings of the previous speaker accurately, and to that speaker's satisfaction.' You see what this would mean. It would simply mean that before presenting your point of view, it would be necessary for you to really achieve the other speaker's frame of reference – to understand his thoughts and feelings so well that you could summarise them for him. Sounds simple doesn't it? But if you try it, you will discover that it is one of the most difficult things you have ever tried to do. (p. 332)

11
WORKING CREATIVELY

INTRODUCING THIS CHAPTER

The need for creative and expressive ways of working with children and young people is explored here through case study material. There is a particular focus on key practitioners such as Natalie Rogers.

The use of such potentially powerful media as art, play, music, drama, stories, books and photographs is looked at, but without ever losing sight of person-centred principles.

TO THE COUNSELLOR

Creative and expressive ways of working present new possibilities for the counsellor working with children and young people. Where you wish to incorporate or diversify into this way of working, it is important to gain additional training and opportunities to practise in this way.

TO THE HELPER

Unless you have embarked upon additional training in creative and expressive approaches, it is important to recognise that these can only be an additional form of communication for children and young people, within your work. Nevertheless, creative and expressive approaches do have the power to enrich your work and offer a different dimension to your practice.

WITH CHILDREN AND YOUNG PEOPLE IN MIND

Whilst the ways of working highlighted in this chapter are facilitative and enhancing for work with adults and young people, they are particularly valuable with younger children and sometimes even necessary as ways of enabling the communication of a child's thoughts and feelings.

A DIFFERENT WAY OF WORKING

The person-centred approach has sometimes been criticised for its over-optimistic and sometimes linear approach, allowing for little deviation from a theoretical norm and orthodoxy. We shall see that this was furthest from Carl Rogers' thinking. However, I have to admit to feeling a sense of freedom as I write this chapter. It is as though creative approaches to working with children and young people offer new and exciting possibilities; a kind of blossoming of the approach which brings new colour and which itself seems to capture the essence of child-centredness.

Case study: Maggie

Maggie (aged 9) had been attending a child counselling service as a result of a traumatic experience she had when she saw one of her school friends killed by a car on a crossing whilst walking home from school with her mother. Maggie's mother had also been badly affected by what she had seen so it was hardly surprising that little Maggie has been left with such horrific memories.

For a number of weeks, her counsellor Andy has struggled to engage her and long silences left Andy feeling that he was at best doing no harm, though at worst he could be damaging Maggie's fragile self. Andy desperately wanted her to talk about how she felt and he sensed that she wanted desperately to share what she had seen and many of the very frightening thoughts and images which whirled around in her head.

Andy also understood that such a painful experience was likely to remain safely hidden away, for to re-live the scene would have been far too distressing and painful for Maggie. Andy also felt unsure that, even if Maggie wanted to talk about what had happened, she would have the right language to express her grief, sadness and distress.

It was policy for the counselling service to leave drawing, painting and art materials in the room. Maggie asked if she could paint her house and family and with Andy's warm agreement she began to paint – anything at first: her home, parents,

(Continued)

(Continued)

brothers and sisters. Eventually, she painted her friend Judy who had died so tragically. At first, the pictures depicted the two children playing together, while later she painted herself playing alone with Judy in 'heaven'. As she painted, Maggie cried and asked, 'where is Judy now?' and also explained how she missed her best friend.

Case study: Richard

Richard was 17 when he first started to attend for counselling at his college where he was studying art. A bright and articulate student, Richard nevertheless found it hard talking about his complicated family circumstances, which seemed to be infused with divorce, re-constituted families, brothers and sisters by different parents and broken relationships with a number of girlfriends in recent months. All this had left Richard feeling quite 'depressed' and without any real sense of personal identity. He told his counsellor he needed to be clear about relationships in his own life, just to begin to get a sense of what he was feeling about each of the people who played such an important part in his life.

Richard repeatedly said how important it was for him to be able to explain who everybody was to Malcolm his counsellor. 'Only then', he said, 'can I talk about what I feel'. Malcolm thought about offering Richard the idea that he was concerned less with understanding the structure of his family and more with how Richard was feeling at that time. Malcolm thought hard on this and began to recognise that what Richard was feeling at the time was frustration and a sense of being unable to move on, as if there were a barrier which needed to be overcome. He reflected this back to Richard who felt that now Malcolm was beginning to understand.

The following week and in subsequent sessions after that, Richard brought in a photograph album, which he desperately wanted to share with Malcolm. Very soon, Richard felt able to explain who everybody was but also to start to talk a little about each of the people who made up his world, past and present.

Case study: Thaania

Thaania (aged 8) loved to play with small figurines (animals, people, dinosaurs) with her favourite worker Gillian at the after-school club which she attended before her father could pick her up at 6pm on his way home from work. Thaania had lived at home with just her father since her mother died of cancer a year before. She would use the small plastic figures to tell all sorts of stories, some happy, some sad, but with what Gillian could see had a common theme, that is: families and people going away and not coming back again. Thaania also liked to play with the soft toys which were stored in the cupboard of the church hall where the club took place. Few of the other children showed any interest in the worn and sometimes quite grubby cuddly toys, but for Thaania they represented not only her way of holding on to Gillian's time but also helped her re-create, in a safe way, some of the difficult feelings of loss which she held so tightly inside.

Case study: Lizzie

Lizzie, now 15, had been sexually abused by her half-brother when she was six. He was 12 when the single instance of abuse happened, on a day when her half-brother was entrusted with the responsibility of looking after her whilst her parents were out.

Lizzie had never spoken to anyone about what had happened but her silence had more recently caused feelings to burn up inside her to the point where she self-referred to the school counsellor. She very soon insisted that she didn't want to talk about the details of what had happened because she felt that there was little purpose in re-living her experience; indeed, her recollections of what had happened were confused and not altogether clear to her.

She was ambivalent about her half-brother Colin, whom she said she felt some anger towards, but also said that 'he was having a hard time' when it happened and that he 'hadn't actually harmed' her. Lizzie, a bright student, with hopes of doing English literature at university preferred to write about her feelings rather than talk a lot. Each week, she would arrive with a new poem or piece of creative writing, normally around themes of trust, mixed feelings and shame.

Lizzie was able to use words well, but chose to express herself through her writing which she told her counsellor gave her time to really get in touch with what she was feeling, week by week.

What links these brief stories of helping and counselling is that Maggie, Richard, Thaania and Lizzie all either preferred or were only able to begin to express their feelings and share their story through means other than exclusively through talk. As stated earlier in this book, working with children and young people therapeutically is different to working with most adults. It was also said that the image of the counselling room, with client and adult sitting for 50 minutes, is to a large extent an adult model and those working with children and young people soon come to realise that media other than talk may be necessary if a therapeutic relationship is to be established and nurtured. There is of course a proviso, that is, that whatever medium is used, the person-centred counsellor does not lose sight of the principles and beliefs which underpin the approach.

It should also be noted that whilst this chapter focuses on the 'creative' dimension, other ways of working though not essentially creative still have a part to play in work with children and young people and are therefore included in this chapter in a way which offers the person-centred practitioner new opportunities and possibilities.

WHY OTHER APPROACHES IN WORKING WITH CHILDREN AND YOUNG PEOPLE ARE USEFUL

Some children and young people find sharing their thoughts, feelings and problems with a caring adult quite easy and some positively crave the time that adults are able to offer. Some children and young people seem able to sit with an adult and talk week after week about their lives, their hopes and fears and their anxieties. However, others do not find talking so easy and finding other ways for children to express their feelings becomes necessary.

A psychodynamic perspective on the difficulties faced in counselling children is offered by Geldard and Geldard (1997), who write:

> Unfortunately, many children who come to counselling have issues which are too painful for them to confront. Sometimes these issues are known to the child, but often they are hidden, or partially hidden, in the child's unconscious. Some children have misconceptions about past traumatic events as a result of information which has been repressed and is missing from their consciousness, because it is too painful. If a child is to become aware of the issues, which are partially or fully buried in the unconscious, then the counsellor will need to raise the child's awareness of these issues. (p. 64)

They go on to say that: 'children are experts at deflecting away from emotional pain and at avoiding the issues, which relate to that pain' (p. 64).

Of course, what is being said here would apply equally to many adults and neither is it surprising that this process of keeping emotions firmly buried should occur. In many ways, it represents an understandable response to unpleasant things in people's lives. The idea that if you are bothered by something it is better to 'get it out' is very much a sophisticated adult position which children and young people sometimes do not share.

Using creative and alternative approaches also helps young people overcome the kinds of language barriers explored elsewhere in this book. Art, music, drama and writing also serve to enable the young person to do what they might do in a more traditional counselling setting. The process is the same, the counsellor is the same, the approach is the same but words are replaced by other chosen forms of expression.

WITH CHILDREN AND YOUNG PEOPLE IN MIND

Using alternative approaches can seem less daunting for the child or young person. Creative approaches also connect with the child's inclination towards creativity, and symbolic representation facilitates communication where words are hard to find. Alternative approaches offer a warm, caring and non-pressured therapeutic environment through which children can express themselves with greater accuracy, expression and personal meaning.

Children and young people often enjoy working creatively and the adult often enjoys the experience too. Creative and alternative approaches can also enable the young client to talk about the problems and issues they face more safely by allowing painful, complicated or confusing feelings to be expressed through colour, sound, role and by investing characters with their own emotions. The child or young person is therefore able to work with the adult in a way which allows some distance, overcoming a psychological immediateness which might otherwise have proved an insurmountable barrier.

Whether it be for children, young people or adults, Carl Rogers (1967) himself saw the potential relationship between therapy and creativity. Creativity and therapy could be viewed as mirroring processes:

> The mainspring of creativity appears to be the same tendency which we discover so deeply as the curative force in psychotherapy – man's tendency to actualise himself, to become his potentialities. By this I mean the directional trend which is evident in all organic and human life – the urge to expand, extend, develop, mature – the tendency to express and activate all the capacities of the organism, or the self. This tendency may become deeply buried under layer after layer of encrusted psychological defences; it may be hidden behind elaborate façades which deny its existence; it is my belief however, based on my own experience that it exists in every individual, and awaits only the proper conditions to be released and expressed. (1967: 350–1)

These beliefs are shared by Natalie Rogers who has continued her father's work and whose ideas we shall explore more fully later.

A PERSON-CENTRED APPROACH TO CREATIVE THERAPIES AND ALTERNATE WAYS OF WORKING WITH CHILDREN AND YOUNG PEOPLE

In his book *The Tribes of the Person-centred Nation*, Pete Sanders (2004) sets out the debate as to the nature of a family of therapies that might consider themselves to have their origins or beliefs located in the person-centred approach. He considers the place of what he terms 'expressive therapies', recognising that this is a plural concept and that there is not just one expressive therapy, but many, and that these might include not only forms of art such as painting, sculpture and collage, but also voice work, drama, movement and writing. All of these, plus others, I do believe, have the potential to enrich and facilitate our work with young people. However, Sanders notes a number of points which need to be debated in relation to their use.

The first of these raises the question as to whether Rogers' core conditions are indeed 'necessary' but not 'sufficient'. This book has taken the position that when working with children and young people, traditional person-centred counselling may indeed require the practitioner to use a number of approaches, which can be creative in design and which supplement more orthodox approaches.

The second debate set out by Sanders relates to modes of communication. He asks the question:

Are arts modes simply methods of communicating, helping access essentially the same material but through non-verbal channels? Is symbolisation of experience accessible (or maybe *better* accessible) through non-verbal modes of expression, like movement, painting, sculpture? Do non-verbal modes of experiencing and expression complement, add to and amplify verbal expressions? (2004: xii–xiii)

My own position here is clear. Unless there are special circumstances where a child is unable to use the spoken word, working creatively does complement, amplify and I would say give voice to those feelings which young people find difficult to express. In this sense, expressive therapy is best used alongside more verbal ways of working, wherever possible.

The third question raised by Sanders concerns the therapeutic value or 'health-promoting' characteristics of creativity. Reinforcing the position stated by Rogers above, and the inclination of young people to want to play, create and move, this point, I believe, has already been made.

The next issue raised by Sanders concerns the concept of working holistically. He states: 'Since Client/Person-centred Therapy is holistic, some argue that only when the client is offered a range of expressive possibilities (music, movement, painting, sculpting, etc.), not just the verbal, can we claim truly to be working with the whole person' (p. xiii). On this point, and with children and young people in mind, I am inclined to agree with this premise.

Two final debates are advanced by Sanders. The first asks whether creative ways of working are better than purely verbal approaches when working at 'the edge of awareness'? I do feel, for the reasons stated above (that is, the likelihood that childhood sometimes masks more unpleasant and traumatic experience, forcing it into the unconscious), that working creatively can often help children and young people access thoughts and feelings that might otherwise remain hidden.

Sanders' final question is an important one. All of the creative therapies mentioned have links to more psychodynamic and cognitive ways of working. Certainly, for those wishing to work in schools and other settings, there is a large range of published materials asking children to draw or paint scenarios, take on pre-determined roles or construct shapes in order to express emotion, or that even ask them to rate their feelings on a kind of continuum. This is not to say that some of these 'activities' do not have their place in helping children and many are used with some effect by people working in roles which emphasise the management or modification of behaviour and by those professionals such as mentors who often work to raise self-esteem in children and young people damaged by life's circumstances.

Sanders, however, asks the question: 'Can the offering of creative/expressive arts methods be done in such a way as to honour the non-directive principle of classical CCT practice?' (p. xiii). My own position is a resounding yes, but the adult working with the child or young person should never lose sight of the key person-centred principles, as set out in this book and other works that advocate this way of working.

Returning to Rogers' (1967) own position on the place of creativity in relation to the person-centred approach, in his advocacy of creativity, we are able to gain some sense of what would constitute a person-centred approach to working through expressive ways.

Firstly, he sets out what he considers to be the conditions within a person which are most closely aligned with a 'potentially constructive creative act'. These may be highlighted as follows:

- An openness to experience: extensionality. This is described by Rogers as the opposite to a defensive position in which when 'we protect the organisation of the self, certain experiences are prevented from coming into awareness except in distorted fashion'.
- An internal locus of evaluation. Rogers writes:

  Perhaps the most fundamental condition of creativity is that the source or locus of evaluative judgement is internal. The value of his product is, for the creative person, established not by the praise or criticism of others, but by himself.

- The ability to toy with elements and concepts. By this, Rogers means:

  The ability to play spontaneously with ideas, colours, shapes, relationships – to juggle elements into impossible juxtapositions, to shape wild hypotheses, to make the given problematic, to express the ridiculous, to translate from one form to another, to transform into improbable equivalents. It is from this spontaneous toying and exploration that there arises the hunch, the creative seeing of life in a new and significant way. (Rogers, 1967: 355)

It will be clear to the reader that Rogers is endorsing a creative dimension to psychotherapy, and his ideas begin to shape what a creative approach to counselling with children and young people might look like.

In *On Becoming a Person,* Rogers (1967) sets out a fundamental principle in relation to this kind of way of working. He states:

From the very nature of the inner conditions of creativity it is clear that they cannot be forced, but must be permitted to emerge. The farmer cannot make the germ develop and sprout from the seed; he can only supply the nurturing conditions which will permit the seed to develop its own potentialities. So it is with creativity. (pp. 356–7)

In further discussion, Rogers proposes a number of 'external conditions' which he felt would 'nourish the internal conditions', and which he describes as:

- Psychological safety. This, he says, can be established in three ways: accepting the individual as of unconditional worth; providing a climate in which external evaluation is absent; and understanding empathically.
- Psychological freedom. This 'permissiveness', he says, offers the individual an 'opportunity to think, to feel, to be, whatever is most inward within himself'. (pp. 357–8)

The reader will of course not be unfamiliar with these ideas. However, they do suggest that working creatively with children and young people in a person-centred way is both possible and, indeed, desirable.

THE WORK AND INFLUENCE OF NATALIE ROGERS

To help us in our understanding of person-centred approaches to working creatively with children and young people, we are fortunate to be able to draw upon the ideas, practice and writings of Carl Rogers' daughter Natalie, who continued her father's work and gave it a particular focus through what she termed Expressive Arts Therapy. Her philosophy and practice is most readily found in her very readable book *The Creative Connection: Expressive Arts as Healing*, published in 2000.

It is important to note at this point that when she talks in her work about 'arts', she is not limiting this to traditional visual art media such as painting, drawing, sculpture and collage. Rather, Rogers has developed a wider concept which also includes music, drama, dance, writing, poetry, imagery and meditation, amongst other forms of expression.

Before we draw from this and other writings and contributions made by Natalie Rogers, let us look briefly at another case study.

Case study: Daniel

Daniel (aged 9) attended a behaviour intervention unit after his exclusion from school as a result of a series of violent attacks against other pupils at his previous junior school, as well as an incident where a chair had been thrown across a classroom which resulted in a minor injury to his teacher Mrs Williams. Daniel's background was very troubled with family disputes, domestic violence and family criminality crowding his short but unhappy life. Daniel had been 'uncontrollable' at school with teachers remarking that he was 'the worst they had ever seen'. One teacher said that he had 'simply no idea about how to behave in a school environment'.

In his new unit, as he had been at school, teachers, despite small group teaching, found it difficult to get him to sit for more than a few minutes. Conflict with other group members was frequent and sometimes quite violent. Poor school attendance had made progress difficult and any attempts at reprimand or indeed encouragement were met with flight from the room and sometimes the centre itself.

His frustrated teacher would often ask Daniel if he would like to talk about things at home but he most frequently would not reply. His teacher knew that he liked to paint:

It's obviously very hard for you to talk about home Daniel, why don't you draw me what you are feeling? You could use dark colours because that normally means that a person is sad.

I know that there are adults in your life whom you trust and others that you don't. Can you paint me an island? Put everybody you trust on the island and those who you don't, out at sea. That will be a very good way for you to tell me how you feel about certain people in your life.

Show me how you are feeling right now – perhaps you could draw me a face.

(Continued)

(Continued)

Very soon, his unit teacher became disheartened. She thought that giving Daniel some ideas would help him express what he clearly could not put into words. Daniel picked up some mathematical shapes from a box and began building a tower. Frustrated and exhausted, Daniel's teacher let him play; at least he was learning something about shapes and how they fit together.

Daniel's teacher had made an heroic effort to engage him but despite her caring intentions, her approach was directive and possibly intrusive.

Natalie Rogers is clear that working creatively with people can bring growth and change. However, she is very determined that the principles and attitudes which underpin the person-centred approach also form the basis of her expressive therapeutic work.

Writing about her approach Rogers (2000) describes the meaning of expressive arts therapy:

We express inner feelings by creating outer forms. Expressive art refers to using the emotional, intuitive aspects of ourselves in various media. To use the arts expressively means going into our inner realms to discover feelings and to express them through visual art, movement, sound, writing, or drama. (p. 2)

It is also important to understand that creative therapies within the person-centred approach are not concerned with analysis or a young person's ability to paint beautiful pictures or cleverly take on roles or compose memorable music. Sometimes, when children and young people are introduced to this way of working, they become defensive or resistant, often saying that they 'cannot draw' or are not very good at writing and spelling. The adult who incorporates creative and expressive ways of working with children and young people is not concerned with quality, accuracy or any purely aesthetic dimension. Natalie Rogers takes up this point:

When using the arts for self-healing or therapeutic purposes, we are not concerned about the beauty of the visual art, the grammar and style of the writing, or the harmonic flow of the song. We use the arts to let go, to express, and to release. Also, we can gain insight by studying the symbolic and metaphoric messages. Our art speaks back to us if we take the time to let in those messages.

Although interesting and sometimes dramatic products emerge, we leave the aesthetics and the craftsmanship to those who wish to pursue the arts professionally. (2000: 2)

In a discussion of the humanistic principles, Rogers (2000) sets out clearly those principles which underpin her approach:

- All people have the innate ability to be creative.
- The creative process is healing.
- Personal growth and higher states of consciousness are achieved through self-awareness, self-understanding and insight.

- Self-awareness, understanding and insight are achieved by delving into our emotions.
- Our feelings and emotions are an energy source.
- The expressive arts – including movement, art, writing, sound, music, meditation and imagery – lead us into the unconscious.
- Art modes interrelate in what I call the creative connection.
- A connection exists between our life force – our inner core, or soul – and the essence of all beings.
- Therefore, as we journey inwards to discover our essence or wholeness, we discover our relatedness to the outer world. (pp. 7–8)

A further insight to Rogers' thinking around a person-centred approach to working creatively is revealed in an answer to a question posed to her by Tony Merry (1997). Her detailed response offers us a real insight into working creatively and how these ways of working can be used with children and young people.

Merry asks her to define a 'psychologically safe environment' and she replies that she has developed a credo which summarises in a personal way, her adaptation of the person-centred approach to her work. She writes the following for her clients:

- I am aware that going on one's inner journey can be a frightening, exhilarating, exhausting adventure.
- I will be present for you but not intrusive.
- I have faith that you know how to take care of yourself. I will not be responsible for you or take away your power.
- Nor will I abandon you.
- I will respect you and your decisions for yourself. I have faith in your ability.
- I will support you and encourage you on your inner journey.
- My efforts to be congruent may challenge you and your belief system, at times, but I will always respect you and your truth.
- I will encourage you to try new things, to take risks into the unknown of your inner world, but I will never push you.
- I will offer you expressive arts media to help you open to your innate creativity and discover your inner essence. You are free not to use these media.
- At times I will give you my opinions and feedback but will always check it out to see if it is meaningful to you.
- I will honour my own boundaries and yours to the best of my ability.
- I will share my value system and beliefs with you so that you know why I am saying and doing what I say and do.
- I am open to learning from you at all times.
- I make mistakes, do things I am not pleased with, and am misguided at times.
- In such instances, I will say so. I am able to say 'I'm sorry'. (Rogers, 2000: 103–4)

While Rogers' approach suggests a greater degree of counsellor activity, the humanity and person-centredness is evident. Using creative approaches with children and young people necessitates understanding feelings, allowing for autonomy, offering choice as opposed to coercion, and valuing reflection and an openness to learning from the child and adult realness, honesty and warmth. With these principles in mind, let us now turn to the range of possibilities available to the person-centred practitioner working with children and young people.

ART THERAPY

WITH CHILDREN AND YOUNG PEOPLE IN MIND

Art is a particularly powerful way of working with young clients, especially young children who are drawn towards creativity and visual representation of complex ideas and feelings.

The fact that art therapy is found in most therapeutic traditions is, Dalley (1984) suggests, an indication of its importance. Art therapy can take a number of forms. Some practitioners use art therapy sessions to assess, direct and analyse or interpret their client's work. In contrast, the person-centred approach, which, as we have seen, is based upon the understanding that people will move towards growth and actualisation, enables the client to understand their own image in a way which is meaningful to them and, in doing so, move towards growth and healing.

Art therapy, which might include working with, amongst other media, painting, drawing, sculpture, model-making or collage, helps children and young people to find natural, new and safe ways of expressing their deepest thoughts and feelings. This is because the focus is on the activity and finding meaning, rather than on the young client's ability to express themselves using talk. Matt Keating in a *Guardian* article (2007) quotes from Carole Welsby, an art therapist working in a secondary school environment. She writes: 'Verbal therapy can often seem quite threatening, particularly for adolescents. Art therapy allows them almost a place to hide, from which they can appear slowly'.

Information from The British Association of Art Therapists (BAAT) (see www.baat.org) stresses the importance of the relationship in art therapy. Clearly, this mirrors the person-centred perspective which, as we have seen, gives weight to the relationship between counsellor and client as being a major factor in change and growth. However, BAAT suggests that art therapy differs from other psychological therapies in that it involves a *three*-way relationship with the image or artefact, completing the triangular relationship.

A key influence in the person-centred art therapy movement is Liesl Silverstone whose book: *Art Therapy the Person-centred Way* (1997) provides a wonderful resource for adults who want to use art therapeutically with children and young people.

In an account of how she came to be an art therapist, Silverstone gives us some insight into her approach and thinking:

Slowly I began to see the benefits of my work as a school counsellor, extending the person-centred approach to young people, watching their self-esteem grow. And yet, and yet – I began to note the limitations of mere words, began to search for some other mode of knowing.

Images. Art therapy. I discovered first (inevitably) for myself the power, the potential, the truth contained in images made visible. I learned that images, like dreams, tap into the world of spontaneous knowing, nothing to do with thoughts. When dialoguing with a picture I'd have those moments of 'aha!' when the image gave up – or rather, I recognised – a message to me. Through art therapy an integration between the thinking and the knowing mode, between conscious and unconscious material, could take place. I brought the person-centred mode of facilitating to the world of art therapy – allowing the *client* to know what the picture meant. No interpretations. No guess work. No me knowing best. The evidence was astonishing, encouraging. (pp. 1–2)

PLAY THERAPY

Play therapy can be both directive and non-directive. In the former, the therapist takes responsibility for initiating, guiding and interpreting the play activities. In this book, we are concerned with a more person–centred model, often known as non-directive play therapy.

Play itself plays an important part in the development of the child and therefore forms one of the primary activities of childhood. A young child who has had little opportunity to play with toys and other playthings may experience difficulties with adjustment later on into childhood.

WITH CHILDREN AND YOUNG PEOPLE IN MIND

Play therapy taps into this natural inclination in the child towards play and as a result play therapy can be an exciting, creative, meaningful and sometimes beautiful way of working with children and indeed with young people.

Virginia Axline (1989), who is a key figure in play therapy, writes:

Play therapy is based upon the fact that play is the child's natural medium of self-expression. It is an opportunity which is given to the child to 'play out' his feelings and problems, just as, in certain types of adult therapy, an individual 'talks out' his difficulties. (p. 8)

Play therapy uses play as the principle form of communication. It is an especially valuable way of working with children and young people who have difficulty expressing their thoughts and feelings through words alone.

Axline is well known for her book *Dibs: In Search of Self* (1964), in which she describes movingly her work with a young boy, judged by many to be disturbed. She recounts how eventually through therapy and love, he was able to find himself and heal the hurt within.

Axline drew much of her inspiration for her play therapy approach from Carl Rogers and much of her way of working is based around Rogers' core conditions and beliefs about growth and change. Rogers' influence is very much evident in what Axline describes as the 'eight basic principles' which underpin her approach and which influence play therapists around the world, and which according to Carroll (1998) provide the 'cornerstone' of current practice. They are:

- The therapist must develop a warm, friendly relationship with the child, in which good rapport is established as soon as possible. ...
- The therapist accepts the child exactly as he is. ...
- The therapist establishes a feeling of permissiveness in the relationship so that the child feels free to express his feelings completely. ...
- The therapist is alert to recognising the *feelings* the child is expressing and reflects those feelings back to him in such a manner that he gains insight into his behaviour. ...
- The therapist maintains a deep respect for the child's ability to solve his own problems if given an opportunity to do so. The responsibility to make choices and to institute change is the child's. ...
- The therapist does not attempt to direct the child's actions or conversation in any manner. The child leads the way; the therapist follows. ...
- The therapist does not attempt to hurry the therapy along. It is a gradual process as is recognised as such by the therapist. ...
- The therapist establishes only those limitations that are necessary to anchor the therapy to the world of reality and to make the child aware of his responsibility in the relationship. (pp. 67–73)

Axline describes the therapeutic value of play therapy. Through play, she argues, the child is able to bring difficult or painful feelings to the surface and by getting them 'out in the open', the child is able to control them or decide to leave them aside.

In describing the process of play therapy further, Axline (1989) writes:

The play therapy room is good growing ground. In the security of this room where the child is the most important person, where he is in command of the situation and of himself, where no one tells him what to do, no one criticises what he does, no one nags, or suggests, or goads him on, or pries into his private world, he suddenly feels that here he can unfold his wings; he can look squarely at himself, for he is accepted completely; he can test out his ideas; he can express himself fully; for this is his world ... (p. 15)

Play therapy normally takes place in a special place set aside for the work but aspects of play therapy can take place wherever the adult and child meet. Play therapy can take many forms and includes activities which encourage expression such as playing with dolls and soft toys, puppets, miniature animals and figurines and also can involve dressing up and role-play. The play therapist may join in the play when invited by the child or at the child's direction.

One of the most celebrated and exciting forms of play therapy involves the use of sand. The sand is confined within a space which is then used by the young person, utilising any objects or figures which have symbolic significance to tell their story. Geldard and Geldard (1997) suggest the possibilities of sand tray work:

> While telling her story, the child has an opportunity to re-create in the sand tray, and in her imagination, events and situations from her past and present. The child may also explore possibilities for the future or express her fantasies in the sand tray. (p. 107)

Bradway and McCoard (1997), despite their more Jungian psychodynamic approach, explain the nature of sand play work. They suggest that it is an 'active form of imagination'. However, the images in sand play make concrete and visual what might otherwise remain 'invisible and intangible'. Sand play also makes available, to both client and therapist, that which would normally be spoken or 'reported' to the therapist.

Joe Woodhouse (2008) offers us a thoughtful look at the work of the person-centred play therapist working with sand. She offers us these insights:

> Offering Sandplay in a person-centred therapy relationship opens many possibilities for enriching the relationship between child and therapist, thereby facilitating the child's process. The vivid visual and physical nature of Sandplay means there are very many ways in which children can share their personal stories and experiences. Sandplay, as 'growing ground', creates opportunities for child and therapist to relate in ways that may not happen in therapy based simply on talking. The relationship gains more dimensions. (2008: 37)

As with other forms of working in a person-centred way with children and young people, play therapy emphasises the establishment and maintenance of a warm, supportive, non-judgemental and empathic relationship.

A modern and refreshing perspective on person-centred play therapy can be found in the practice and writings of Tracey Walshaw (2008). In her training work, she records how: 'Play therapy students come with constraining mantras about what is and what is not person-centred'. She notes how students arrive, 'having internalised rigid conditions of worth about being person-centred, which puts them into a straightjacket, which limits creativity' (p. 4). She says that the biggest asset she brings to her work with children as a person-centred practitioner is her ability to co-create relationships, 'engaging my spontaneity and creativity'. The reader is asked to reconsider whether a 'discerning practitioner' holds certain boundaries in play therapy because they are an ethical choice rather than a 'rule or familiar pattern'. Walshaw asks us to reconsider orthodoxy, questioning whether the therapist can ask questions of the child, become involved in the play work directly, offer advice, choose media and so on.

Her conclusion is that the discerning child practitioner can challenge traditionally held positions as long as what they do is 'underpinned by a strong theoretical and philosophical understanding of the person-centred approach' (2008: 5).

The British Association of Play Therapists (BAPT) and Play Therapy UK (PTUK) are two useful organisations for counsellors and therapists who wish to incorporate play into their work with children and young people.

MUSIC THERAPY

Making and experiencing music is a universal experience. It offers a young client an opportunity for creative expression and we know that children love to experiment with a large range of sounds and rhythms. Music therapy also recognises that everybody has the ability to create or respond to musical sounds, at whatever level. Music has the capacity to touch our deepest emotions and feelings and enables a child or young person to communicate with few, if any, words.

All of us have felt moved or touched by a particular song or musical piece which conveys personal meaning, evokes a nostalgic response or touches our innermost emotional self. Music touches upon all aspects of human experience, including the depths of depression or elation and joy. In this sense, music is a perfect medium for working with young people in therapeutic settings.

WITH CHILDREN AND YOUNG PEOPLE IN MIND

Music therapy enables a child or young person to express feelings that are too difficult to express in words. This approach also provides a safe environment for a young person to say how they feel and to express their confusion, hopes and fears.

In music therapy, the adult normally participates in the music making, which may involve the use of instruments or singing or generally any sound that has meaning for the young person. Music therapy does not involve the adult teaching the child or young person to play a particular instrument or improve their singing. Rather, the music enables the young client to explore the nature and diversity of sound, including their own voices. Music therapy encourages the young person to create a musical language of their own.

Music therapy can be delivered from a number of theoretical orientations but the person-centred therapist emphasises their relationship with the young person. Music-making instruments and objects are made available to the child or young person and little direction is given. The young client is encouraged to improvise and express themselves freely and with their individual needs in mind.

DRAMA THERAPY

Drama therapy offers children and young people an opportunity to express themselves creatively, increase their self-awareness and explore their relationships with others. Drama therapy uses a variety of processes including games, improvisation, role-play, masks, voice work, myth and ritual. It makes significant use of imagination, metaphor and symbolism. Sometimes, the drama therapist will bring stimulus material or begin sessions with a story. The drama therapist adopting a more person-centred approach is more likely to offer freedom to the child or young person to develop their own story, with the therapist reflecting back what they see and experience.

Whereas more traditional counselling involves the use of talk and listening, drama therapy involves action and actually doing things. This makes drama therapy a particularly valuable and accessible medium for young people to explore and express their thoughts and feelings. The drama therapist creates a safe environment in which young people feel that they can express their emotions, at their own pace and without judgement. It is this process which facilitates growth and development.

Warren (1984) sees drama as human interaction and a way of communicating with others 'verbally, physically and emotionally'. He also views drama as a process, which transforms imagination into action. In this way, through facial expression, body language, movement and speech, deep emotions and feelings can be communicated to others. Drama therapy encourages the young client to experiment with different and new ways of thinking, feeling and experiencing the world and their relationships with others. Drama therapy may also serve to increase confidence in the child or young person and, through role-play, encourage the development of empathy.

ADDITIONAL WAYS OF WORKING WITH CHILDREN AND YOUNG PEOPLE

Children and young people who find it difficult to express themselves through the spoken word sometimes choose to write. For example, they may bring a journal along to sessions to share with the helping adult. This may include what is happening in their life but may also contain much feeling and emotion. Some children and young people like to write poetry in an attempt to let the adult helper know what they are experiencing. Children also like to write stories which have personal meaning, and sharing these with an adult can be quite therapeutic.

Of course, telling stories to children can also be a useful approach. Margot Sunderland (2000), in her book *Using Story Telling as a Therapeutic Tool with Children*, explains the rationale about this way of connecting with a child or young person:

> Using story recognises the limitations of talking about feelings to children in everyday language. Stories can speak to children on a deeper and far more

immediate level than literal, everyday language. Talking about feelings in everyday language can mean going round and round in circles. This is because everyday language is a 'language of thinking', whereas speaking through a story … means that you are using a language of imagining. (2000: 4)

Sunderland says that telling stories to children or children telling stories to adults 'can speak about feelings with amazing richness'. She continues:

> In fact, the mind naturally speaks about emotional issues through story, as we see in dreams. In dreams, image and metaphor are the mind's chosen way of processing powerful feelings in our past or present, as well as our fears or hopes for the future. A story is simply like having a dream while being awake. (2000: 5)

Related to the use of stories is the wider approach known as Bibliotherapy which involves a child or young person reading a book and sharing their thoughts and feelings with a caring adult. Normally, a book is chosen which relates either in content or emotion to the child or young person's current situation. In this way, the young client is able to connect with or relate to the characters in the book, and explore their emotional reaction to the story and those who figure in it. Initially, the focus is on the book but inevitably will begin to turn to the problems and difficulties which brought the child or young person to seek help in the first place. Bibliotherapy normally happens alongside the main process of counselling.

In a similar way, some adults working with children and young people adopt an approach involving the use of film. Film, cinema or reel therapy works in the same way as bibliotherapy but the visual image makes stories more accessible to children and young people. Film therapy hopes that by watching movies, the young client will relate to the characters in the story and the plot itself. This may encourage the child or young person to become aware of and express their own feelings and internal processes.

Another powerful way of working with young clients is through the use of pictures and images. The child or young person is free to choose which pictures they want to talk about. Without judgement, the adult listens, reflects feelings and thereby encourages deeper exploration.

Finally, photographs can play an important part in work with children and young people. My own experience of working with young clients has shown that children are often keen to share family, friends and events by bringing in photograph albums or individual pictures. Linda Berman (1993) has written an interesting book in this area of work; she writes about how her interest in the therapeutic use of photographs began:

> During my work as a therapist, many patients have brought to me photographs of parents, spouses, siblings, children. Often, having responded with interest, I felt uncertain about using them therapeutically and would be left with a sense of missed opportunity. Gradually, however, I began to explore ways in which the photographs could be utilised in the session and my interest in them began to grow …

She goes on to describe the process in this way:

> I feel privileged to have been allowed into several people's personal worlds through sharing their photographs. I have 'met' their relatives and friends and 'watched' them through the growing up process. I have shared the intense pain and joy as repressed memories cascade through time into consciousness, and I have witnessed the subsequent dawning of new insight. (1993: vi)

IN CONCLUSION

There are some person-centred therapists who take a more purist approach to counselling. They might argue that some of the ways of working briefly explored in this chapter are drawn from other psychological and therapeutic traditions. This may hold some truth but as stated earlier in this book, working with children and young people is different and therefore requires the adult helper or counsellor to think creatively. I believe that all the approaches described here can be incorporated into the person-centred approach as long as the practitioner does not lose sight of the core conditions and their philosophical underpinnings. In many ways, art, drama, music or writing are only means of communication. The attitudes, beliefs and ways of working of the person-centred counsellor remain the same.

EXERCISES

1. Through which creative activities do you find that you can express yourself most effectively?
2. Discuss with a partner the emotional impact of a song which evokes nostalgia; a special painting; a toy from your childhood; a play that you have seen; or a book or poem that you have read.

12
DEVELOPING PERSON-CENTRED SKILLS, ATTITUDES AND QUALITIES

INTRODUCING THIS CHAPTER

This chapter raises important questions about the very place of skills and techniques within the person-centred approach. It touches upon some key concepts such as 'presence', 'frames of reference', immediacy, challenging and silence and takes a person-centred view of these. The ideas most relevant to working with children and young people are illustrated with a number of practical examples. The chapter closes with a brief look at some of the most important qualities and attitudes which are likely to be found in the person-centred practitioner.

AVOIDANCE OF TECHNIQUE

As I contemplate the writing of this chapter, my memory is drawn to my early training in counselling. I recall how the tutor talked for a few minutes after which we were asked to write a summary of what he had said and read this to the rest of the group. I was confident that my summary was accurate and was pleased when the group confirmed this. Feeling inwardly proud but trying not to show it, lest I appear boastful, I became increasingly confident in my belief that I could make a go of this counselling thing.

I also call to mind the assessment process which was based upon my ability to demonstrate the use of a number of counselling 'skills' such as 'paraphrasing' and asking 'open' and not 'closed' questions.

The use of 'skills' is often at its most basic when observed at the beginning of counselling courses. Trainees can be observed religiously attempting to demonstrate a range of techniques and skills, which have been discussed and demonstrated.

WITH CHILDREN AND YOUNG PEOPLE IN MIND

If a stilted, albeit 'skilled', approach is carried over into work with children and young people, the result is often a play of roles between the adult and young client. At best, an over-reliance on skills can hamper the development of a therapeutic relationship with the child. In some cases, it can serve to alienate the young person, as the experience appears to mimic non-therapeutic relationships and is often experienced by the young child as false and fabricated.

Here, we are talking about the development of techniques, a concept that is, to a large degree, at odds with the person-centred approach. As we have seen, Rogers regarded his core conditions of unconditional positive regard, congruence and empathy as both 'necessary and sufficient'. These conditions represent an attitude within the counsellor rather than a set of skills to be deployed in the therapeutic session. It is this which differentiates person-centred ways of working from other approaches. Person-centred counselling places emphasis on the relationship between the client and counsellor, rather than on a set of learned techniques.

Rogers commented widely on this matter. In 1951, he wrote:

It is common to find client-centred therapy spoken of as simply a method or a technique to be used by the counsellor. No doubt, this connotation is due in part to the fact that earlier presentations tended to overstress technique. It may more accurately be said that the counsellor who is effective in client-centred therapy holds a coherent and developing set of attitudes deeply imbedded in his personal organization, a system of attitudes which is implemented by techniques and methods consistent with it. In our experience, the counsellor who tries to use a 'method' is doomed to be unsuccessful unless this method is genuinely in line with his own attitudes. On the other hand, the counsellor whose attitudes are of the type, which facilitate therapy, may only be partially successful, because his attitudes are inadequately implemented by appropriate methods and techniques. (pp. 19–20)

Rogers believed that techniques and skills were only relevant within the person-centred approach if they served to enhance the relationship which is based upon the core conditions. In this sense, they do not exist in their own right.

In a wonderful collection of Rogers' writings edited by Kirschenbaum and Henderson (1990), we find Rogers reflecting upon this very point:

For the practice of psychotherapy, the theory also offers significant problems for consideration. One of its implications is that the techniques of the various therapies are relatively unimportant except to the extent that they serve as channels for fulfilling one of the conditions. In client-centred therapy, for example, the technique of 'reflecting feelings' has been described and commented on. In terms of the theory here being presented, this technique is by no means an essential condition of therapy. To the extent, however, that it provides a channel by which the therapist communicates a sensitive empathy and an unconditional positive regard, then it may serve as a technical channel by which the essential conditions of therapy are fulfilled. (1990: 233)

Adults working with children and young people sometimes defer to technique when they experience problems with the counselling relationship. Merry (1999) illustrates this point:

A problem in person-centred counselling (and all other counselling) occurs when the counsellor reaches for a technique either when the going gets tough (when the client seems 'stuck' for example), or simply because the counsellor knows a lot of techniques and wants to use them. (p. 115)

Merry goes on to say that in such circumstances, rather than deploying a technique which serves to 'gloss over these problems', the counsellor may well ask themselves whether they are being fully accepting, congruent and offering a high degree of empathy to their client.

I have seen this process so many times in supervising counsellors working with children and young people. The counsellor, feeling inadequate and insecure, turns to 'tried and tested' techniques to relieve the anxiety in themselves, but in a way which is presented as helping the young person move on. In many ways, this is understandable, and I am sure this has been evident in my own work with children and young people over the years. The key here is holding on to the core beliefs in the ability of the client to find their own way and, ultimately, to trust in the therapeutic process.

This emphasis on and acceptance of the pre-eminence of the relationship in person-centred work is found in Cooper et al. (2007):

Among other things, this implies a strict rejection of both an abstinent attitude and the use of preconceived techniques. It rules out the therapist considering himself or herself as an expert in the correct usage of methods and means, and even excludes the use of any methods and techniques that are not rooted in the immediate experience of the relationship. The only 'means' or 'instrument' employed is the person of the therapist him- or herself. (p. 41)

The reader who is interested in the development of counselling skills can turn to the vast array of books on this subject, but may wish to explore and practise these with the person-centred principles set out in this book, and with the argument set out above, firmly in mind.

TO THE COUNSELLOR

You may have begun your training in counselling following generic skills-based courses. However, it can sometimes be difficult to re-asses these and give up ways of working which feel both familiar and safe. The person-centred approach requires more of you as a person.

TO THE HELPER

You may have had opportunities to develop your counselling skills in ways designed to improve your effectiveness in working with children and young people. These are to be valued and will improve your efforts to listen and respond. Your relationships with children and young people will, however, be enhanced the more person-centred you are and the more willing you are to give of yourself, rather than relying upon techniques alone.

Whilst not considered techniques, I do wish to turn to a number of concepts and experiences faced by the adult working with children and young people in a person-centred way.

PRESENCE

Feltham and Dryden (1993) note how Carl Rogers almost came to see 'presence' as a fourth core condition. This is how Rogers described it:

> When I am at my best, as a group facilitator or therapist, I discover another characteristic. I find that when I am closest to my inner, intuitive self, when I am somehow in touch with the unknown in me, when perhaps I am in a slightly altered state of consciousness in the relationship, then whatever I do seems to be full of healing. Then simply my 'presence' is releasing and helpful. There is nothing I can do to force this experience, but when I can relax and be close to the transcendental core of me, then I might behave in strange and impulsive ways in the relationship, which I cannot justify rationally, which have nothing to do with my thought processes. But these strange behaviours turn out to be 'right', in some odd way. At those moments, it seems that my inner spirit has reached out and touched the inner spirit of the other. (quoted in Mearns, 1994: 7)

Mearns helps us to understand the concept of 'presence' further. He sees person-centred counselling as more to do with 'being' than with 'doing'. Presence is seen as a powerful experience for the client, when a counsellor or therapist has been 'present with him in parts of his world'. This 'fearless' support offered to the client when he or she is most in fear, is seen as being especially important.

Mearns sees presence as a combination of two circumstances. The first refers to presence in terms of the 'blending together' of the core conditions to a significant extent, and the second is when:

> The counsellor is able to be truly 'still' within herself, allowing her person to fully resonate with the client's experiencing. In a sense, the counsellor has allowed her person to step right into the client's experiencing without needing to do anything to establish her separateness. (Mearns, 1994: 8)

This closeness to experiencing is at the core of presence in the counselling relationship. Developing Mearns' (1994) discussion on this point, the closeness between the counsellor working with a child or young person can be hindered by the adult's preoccupation with understanding and knowing. This is often where counsellors new to the profession find themselves, putting much of their energy into making sense of their young client's story, relationships and circumstances at the expense of actually experiencing and being experienced by the young person. As Mearns argues, understanding can come later. It is the power of presence which is a key feature of the helping or therapeutic relationship.

STAYING IN THE CHILD OR YOUNG PERSON'S FRAME OF REFERENCE

Working within a young client's frame of reference is strongly linked to the concept of empathy. The person-centred approach stresses the importance of valuing the personal world of the client. In this way, the person-centred therapist tries to experience the client's world, from the client's point of view.

It is important to distinguish between the young person's internal frame of reference and the adult's external frame of reference. In the latter, the adult sometimes, often through personal related experience, feels that they know and understand what the child or young person is feeling, thinking or remembering. This then creates a temptation to be less empathic and out of touch with the client's world, as they perceive it.

The following represents some statements that may be seen as emanating from the adult's external frame of reference:

- You say that you are overweight, but I think you are just right.
- Your life may look pretty desperate now, but things always change and you will look back one day and wonder what all the fuss was about.
- I'm sure that your mother does care about you. She just doesn't know how to show it.
- You have your whole life ahead of you.

WITH CHILDREN AND YOUNG PEOPLE IN MIND

Staying within the child or young person's frame of reference means that we are displaying empathy and avoiding judgement. The more we are able to really listen to our young clients, the more their world will make sense to us.

IMMEDIACY

The word immediacy causes us to think about a lack of delay, speed, and instant effect without mediation. Children and young people often talk about events and feelings in the past. Immediacy means focusing on the 'here-and-now' in the relationship or what Sutton and Stewart (2002: 88–9) refer to as 'you–me talk'. They describe immediacy as 'open and honest communication' which requires an awareness of what is happening in the counselling relationship at any time and 'reflecting this back to the client tentatively and sensitively'. Put simply, they see immediacy as when the counsellor discusses the relationship directly with the client, in the present tense.

Mearns and Cooper (2005) in their exploration of 'relational depth' in counselling see immediacy as 'the more proactive facet of transparency'. The ability to work in this way has been held in esteem and they suggest it is what distinguishes more experienced practitioners from less experienced ones. Immediacy is seen as a distinguishing feature of the person-centred approach.

Mearns and Cooper suggest that disclosure of here-and-now feelings may take a variety of forms, the most significant of which is:

> The disclosure of feelings that seem to emerge from an empathic attunement with the client. Where a therapist ... really allows herself to 'breathe in' her client being, it is likely that some of that will be re-invoked within the therapist. In other words, she may begin to develop an in-depth, advanced empathic sense of what the client is experiencing; and this will not just be a cognitive understanding, but one that is also emotional and bodily in nature. (2005: 130)

WITH CHILDREN AND YOUNG PEOPLE IN MIND

The use of immediacy in work with children and young people forces us to acknowledge the emotional maturity of the young client. Working in the here-and-now in this way is most powerful when a relationship has been established with the young person. It is important to recognise that the adult–child therapeutic relationship does not exist without a wider context, and being open and honest with a young client may be experienced as mimicking other more authoritative and parent-like relationships.

Immediacy does not mean saying whatever comes into the adult's head; it requires a degree of tentativeness and sensitivity and, of course, self-awareness in the therapist or helper.

Examples of immediacy include:

- When the counselling relationship is affected by other relationships, for example:

  When you talk about being angry with your dad for letting you down, I feel some of that anger is for me. I'm wondering what is going on between us.

  Laura, I notice that whenever you begin to express your feelings about your mother, you change subjects and go in a different direction.

- Exploring problems and issues within the counselling relationship itself, for example:

  I know that last week you said you wanted to talk about what happened to you when you were small. I'm wondering if you are finding it hard to talk freely with a male counsellor?

  I'm feeling quite frustrated at the moment – when we start to talk about school you talk openly about your feelings, yet when you speak about home you appear to go into head mode and I don't get any real sense of what it is like for you.

  Earlier you told me how important counselling is for you and how it gives you a place to talk about your feelings. Often, however, I feel as though you are waiting for me to ask you questions and even come up with the answers. It seems as though you want me to take control of your life and solve your problems for you.

- Exploring what is happening in the relationship right now, for example:

  When you talk about your grandma dying, I feel sad too.

  Diana, we have been working together now for six weeks and, today, something feels different. I feel a little warmer towards you. I'm wondering if you are experiencing anything different today?

  I'm feeling really confused right now. Is that what it feels like to you, Derek?

  A few times today, Salma, you have said 'honestly' or 'truthfully'. I'm wondering if you feel that I don't believe what you say.

WITH CHILDREN AND YOUNG PEOPLE IN MIND

Used with care, immediacy can be a powerful experience for the young client. The therapeutic impact lies in the willingness of the counsellor to share what they see and feel with the young person and offer the kind of feedback not normally experienced by children and young people in their everyday relationships with peers and other adults.

CHALLENGING

Stewart (1997) defines challenging as: 'to help the client face reality, as it is seen through the eyes of the counsellor' (p. 55). The emphasis on the counsellor or helper's reality might suggest that the idea of challenge does not sit happily within the person-centred approach. It would appear to be in conflict with working within the client's frame of reference and reality as perceived by the young person. In this sense, challenging or confrontation would appear to be incompatible with the person-centred approach. Indeed, it is very hard to find reference to these two concepts in the person-centred literature.

As Vincent (2005) notes, challenging and confronting figure prominently on many counselling skills courses. He writes:

> At its 'worst', confrontation would seem to assume a hectoring quality, in that the 'implementer of the skill' is seemingly determined to get the client to see things as the counsellor does. At its 'best', the user of counselling skills perceives client incongruence, for example, and is determined to confront the client with this observation in order to ensure that the client sees it, too. (2005: 52)

Challenging and confronting in counselling is normally designed to draw attention to discrepancies and distortions in thoughts, feelings and behaviours. Vincent helps us to unravel this problem and find reconciliation between the idea of challenge and confrontation and the person-centred approach. He presents a powerful argument for the process in the following way: 'Is there anything more "confrontational" than authentic unconditional positive regard and genuine (and accurate) empathic understanding?' (p. 52), and goes on to offer the following example as an illustration:

> If clients have low self-esteem as a result of their conditions of worth, introjected values and needs for positive regard (and so on), and the therapist offers unconditional acceptance and empathic understanding of them, then their very self concept is effectively 'challenged' or 'confronted'. (Vincent, 2005: 52)

Vincent sees the difference as to do with counsellor 'intent'. That is, that challenge and confrontation might occur as part of the therapeutic process but the therapist seeks only to offer the core conditions, 'simply and only that'.

Vincent records how through his work, he has noticed person-centred counsellors resorting to the techniques of challenging or confronting. He regards it as a result of counsellors feeling as if they, the client or the process has become stuck, or as a failure of supervision.

Most books on counselling skills suggest that challenging and confrontation need to be delivered with care and in a suggestive rather than factual way. Challenge and confrontation within the person-centred approach requires no such safeguards as long as the core conditions prevail, for as Tolan (2003) remarks:

If the challenge is too great, the client will not acknowledge, or will deny the validity of, the counsellor's response. The counsellor in turn will accept that her client is the final arbiter – he is the only person who knows himself 'from the inside'. (p. 149)

WITH CHILDREN AND YOUNG PEOPLE IN MIND

Challenging and confrontation are not techniques to be learned and administered to the child or young person. They just happen as a consequence of offering the core conditions. They are not things that we 'do' to our young clients, however tentatively.

SILENCE

Silence in counselling presents one of the greatest challenges to those new to counselling and even the most experienced. This is not surprising since relationships are normally characterised by talk. Prolonged silence can begin to take on meaning for those involved. It can suggest anger, awkwardness, embarrassment, fear or confusion. For many children and young people, silence may have become the way that they cope with authority and power, and remaining silent whilst a parent or teacher talks shows respect to those who demand it. In the child's social world, not talking to them can be a form of bullying, creating a sense of separateness, isolation and exclusion. Conversely, a silent child can also mean insolence and therefore it is not hard to see why sometimes children get it wrong. Corey and Corey (1989) suggest that silence can be caused by fear and the expectation that the helper is the expert and is therefore waiting for the adult to ask a question or tell them what to do. They suggest that the client may also feel inadequate or be responding to 'past conditioning' of being 'seen and not heard'. They also postulate that silence may have cultural meaning and expectations or that the client may have learned to be 'quiet and invisible' because this pattern has served to protect them in childhood.

Children and young people entering into a person-centred helping relationship with an adult may therefore find silence difficult, whilst work with professionals in supervision often reveals a concern that when silence occurs within the therapeutic relationship, it can feel like punishing.

Let us look at an example.

Michelle (aged 12):   Sometimes my friends can be real bitches. They say they're your friend but then go and talk about you behind your back. I have to pretend I don't know and keep smiling so they won't suspect that I know. I don't know what to do. I know that if I say something wrong, that will be it and I'm gone. I think about it all the time; I'm just not sure what I should do.

(After a minute of silence)

Bob: Sounds like you have a difficult decision to make. You are frightened to do the wrong thing.

In this example, Michelle is beginning to explore her dilemma. It may be that she needs time to consider her choices and the way she feels. Bob may have responded too quickly, denying his young client time to feel and experience. It may be that Bob is making a genuine attempt to clarify things for Michelle but it seems that she is already aware of having to make a difficult decision. It could be that Bob feels a compulsion to fill the 'gap' in their conversation.

Hough (1996) suggests that new counsellors sometimes find working with silence hard: 'Silence in counselling can seem intolerable for students, especially since they may associate it with feelings of personal impotence and an inability to help "solve" a client's problems' (p. 31).

Allowing a child or young client to be silent creates the space for thinking and processing. It enables the child to begin to make associations that are personal to them, rather than those experienced in dialogue. It can help a client such as Michelle explore solutions and problem-solve. Intervening too early deprives both adult and child an opportunity for deeper exploration and experiencing, so often not found in normal day-to-day conversation where people take turns in speaking and where silence is rare or imbued with meaning.

Margaret Crompton (1992) in *Children and Counselling* offers us some thoughtful and sometimes beautiful insights into the relationship between children, counselling and silence. She writes how children have so few opportunities for silence, especially shared with an adult. Where the adult makes no demands on the child, the young client is under no pressure to 'do' anything: 'If children feel any kind of pressure, they don't feel free to offer what they can' (p. 70).

The importance of silence for children, Crompton suggests, is that it enables 'clear thought and attention to inner voices'. By way of illustration through a number of case examples, Crompton adds: 'The environment of accepting silence enabled these children to work, silently and internally and, without discussing whatever problems were perceived by themselves and/or the concerned adults, to change. (1992: 72)

Crompton also draws from the writings of Dorfman (1951) who, in her discussion of play therapy and the case of a silent child, writes: 'Perhaps the child will sit in silence. If the therapist is truly convinced that the hour belongs to the child, he will not feel the necessity of urging the child to play or talk' (p. 72).

As we have seen, in the person-centred approach, the young client is clearly at the centre of the relationship. The client is trusted to work at their own pace and in a way that is meaningful for them. The adult makes every effort to avoid interpretation or offer reassurance in an attempt to 'rescue' their young client from difficult or confusing feelings. Silence within a helping relationship allows both the adult and young client to explore deeper meanings and, rather than it being a negative experience, silence can deepen the therapeutic relationship. The role of the adult working in a person-centred way, is to listen to silences as well as words.

With reference to the writings of Elizabeth Bowen, Crompton writes how:

> External noise is reflected in and reflects the internal noise which inhibits true growth and development, leaving no space for inwardness. The desperate need of a young woman mirrors that of many children:
>
> 'If she only had a few feet of silence of her own, to exclude the world from, to build up something of herself' (Bowen, in Wilson, 1983). (Crompton, 1992: 80)

Crompton concludes: 'One of the greatest gifts a counsellor can offer is a few feet of silence. So simple. So difficult. So rare' (p. 80).

USING METAPHOR AND SIMILE

At first sight, the difference between these two figures of speech can sometimes be quite subtle; they are both used in writing and speech to draw comparisons, often by making connections between items which might not otherwise be connected. However, there are differences and grammatical rules which govern their use. A metaphor is where one thing is compared to another and is said to be that thing. Examples of metaphors therefore might include:

- My life is a prison
- Lost in my grief.

In contrast, a simile is a figure of speech where something is compared to another, using the words 'as' or 'like'. Examples of similes could be:

- Cold as ice
- I felt like a volcano about to erupt.

With the person–centred approach in mind, I particularly like Tudor and Worrall's examination of these related ideas: 'In strict rhetorical terms, a metaphor (Rogers was a pioneer) is a more concentrated or elliptical form of simile (Rogers was like a pioneer)' (Tudor and Worrall, 2006: 41).

Like Tudor and Worrall, I would like, for the purposes of this section, to use the word metaphor generically and interchangeably as meaning a figure of speech 'that works by associating or comparing one thing with another'.

With writing in mind, Kopp (1998) offers us some reasons why metaphors are useful in language. These include:

- They enlighten ordinary language.
- They are more efficient and economical than ordinary language.
- They create new meanings; they allow you to write about feelings, thoughts, experiences, etc. for which there are no easy words.

These ideas are relevant in counselling children and young people too. It is also important to observe that metaphors are not confined to verbal forms of expression. Children express themselves through metaphor during play and in a number of the ways explored in the previous chapter.

Metaphor enables children and young people to explore thoughts and feelings at a symbolic level. By using such comparative imagery, they are able to communicate feelings and emotions which might otherwise prove too distressing or confusing.

Counsellors sometimes use metaphor in their work with young people in an attempt to help to access what is happening for them during a session; to reach thoughts, feelings and emotions which might otherwise prove inaccessible.

Children and young people frequently generate their own metaphors and these enable the client to communicate their inner world whilst helping the adult working with the child or young person to connect with their young client's view of their world.

Let us look at two brief examples.

Saif (counsellor):	You are lost in a wood and cannot find your way out?
Uma (client, aged 19):	Yes, not only am I lost, but it's getting dark and I'm frightened.
Saif:	You are frightened, time is running out and you cannot find a way to escape?

In this example, the metaphor is created by the counsellor who is trying hard to get a feel for what it might be like for Uma at this point in her life.

In the following dialogue, the young client attempts to convey what they are experiencing through the creation of their own metaphor and the counsellor responds empathically, working with the client-generated imagery:

Isaac (aged 14):	My parents fight all the time. I sit at the top of the stairs and watch. I feel sick. I know what happens next. They will both try to get me on their side. I don't know what to think. Sometimes I hate them both. I feel like I'm being torn apart.
Tom (mentor):	You are angry with your parents. You feel like you are splitting down the middle.
Isaac:	Yes, the pain is killing me.

Metaphors are found in children's stories, myths, legends and fairy stories and are therefore readily accessible to young clients. Berman and Brown (2000), in their work on the use of metaphor in storytelling and guided imagery, see the ability to make metaphorical connections as an essential component of learning and key to personal change. They write: 'It has been suggested that if a picture is worth a thousand words, then perhaps we can regard a metaphor as being worth a 1,000 pictures' (p. 4).

The adults' willingness and ability to work with the metaphors of children and young people helps build trust and plays an important part in building an empathic relationship with young clients.

COUNSELLOR QUALITIES AND ATTITUDES

TO THE HELPER

Whilst this section is written with the professional counsellor in mind, I firmly believe that the qualities and attitudes described here are equally relevant to the non-specialist who wishes to work with children in a helping capacity. Just as the trained counsellor aspires to these goals, so should the non-counsellor aim to develop themselves personally and professionally.

In Chapter 1, reference was made to the British Association for Counselling and Psychotherapy's *Ethical Framework for Good Practice* (2007a). This respected document sets out the principles and personal qualities of an ethical counsellor. This ethical code or Framework helps us to identify the kind of qualities and attitudes necessary for effective counselling. This section will look at these and attempt to identify additional qualities that are necessary for working with children and young people. The values identified by BACP include:

- respecting human rights and dignity
- ensuring the integrity of practitioner–client relationships
- enhancing the quality of professional knowledge and its application
- alleviating personal distress and suffering
- fostering a sense of self that is meaningful to the person(s) concerned
- increasing personal effectiveness
- enhancing the quality of relationships between people
- appreciating the variety of human experience and culture
- striving for the fair and adequate provision of counselling and psychotherapy services.

The *Ethical Framework* introduces a range of practitioner qualities that the BACP considers to be important to clients. However, the BACP is concerned that these 'personal moral qualities' are not presented as a requirement: 'It is fundamental that these personal qualities are deeply rooted in the person concerned and developed out of personal commitment rather than the requirement of an external authority' (2007a: 4)

The counsellor qualities identified by BACP are:

- empathy
- sincerity
- integrity
- resilience
- respect

- humility
- competence
- fairness
- wisdom
- courage.

The person-centred practitioner would of course value the importance of empathy and the counsellor communicating their understanding of the client's world, from the client's perspective. They would also wish to emphasise the other core conditions of unconditional positive regard and the acceptance of themselves and others, as well as congruence or genuineness. Indeed, the reader will get a sense of what is important within a person-centred relationship and the qualities most valued by clients from much of the philosophy and principles which underpin the approach set out elsewhere in this book.

In completing this chapter, I have thought deeply about those skills, attitudes and qualities which I believe to be most important to young people when they choose to share their life and feelings with a caring adult, in whatever role. Whilst they may not all be recognised counselling terms, I feel that each is important to the young people we work with. They include:

- an understanding of what it is like to be young; that is, to be in touch with your own childhood
- being welcoming, especially at the start of the process, when anxiety is at its highest
- warmth and tenderness; sensed by the young person. A smile can convey such warmth
- a real empathy and desire to experience the client's world as they experience it
- being a human being, and not an adult in a familiar parental or professional role, but accepting that the relationship is still an adult–child one
- an enjoyment of working with children and young people; children and young people can normally tell
- a preparedness to say sorry when something goes wrong in the relationship
- friendliness and a non-authoritarian stance
- an acceptance that the child or young person is unique, with their own thoughts, feelings and beliefs
- acceptance and non-judgementalism. This means not reacting with shock, horror, disapproval or embarrassment to what the young person tells us
- a willingness to be genuine and open
- the ability to create a psychologically safe place in which to listen and work with the young client. The child needs to feel that you are strong and able to 'hold' all that they bring to sessions
- a deep respect for the child's rights and confidentiality and an openness and honesty about limitations
- energy and spontaneity
- a sense of humour and being able to laugh with the child
- trustworthiness and reliability.

The child or young person also needs to recognise that the adult is culturally sensitive and respectful. We turn to issues of diversity and difference in our next chapter.

EXERCISES

1. How do you experience silence? When are you most in need of silence? Try listening to someone, without interrupting.
2. Think of as many metaphors as you can. Be conscious throughout the day of your own and other people's use of metaphor. How could you develop these metaphors?
3. It is quite likely that as you read the last part of this chapter, you reflected upon the qualities identified. Share your qualities with another person in the group. If you are working with colleagues, talk about the qualities that you recognise in each other.

13

KEY QUESTIONS ABOUT WORKING WITH CHILDREN AND YOUNG PEOPLE

INTRODUCING THIS CHAPTER

This chapter poses three important questions for consideration by the person-centred practitioner working with children and young people. The first recognises the stresses and problems that young people find in their lives and asks whether the person-centred approach can lead to acceptance and conformity.

The second question tackles the idea of the 'unconscious' and asks how such understandings, most commonly given emphasis within other approaches, are understood by the person-centred practitioner.

Finally, we will look at diversity and difference in counselling and helping. Such issues are of increasing importance for those working with children and young people, especially in multi-cultural and multi-faith contexts. We ask the question: to what extent is 'knowledge' important?

IS THE PERSON-CENTRED APPROACH POLITICAL ENOUGH?

Very soon, those who begin working with children and young people in difficulty begin to recognise the range of circumstances in which they live. Sometimes, presenting problems include relationship breakdown and loss in what might otherwise be healthy conditions in which to grow and thrive. Other children and young people live in poverty, experience violence to themselves or to someone close to them, or experience discrimination, bullying or abuse.

It has been argued that counselling in general and the person-centred approach in particular can lead a child towards acceptance of their lot or encourage conformity when they might otherwise challenge or at least be very angry at their circumstances; the difficult environments and relationships over which they have little control or influence.

In recent years, there has been a growth in a more politicised kind of therapy for clients that recognises that counselling does not exist just within the confines of the counselling room, but happens within a wider socio-political environment.

Many of these arguments are explored in Procter et al. (2006) and Merry (2000). In her 'Opening Remarks' to the book, *Politicising the Person-centred Approach*, which she co-edited, Gillian Procter sets out some of the issues involved in this discussion. She writes:

> Surely an approach based on challenging hierarchies and authorities and advocating trust in oneself is political? Surely an approach that aims to liberate us from internalised messages from others (conditions of worth), to be able to grow as individual unique people, is political? Surely an approach so concerned with avoiding taking power over people, and promoting personal power is political? Surely a theory that suggests that distress is not the result of internal individual dysfunction but a result of dysfunctional relationships is political? (Procter et al., 2006: 1)

However, Procter questions many of these assumptions, suggesting that politics is linked more to sociology, and emphasises the collective, as opposed to psychology, which is most likely to be based upon the individual. Politics is seen as concerned with the 'we', which is, largely, not part of the language of person-centred theory. She says:

> It could be that an emphasis on the uniqueness of each individual and a phenomenological approach seems to lead to a denial or missing of commonalities among people. It could be that a focus on all persons as equal regardless of role or status leads to an obscuring of inequalities and the effects of this in society. (2006: 1)

It could be, then, that the person-centred approach, by working with the individual fails to recognise that throughout history, change has occurred collectively, and an approach which emphasises the individual prevents such change occurring, confining anger, frustration and unhappiness to the counselling room.

Certainly, there are many things about children and young people's lives which need changing, but what is the role of the person-centred counsellor in all this?

Carl Rogers has often been associated with the concept of revolution and his ideas seen as revolutionary, both in the sense that his ideas brought change to the world of psychotherapy, but also because his approach had the potential for initiating social change. On the relationship between the person-centred approach, his work and the political dimension, Rogers (1977) wrote:

> Gradually I realised my experience ran parallel to the old story of the uneducated man and his first exposure to a course in literature. 'You know' he told his friends later, 'I've found out I've been speaking prose all my life and never knew it.' In a similar vein I could now say 'I've been practicing and teaching politics all my professional life and never realised it fully until now.' (pp. 3–4)

Rogers sees politics as to do with power and control, that is a 'person's desire, attempt to obtain, possess, share, or surrender power and control over others and/or themselves (cited in Kirschenbaum and Henderson, 1990: 376). Politics is also concerned with strategy and how decisions are made, and by whom. Inevitably, politics is also concerned with the effects that these decisions have over people, individually or collectively.

Rogers goes on to argue in some depth that the person-centred approach, which emphasises and prizes the notion that the individual can be trusted, runs counter to the accepted norm that people need to be 'guided, instructed, rewarded, punished and controlled by those who are wiser or higher in status' (cited in Kirschenbaum and Henderson, 1990: 381). For this reason, Rogers states that: 'Simply describingthe fundamental premise of client-centred therapy is to make a challenging political statement' (p. 381). Rogers makes the point that the person-centred counsellor by consciously renouncing control over their client, places the responsibility for decision-making and its effects, firmly within the client. He tells us that it is 'politically centred in the client'.

I remember a tutor of mine, some years ago, suggesting that I had a tendency towards 'polarised thinking'; that is, taking an extreme position to win an argument. I recognised that trait within myself, and worked hard to adopt a position where I was able to embrace many sides of an argument.

Like Rogers, I believe that the person-centred approach can empower children and young people to take control of their lives and challenge the status quo. Importantly, these attitudes may continue into other aspects of their lives or be utilised in the future. However, I also understand that young people find themselves in circumstances which need to change but I believe the role of the counsellor or adult working in a person-centred way is political in the way suggested by Rogers.

Procter et al. (2006) note how professional bodies have advocated that counsellors and therapists remain 'apolitical'; this need not be the case.

I would like to make it clear that the person-centred practitioner is not a therapist, all their waking hours. It is therefore highly commendable that adults who work with children and young people, who witness and experience the great injustices and inequalities faced by their young clients, may wish to be politically active in other aspects of their lives. Indeed, the adult who works with children and young people is often able to feed back to the organisation and other professionals, themes and concerns which emerge from the overview gained by working with a range of young clients.

The person-centred practitioner may seek to challenge orthodoxy, tradition, paternalism and discrimination, but when working with and supporting the child or young person, the focus is very much on the needs of the young person, as defined by them.

WITH CHILDREN AND YOUNG PEOPLE IN MIND

The last decade has seen an increasing interest in the rights of the child and the voice of young people. Schools, for example, are expected to take into account the views of young people on a range of issues of direct interest to them. These

(Continued)

(Continued)

changing attitudes, alongside the nature of the person-centred approach, which seeks to empower children and young people, and the campaigning spirit of those who work professionally to change young people's lives for the better, makes for a powerful mix, which allows for a degree of optimism.

WHAT ABOUT THE UNCONSCIOUS?

Any professional working with children and young people will recognise that, like adults, behaviour may appear inconsistent, unusual or driven by emotions which do not appear to be evident. Psychodynamic theory would suggest that this is because of unconscious forces within each of us and which determine much of our ways of relating. The question here then is, to what extent is the unconscious relevant to the person-centred practitioner? Before we continue with this discussion, some basic definitions are needed.

The related concepts of consciousness and the unconscious are complex and have been written about in depth in disciplines such as philosophy and psychology, as well as the arts and biological sciences. For the sake of brevity, we will adopt the psychotherapeutic perspective offered by McLoughlin (1995):

> The field of psychodynamic counselling has developed from the psychoanalytic tradition inaugurated by Freud. At its core is a belief in the role of the unconscious in the development of conflict and disturbance. Through the careful unfolding of the therapeutic relationship, within a defined setting, it is understood that resolution of conflict and disturbance may be achieved. (p. xi)

Among the key ideas in psychodynamic theory of the unconscious are 'transference' and 'counter-transference' and the deployment of 'defence mechanisms'.

WITH CHILDREN AND YOUNG PEOPLE IN MIND

Transference may be said to be in operation when a young client displaces feelings, attitudes or human qualities that have their origins in the young person's previous experience of significant people in their past or current lives. The child or young person then begins to relate to the helper or counsellor as though they were that person. Counter-transference occurs where a therapist begins to relate to a young person in ways which have been evoked by that young person.

Defence mechanisms, many of which have been identified and explored in the psychodynamic literature, are seen as the unconscious ways in which our minds protect us from unpleasant or unacceptable feelings and emotions. Without these defences, such as denial, projection, rationalisation, regression, displacement and repression, we would be filled with anxiety and our mental well-being would be severely affected.

In relation to the concept of the unconscious in general, Jacobs (1988) writes:

> There is no need to mystify the term 'unconscious'. It is a useful image with which to describe certain phenomena, and even to conceptualise the dynamics of the psyche, in which some feelings, certain ideas and even whole experiences appear to be pushed into hiding, because they are too threatening or too painful for the conscious self to acknowledge or experience at the time. (p. 9)

At first sight, it would appear that ideas about the unconscious and person-centred helping or counselling, which emphasises a focus on the client's frame of reference, are incompatible. However, more recently, writers and theorists have returned to a discussion about these two apparently conflicting ways of working.

In relation to the concept of transference, Carl Rogers (1987) was, as Merry (1995) comments, 'quite hostile' to the idea playing a central role in psychotherapy:

> To deal with transference feelings as a very special part of therapy, making their handling the very core of therapy, is to my mind a very grave mistake. Such an approach fosters dependence and lengthens therapy. It creates a whole new problem, the only purpose of which appears to be the intellectual satisfaction of the therapist – showing the elaborateness of his or her expertise. I deplore it. (Rogers, 1987: 183–4)

However, Feltham and Dryden (1993) see the interpretation and 'working through' of transference and counter-transference as central to psychoanalysis. McLoughlin (1995) emphasises the role of the therapist within the psychodynamic approach:

> Through the maintenance of the setting and the cultivation of her stance she becomes available for the client to use. In a sense, she offers herself for usage in the hope that the client will be able to make use of her to communicate what he needs to say about the nature of his inner world. (p. 47)

Here perhaps lies the difference between the person-centred and psychodynamic approaches. Mearns (1994), in a discussion of how clients sometimes give away power to the therapist, says that whilst the person-centred counsellor will not 'encourage' the development of transference, they will work with any transference that emerges within the relationship. The counsellor does not attempt to be a 'blank screen' upon which the client projects her transference in the way described above. Mearns explains his thinking thus: 'The person-centred counsellor is a real person involved in a real relationship. She is not keeping herself out of the relationship but being fully present within it' (1994: 78).

In this way, the person-centred counsellor acknowledges the existence of the unconscious as did Rogers himself. Thorne (1992), in his popular study of the life and work of Carl Rogers, says that the person-centred thinker and practitioner was very wary of 'embracing any of the maps of the unconscious', recognising that 'we are all to some extent influenced by forces outside our awareness'. Thorne writes:

> Far from pleading guilty to the charge that he ignores the unconscious, Rogers would assuredly claim that his respect for the unconscious compels him to refrain from adopting any map of this essentially unknowable terrain which might lead him to impose his view or interpretation on his client. In short, Rogers accepts both the reality of social conditioning and of the unconscious but refrains from elevating either to a position where they threaten to deprive individuals of the freedom to trust their own subjective experience and the mystery of their own natures. (1992: 82)

The unconscious has been examined in relationship to two key person-centred concepts, that is: awareness and congruence. Mearns and Thorne (2000) disagree with those who: 'would argue that awareness may be limited and that the therapist's congruence is therefore imperfect and, in this sense, lacks a meaningful authenticity' (p. 95). They argue that even within the psychodynamic field, originated by Freud, 'the unconscious can never be made fully conscious' (p. 96).

Paul Wilkins (1997) feels that there are few problems 'with acknowledging the existence of an unconscious dimension to the mind'. He writes:

> It seems clear that, under the right conditions, we have an ability to 'recover' (and I suspect create) experiences, ideas, feelings of which we have been unaware. It follows that we must be equally able to 'lose' these from awareness to an unaware part of our mind. (1997: 204)

Wilkins sees positive benefits of the 'unconscious' to the person-centred practitioner, for example in increasing our understanding of Rogerian concepts such as 'presence' whilst allowing us new insights into work with dreams, visions, fantasies, intuition, imagination and creativity. It is also suggested that the unconscious dimension to therapy has the potential to help us understand the core conditions a little more.

TO THE COUNSELLOR

The difference between the psychodynamic and person-centred perspectives on the unconscious appear to be related to what actually happens between the adult or counsellor and the child or client in a session, with the former methodology concerned with 'working with' and the latter 'being aware of' and increasing our understanding of the therapeutic relationship.

TO THE HELPER

It is unlikely that you will need or be expected to have any extensive knowledge of unconscious processes or to work with them, but it is important to be aware of their influence and their impact on your relationship with the child or young person you are working with.

DIVERSITY AND DIFFERENCE: HOW IMPORTANT IS KNOWLEDGE?

Some years ago, I was working with a young client, aged 18 – we will call her Darvinder. She had left home a year or so before coming to counselling, after disputes with her parents over a boyfriend that she had been seeing whilst at school. She was now separated from her boyfriend and living alone in a one-bedroom flat, feeling quite isolated and rarely speaking to another person, as each day passed. She explained how she felt unable to return home and that shame and acceptance were key issues. Whilst she still saw herself as a young Sikh woman, she explained that it would not be possible, as a single woman, estranged from her family, to become involved with the Sikh community in the city where she had now settled.

She talked at length about how important her faith and community had been to her and her sense of loss at what had disappeared from her life. Whilst I was able to get a sense of her isolation, detachment and loss, I struggled to understand why she could not regain her place within the new Sikh community where she now lived. I used whatever multi-cultural and multi-faith knowledge I had to make sense of the barriers she faced. Up until this point, Darvinder had been using general terms to describe her religion and culture to me. However, I remember clearly the session where she referred to 'our places of worship'. I replied, 'ah yes, a Gurdwara'. She looked surprised and then said – and I can remember her exact words – 'Oh Mark, now I think you are starting to understand me'. The significance of this moment is indicated by my clear memory of what was said and even the expression on Darvinder's face. We had connected and somehow I had entered her special world of belief, family and culture.

Many of you reading this book will be working with children and young people from a wide variety of ethnic, religious, national and cultural backgrounds, often in towns and cities across the country. The example of my work with Darvinder raises an important issue: how important is it to have knowledge about our young clients' culture, faith and community?

My person-centred training had taught me that knowledge was of little value and could possibly be detrimental. Extending this argument further, I also knew that I didn't need to be self-harming myself, to listen to a young person for whom this had become a way of coping with difficult feelings. I knew that I could not have experienced all the life events and experiences that children and young people were likely to bring into the counselling room. However, I knew that I had most probably experienced the range of feelings and emotions that might underlie these events and circumstances and, besides, this was about my client's world, not my client's world in relation to my own. I also understood that diversity came in many forms: social class, gender, sexuality, disability, age, religion and belief, and whilst I may not share the many dimensions to my young client's lives, I knew this did not prevent me from being a good, empathic counsellor.

The issue around working multi-culturally is, itself, complex and diverse and the reader might well be drawn to the additional reading highlighted below. However, for our current purposes, let us look briefly now at the question of diversity in relation to culture, religion and faith.

Further reading and study in this area suggests that the idea of cross-cultural counselling and helping is more complex than perhaps the above example might suggest. D'Ardenne and Mahtani (1989) point us in the right direction. They describe how Smith (1985) has referred to the 'myth of sameness' where counsellors 'bury their heads in the sand' and protest that: 'The only essential attitude required in counselling is one that contains empathy' (D'Ardenne and Mahtani, 1989: 36).

However, they see empathy as: 'a necessary quality for counsellors, but it is certainly not sufficient for efficient trans-cultural counselling' (p. 36).

D'Ardenne and Mahtani implore us to look into our own prejudices. They write: 'Counsellors should be very careful when insisting that they are non-judgemental with all their clients, regardless of colour or creed. You may be rationalising and avoiding different cultural and racial conflicts within yourself' (1989: 36).

Feltham (1999) even goes so far as to suggest that in counselling across cultures, a lack of awareness can lead us to become 'an agent of assimilation'. He writes:

> It is possible then that, cross-culturally, counselling may become, through the very 'relationship', that is, way of relating, that it espouses, an agent of assimilation to dominant western culture. In other words, at a micro-level, counselling might ostensibly be respecting difference while imposing a dominant culture notion of self and western ideals of how we should relate, simply because of the theories which inform it and the context in which it has developed. (1999: 192)

As counsellors and helpers working with troubled children and young people, we should understand that there may be significant differences in the assumptions we make around family life and relationships, belonging and identity. For example, in some 'collective' cultures, the idea of turning to someone outside the family for help, such as a teacher, mentor or counsellor, can be seen as alien. We also need a heightened awareness of the experience of racism which some of our clients may have been exposed to directly or indirectly. Some of the practical questions D'Ardenne and Mahtani (1989) ask us to consider include:

- how your cultural or racial background affects your attitude to your client
- whether or not you see the client's culture or race as a cause of the present problem

- whether or not you see the client's culture as part of the solution to the present problem
- whether or not you can accept, acknowledge and understand your client's culture
- whether or not your expectations about the client's culture affects the counselling outcome
- whether or not your cultural prejudice has a bearing on the counselling relationship; and whether or not any cultural prejudice or racism experienced by you affects the counselling relationship. (p. 37)

I have no doubt that some cross-cultural knowledge can be helpful when working with children and young people. I know that knowing a little about Sikhism was respected and valued by Darvinder and enhanced the quality of our relationship. However, over-confidence can lead to me making cultural assumptions which are, in effect, cultural stereotypes, the danger being that I relate to my young client's world but only through my own ingrained assumptions and attitudes.

WITH CHILDREN AND YOUNG PEOPLE IN MIND

I am mindful of the fact that I have been exposed to many years of prejudicial and stereotypical attitudes, which, despite every effort on my part to internally challenge them, nevertheless leave their mark. These deeply ingrained ideas will exist; the task is to recognise that they may well affect how I work with my young people. To take the attitude that I treat all the children and young people I meet as being the 'same', is to court the dangers of 'cultural blindness' and therefore of failing to acknowledge difference.

Colin Lago (2007) has written extensively on the subject of race, culture and counselling. He helps us to clarify our thinking in the following way:

Counselling across difference and diversity demands that therapists enhance their awareness of their own identity and attitudinal base as well as developing their knowledge of the specific minority client groups with whom they work. Implicit in this enhanced sensitivity and knowledge will be an understanding of the myriad of discriminatory mechanisms that pervade society (and thus individuals within it) and a commitment and willingness to seek new language/s and behaviours that are respectful and anti-discriminatory for all clients. (2007: 252)

Knowledge can be helpful, if used with awareness. However, knowledge without a concern for our own attitudes and socialisation may cause us to repeat wider discriminatory processes which permeate society and adversely affect the lives of children and young people who are culturally different.

EXERCISES

1. What social or political issues do you feel strongly about? How would it feel counselling a young person who held either very different or similar views to your own?
2. What socio-political issues are currently most important in affecting the lives of children and young people?
3. What defence mechanisms have you seen people deploy?
4. Where do you get your multi-cultural knowledge? How reliable are these sources?
5. Are you aware of any cultural stereotypes you may hold?
6. What might be the arguments for and against culturally matching client and counsellor?
7. In what ways do you attempt to address any racial or cultural assumptions or prejudices in your own life and in your work with children and young people?
8. How might you respond to a young client who is expressing racist or offensive cultural views?

14
TRAINING, SUPERVISION AND WELL-BEING

INTRODUCING THIS CHAPTER

This chapter begins with a personal reflection of my own counselling training, and how it left me feeling ill-prepared to work with young clients. We then identify some of the key features of person-centred training and what you might expect from a good course. We then turn our attention to training to work with children and young people specifically. We look briefly at the ethos of such a course and what elements it might contain.

The nature and process of person-centred counselling supervision is examined and the chapter concludes with a discussion about how the professional can ensure their own emotional health and well-being.

TO THE COUNSELLOR

You will already have undertaken a course of training and will have developed some idea as to how well it has prepared you to work with clients. The process of learning continues throughout a counsellor's career and because there are so many contra-influences acting upon the person-centred counsellor, it is important to expose yourself to person-centred professional development opportunities and also to keep in touch with like-minded practitioners.

PERSON-CENTRED COUNSELLING TRAINING

In writing this final chapter, let me begin with a personal reflection on my own initial experiences of being a trainee. Before embarking on a full diploma course,

I tested out my interest and enthusiasm for working as a counsellor by taking part in a number of short- and medium-term courses in 'counselling skills'. On looking back, I think that I learned very little except to play the role of counsellor and to demonstrate skills which I thought might impress my tutors or colleagues. Very little of 'me' was expected, rather the courses often focused on demonstrable competencies. Whilst I believe a lot was going on inside my head, I'm not sure I had any idea what to do with the many feelings that I experienced and probably spent time and energy trying to disguise what was really going on for me.

When I started to work with children and young people, I felt very unprepared and I recognised the gap between my training and the reality of working with young clients.

I am aware that much counselling training has moved on since the early 1980s and, in particular, training in person-centred approaches has achieved a new depth and vitality. Hopefully, this brief section will introduce the reader to how good person-centred training might be experienced and, especially, what additional training is desirable for those working with children and young people. Training in person-centred approaches to counselling children is essential to those who wish to develop professionally as counsellors, but it is also valuable for those who intend to use the approach as a part of their work with children and young people.

Tudor (2007) suggests that the person-centred approach is unusual in the sense that it is not only a form of therapy, but also an approach to education. He describes Rogers' own interest in education which culminated in the celebrated *Freedom to Learn* first published in 1969 and again in 1983. In these works, Rogers emphasises the importance of learning through experience rather than a reliance on course content. In a comparison between traditional education and student-centred approaches, Tudor identifies process- and student-led curriculum over a 'prescribed curriculum'. He also highlights student control over learning, learning through experience and negotiated and agreed learning outcomes. Tudor goes on to set out key elements in a person-centred approach to training counsellors. These include:

- learning through experience
- learning through personal development
- learning through relationships
- learning through self-directed work, assignments and self-assessment (2007: 382–4).

Dryden and Thorne (1991: 9–11) state how important it is to have an appropriate and facilitative learning environment in which to develop as a counsellor. They call for a consistency between the course ethos and the philosophy of the approach. In other words, with person-centred counselling in mind, we would expect to see course facilitators demonstrating the core conditions and showing a deep respect for the student as a person in their quest for personal growth and development.

It is suggested that a general course in person-centred counselling at diploma level might include the following elements:

- the work of Carl Rogers and more recent developments and ideas in the approach which have challenged and developed Rogers' original thinking
- theory around the core conditions and the person-centred perspective on personality, change and personal growth

- an opportunity for personal development and increasing self-awareness
- skills development
- an expectation that the student will work with clients with appropriate levels of supervision
- a requirement in some courses that course members undertake a period of personal counselling themselves
- ethical and legal issues.

Person-centred training courses give status to the practice of personal development, often facilitated through the group experience. Buchanan and Hughes (2000) in their study of the experiences of counsellors in training place importance on the creation of opportunities for personal development within the person-centred approach. Personal development is seen as central to the process of becoming a counsellor. They see a learning environment that 'feels right and safe' as being essential for personal growth and increased self-awareness. They write: 'In the same way that a counsellor wishes to provide a safe environment for the client, a trainee is also seeking a place which will offer the right conditions for them to develop' (Buchanan and Hughes, 2000: 25).

Opportunities for personal development enable the trainee to reflect upon:

- personal needs and expectations
- relationships with others such as course members, family, colleagues and friends
- life issues, past and present which impact upon their thoughts and feelings
- new ways of being
- personal values and beliefs which affect our view of others and our relationships with others
- feelings and emotions experienced in the present
- the internal dialogue, which affects our perception of ourselves, our conditions of worth and consequent self-esteem.

The relationship between skills and techniques and the person-centred approach has already been touched upon in this book. Mearns (1997) reminds us that the person-centred approach is not centred on skills development. He seeks to differentiate between some counselling courses which have a *reductionist* emphasis, breaking down skills into smaller components and which can be taught and practised, and a more holistic emphasis where the focus is on the experience of actual counselling or role-play and where feedback is offered to the counsellor within a context.

Buchanan and Hughes (2000) argue that some theoretical input into person-centred training is essential for the following reasons:

- It provides us with the foundation to become proficient and competent counsellors.
- It can give the counsellor a firm foothold from which they can develop their own ideas.
- It can assist the counsellor in times when he/she feels they are losing their client or they are unable to understand the process the client is going through.

- Theory creates a common language through which counsellors can discuss their ideas.
- Theory offers a clear starting point for research.

However, Buchanan and Hughes also set out some of the dangers of theory for the counsellor or helper in training: 'Some people believe that theory can foster a rigid way of working and creates a counsellor who adheres to an inflexible rule book' (p. 50). The trainee may also 'become over-dependent upon the approach and not listen to their own developing ideas, which could be potentially moulded into their individual style' (Buchanan and Hughes, 2000: 50)

Some courses require that trainees engage in their own person-centred therapy, despite the suggestion that there may not be a relationship between personal therapy and counsellor development. However, the experience of being counselled by another person may offer the trainee new personal insights, helping them to understand what it might be like to be a client and also to see, at first hand, how another counsellor works.

TRAINING TO WORK WITH CHILDREN AND YOUNG PEOPLE

Whilst it is important to gain some experience of counselling real clients during training, it is also important to work with children and young people. Sometimes professionals who want to work with young clients train to work with older clients and then take advantage of the growing number of training opportunities for counsellors and helpers who want to specialise in working with a younger client group.

It would be expected that the counsellor or helper wishing to work with this age group would already have or be able to have access to young people. I cannot overstate the importance of working experientially through role-play and professionals taking on the role of counsellor and client while being observed, and then offered constructive feedback by others in training and those facilitating the course. It has already been stated in this book that working in a person-centred way does not rely upon knowledge. However, counselling and support for young people most often occurs in formal settings such as schools, youth centres, hospitals, and in voluntary agencies who, whilst they vigorously protect their independence, are increasingly expected to work within externally set guidelines and expectations.

Those wishing to work, or already working, with children and young people in a person-centred way might expect training of the kind described above but more specifically be offered the opportunity to explore academically and experientially many of the following:

- a working understanding of the ethical and legal issues which relate specifically to children and young people
- an understanding of child protection procedures and how to balance legal and professional requirements and the young client's right to confidentiality

- an awareness of youth culture and an understanding of the place of children and young people in society
- an awareness of issues and stresses which face children and young people growing up today
- an awareness of the influences upon children and young people through the peer group, family and the media
- the basics of early child development and the nature of adolescence and transition
- how counselling has developed for children and young people
- the child's place within the family
- an opportunity for the trainee to reflect upon their own experiences of growing up and an awareness of how this might impact upon their work with children and young people
- how a person's current role as adult, parent, teacher or nurse, etc. might affect their work with young clients
- the nature and quality of the child–counsellor relationship
- the differences between working therapeutically with children, young people and adults
- an understanding of mental health issues affecting children and young people such as depression, anxiety, self-harm and suicide
- what research has told us about counselling and working therapeutically with children and young people
- an introduction to the process and potential of working creatively and expressively with children and young people
- working with diversity and difference in children and young people, including race and gender issues
- some understanding of children with additional needs, including language and learning difficulties
- using supervision productively.

A comprehensive list of the kinds of components which should be included on counselling courses for those working with children and young people can also be found in the Welsh Assembly Government's (2008) strategy for counselling in schools.

I believe that work around self-awareness is especially important when working with children and young people. Self-awareness refers to a consciousness of what a person experiences. It involves an awareness of our needs, strengths, qualities and weaknesses, personality and identity. Self-awareness implies the ability to reflect, in the here-and-now, upon our relationship with others. It is also suggestive of our ability to be aware of and in touch with what we are feeling, why we feel like we do and how this affects the way we relate to others.

The development of self-awareness in those who work with children and young people is essential because inherent in this work are potential dangers of over-identification; the playing out of adult–child roles including issues around power; and the need to care for and protect, particularly as if in a parental role. Everybody reading this book has been a child and therein exists both the pitfalls and possibilities of working with children and young people – the idea that we see the world as *we* experienced it, or empathically that we see the world through the young client's eyes in a way that we might begin to understand.

PERSON-CENTRED SUPERVISION

TO THE COUNSELLOR

Good counselling supervision by an experienced practitioner is not only desirable but an essential requirement of the profession. Although sometimes difficult to find, it is important that your supervisor has some experience of working with the younger age group, especially young children.

TO THE HELPER

You will probably already have access to line management as part of your wider professional role. If you are working as a counsellor within the voluntary sector, you are entitled to supervision of the same quality as a professional counsellor. Where you are using counselling skills and working in some depth with children and young people and supervision is not available, it is important that you find suitable colleagues with whom you can share your work.

Supervision is a vital aspect of the work of the counsellor working with children and young people. Indeed, the receipt of regular supervision whilst working with young clients is a requirement of The British Association for Counselling and Psychotherapy. Mearns and Thorne (2000) draw a contrast with counselling supervision and supervision found in other helping professions which they describe as 'little more than thinly disguised management monitoring'.

Whilst supervision may be mandatory for counsellors, my own experience of supervising counsellors working in schools and related agency settings with children and young people reveals that supervisees do not see supervision sessions as burdensome or time-consuming but as a welcome opportunity to discuss and explore their work in a safe and supportive environment. This enables both the new and experienced counsellor to address many of the doubts, concerns and anxieties that emerge almost as a matter of course for those working with a younger client age group. Good counsellors are committed to their own supervision and see it as valuable quality time.

Supervision takes a variety of forms such as co-supervision or peer supervision, where experienced counsellors offer each other time to explore their work, each taking on the role of supervisor and supervisee at various times during the session, and group supervision which involves a group of peers, with the group facilitated by a supervisor. Each kind of supervision offers something different and it would be wrong to recommend one over another. However, for the purposes of discussion here, I will be referring to individual or one-to-one supervision which involves a supervisee working with a supervisor who will be an experienced counsellor who continues to work with clients.

Mearns and Thorne (2000) celebrate the kind of one-to-one supervision which is ideally found within the counselling profession. They refer to:

> a strong empowering and developmental dimension to supervision, emphasising the creation of a supervisory relationship in which the therapist feels sufficiently safe to explore the most difficult and potentially threatening dimensions of her work. The job of the supervisor is not to judge, nor to sanction, but to act as facilitator to the therapist's exploration and development. (2000: 22)

As Feltham and Dryden (1993: 186) state, supervision, especially within organisational settings has more formal aims in mind too. These include:

- the overseeing of the counsellor's work
- protecting the client and supporting the counsellor
- addressing professional and ethical boundaries
- counsellor competence
- the counsellor's personal development
- the skilful and purposeful use of therapeutic techniques
- client material and client–counsellor interaction
- the well-being of counsellors themselves.

Tudor et al. (2004) offer us a succinct but insightful summary of what supervision is for:

> Supervision is a process in which therapists and other practitioners talk about their work with another colleague, whose function it is to help them explore their relationships with their clients. At its best, supervision offers support, challenge and professional refreshment. It's a place where therapists can talk about the joys and difficulties of their work, revisit familiar theoretical concepts, test new ones, explore ethical dilemmas and agree a course of action. It's one of the ways in which therapists live and learn to thrive among the paradoxes, uncertainties and intangibles of their work. (p. 71)

A supervisor helps the supervisee see things which may be not immediately apparent or hidden from awareness and, as Tolan (2003) notes, supervision enables spontaneity in the counsellor who knows that their work is being sympathetically monitored. In this sense, supervision encourages the counsellor to bring more of themselves into the counselling relationship.

The person-centred counsellor will expect to receive person-centred supervision. This, Bryant-Jefferies (2004) says, is characterised by an exploration of 'the relationship that the supervisee has with her client and the feelings, thoughts and experiences that the supervisee has within that relationship' (p. 37).

Bryant-Jefferies sees person-centred supervision firmly centred around Rogers' core conditions. He writes:

> The emphasis is on helping them [counsellors] to reflect on their congruence, the quality and nature of their empathy and their ability to be warmly accepting of the client, and what may interfere with any of these – the intention being to clarify and to ensure that the supervisee is able to offer those aspects of the 'necessary and sufficient' conditions for which they have responsibility. (2004: 37)

In the light of this association with the core conditions, Tudor and Worrall (2004) consider the relationship between therapy and supervision. They conclude that rather than being a *parallel* or 'precise similarity', counselling and supervision should be viewed as *analogous* 'because parallel lines only meet at infinity'. They believe that at times the two processes are 'indistinguishable'. This is not to suggest of course that supervision *is* therapy, but the processes, with the core conditions at their heart, are similar in 'some' respects.

After some discussion of the core conditions in relation to the process of supervision, Tudor and Worrall suggest that whilst the core conditions are sufficient, they offer a number of other supervisor 'qualities' which, whilst not essential, will significantly enhance the process. These are:

- knowledge
- experience
- currency
- generosity.

By knowledge, they do not mean that the supervisor has to know more than a supervisee but that they should have a good knowledge of the person-centred approach and generic professional knowledge around legal and ethical matters and feel confident about these. This knowledge base is particularly important where the supervisor is working with a counsellor whose focus is on children and young people because the area is quite complex and more likely to be affected by guidance and regulation.

Experience in the supervisor refers to their working in a particular field and having reflected upon that experience in a way that they can respond appropriately to what the counsellor may bring to sessions. With regard to children and young people, it is essential that the supervisor not only has general counselling experience but has worked with young clients, preferably within organisational settings where issues around information sharing and boundaries can be very specific.

By 'currency', Tudor and Worrall (2004) indicate that the supervisor's knowledge and experience is up-to-date. This characteristic of the supervisor's repertoire is important where counsellors are working with children and young people, as this area is constantly developing and is set within a wider arena of change in relation to the protection, welfare and mental health of children and young people.

Finally, Tudor and Worrall suggest that 'generosity' is a valuable quality for the supervisor to possess. Here they are referring to the supervisor's willingness to share what they know and their experiences in order to facilitate the counsellor's growth and development.

Lambers (2007) maintains that supervision from the person-centred perspective should focus on 'the experience of the therapist and on the therapeutic ability of the supervisee through the supervision relationship' (p. 367). This perspective on person-centred supervision is further developed:

> Central in supervision is the experience of the therapist and the reflection on the relationship between client and therapist, rather than the exploration of the client's 'case'... the supervision relationship offers a context where the therapist can bring into awareness experiences and processes emerging in her relationship with her client, and where she can explore the relationship qualities necessary for her therapeutic work. (Lambers, 2007: 370)

WITH CHILDREN AND YOUNG PEOPLE IN MIND

All supervision requires a high degree of skill and particular qualities in the supervisor. Where the supervision takes place in the context of work with children and young people, this is particularly the case.

Whilst there has been some attempt to reconcile the person-centred approach with psychodynamic theory, with its emphasis on the influence of the unconscious, the person-centred practitioner is, as we have seen, largely concerned with the present; the experience of 'now'. However, work which focuses on the relationship between the counsellor and a child will inevitably touch upon how the young client may impact upon the counsellor's deeper feelings and also how the counsellor responds to these new experiences. Whether we refer to these as 'transference' and 'counter-transference' or not, they may become evident in all sorts of ways during supervision.

For all of us, the experience of childhood and adolescence remains just below the surface and sessions with young clients may evoke strong or complicated emotions associated with the counsellor's past and which may begin to have an impact on the work. For example, the counsellor may find in supervision that they have begun to relate to a client in say a protective or parental way, which connects with their own experience of parenting as a child or as a parent in the present. When working at depth, sessions with children and young people may cause feelings such as fear, neediness, love, loss and jealousy, amongst many others, to surface.

Supervision may well bring these emotions into awareness and these new insights have the potential for significant learning and development in the counsellor as well as for facilitating the relationship with the young client. However, the supervisor is entrusted not to 'point out' or judge when the worlds of the counsellor and client connect in this way but rather to see these experiences as an opportunity to develop the counsellor's empathy, realness and her openness to experience.

An open and honest case study focusing on the use of supervision in relation to a young client, Sally, can be found in the writings of Gill Clarke (2008): 'Supervision was my lifeline and a safe space to be open to myself and explore what was happening in the relationship between Sally and myself' (p. 41).

LOOKING AFTER YOURSELF

Stress and burnout are over-represented in the caring professions. Despite its apparent 'simplicity' or even beauty, the person-centred approach is, because it involves the whole person and emphasises the relationship, probably the hardest way of working. It could also be argued that working with children and young people is perhaps the hardest group to work with, but I believe the most rewarding too.

WITH CHILDREN AND YOUNG PEOPLE IN MIND

As well as being exciting, meaningful and rewarding, counselling and helping children and young people can be extremely exhausting, demoralising and sometimes anxiety producing. Counsellors and helpers who work with children and young people often see many 'clients', often for reduced periods of time, and the adults' feelings are sometimes more akin to a ride on a roller coaster. Professionals whose primary work is with children and young people often feel a particular sense of responsibility for their young clients and may also experience some of the hopelessness and frustration that children and young people feel when they so often have little in the way of resources or power to change their lives.

Geldard (1998) makes the point that the counsellor's well-being is of 'paramount importance', simply because a counsellor who is not feeling well, physically or emotionally, is unlikely to be effective in the counselling environment. He outlines some of the key indicators of burnout. These include:

- physical and emotional symptoms
- negative attitudes, especially towards clients
- disillusionment with the counselling process
- personal consequences, where diminished self-esteem puts pressure on relationships and where feelings of anger, frustration, helplessness and hopelessness are projected onto others (1998: 240–1).

He also stresses the dangers of counsellors becoming over-involved with their clients and their issues. Working with suicidal clients is naturally particularly emotionally draining, whilst many counsellors and helpers work in isolated settings. For example, peripatetic school counsellors may see many clients but have very little contact with colleagues before moving on to other schools or settings.

Looking after yourself means just that. It means getting your work into perspective and having realistic expectations about what counselling can achieve and just what is expected of you as a professional, and most importantly, as a person with your own needs. Do not be over-critical of yourself and your work; rather see yourself always as a counsellor or helper in the making – you do not need to be perfect or the finished article. Time needs to be managed and boundaries maintained; you are not expected to be available to listen to and support children at all times. It is also important to know when things are getting on top of you and recognise that there will be occasions when you need to take some time out.

Your own family relationships and friendships need to be nurtured and maintained. Taking time for you is important too and having fun relieves stress and tension. It is important to eat a balanced diet and get enough exercise; the fitter you are physically, the fitter you will be mentally. A concern for your own well-being, far from detracting from your energies and enthusiasm for working with children and young people, actually means that you can be more present for your clients and more able to demonstrate and feel the core conditions.

Most importantly, it is crucial to find someone to listen to you. It would be contradictory to value the kind of listening relationships we seek to provide for children and young people, and yet deny our own needs to be accepted and understood.

A FINAL WORD TO THE COUNSELLOR AND HELPER ALIKE

It is likely that you chose this book to read because of your interest in working with children and young people and a desire to offer help either professionally as a counsellor or as part of some other role. It is also probable that you have an interest in the person-centred approach or at least want to know more about this way of working.

With the very best intentions, we intervene in many ways in the lives of young people in difficulty. The person-centred approach seeks to empower children and young people and help them find their own direction in a way that is meaningful to them. This kind of work is so greatly needed and so valued by young people. Becoming the kind of counsellor or helper highlighted in this book, for most of us, remains an aspiration. Where I have been privileged enough to see or experience the person-centred approach in action with children and young people, it has been a spiritual experience, one of beauty and humanity.

APPENDIX

Abandoned abhorred able abnormal above average absent-minded absorbed abused abusive abysmal accepted accepting accountable accused aching acknowledged active adamant addicted admired adored adrift adult adventurous affectionate affirmed affluent afraid against aggravated aggrieved aggressive agitated agony agoraphobic alarmed alive alienated alone aloof amazed ambiguous ambitious ambivalent ambushed amorous amused analysed anchored anaesthetised anguish angry angst annihilated anonymous annoyed antagonistic anti-social anxious apart apathetic apologetic appalled applauded appreciative apprehensive approachable approved of argumentative aroused arrogant articulate artificial artistic ashamed asphyxiated assaulted assertive assured astonished at a loss at ease attacked attracted attractive authoritarian available avenged average avoided awake aware awe awesome awful awkward

Babied babyish backward bad bad-tempered baffled balanced bamboozled banished bankrupt banned bare barred barren bashful battered battle-weary bawled-out bear-able beaten beautiful belittled befriended begged behind belligerent belonging below beloved benevolent benign bent berated bereaved besieged betrayed better bewildered bewitched biased big bitchy bitter bizarre blamed blameless blaming bland blank bleak bleeding blessed blind blissful blocked bloody bloody-minded blossoming blown-apart blown-around blue blurred boastful boffin boiling boisterous bolstered bold bombarded bored boring bossed-bossy bothered bought bouncy bound-up boxed-in brainwashed brainy breathless bright brilliant broken broken-hearted browbeaten brushed-off brutalised bubbly bullied buoyant burdened buried burned-out bursting business-busting busy by-passed bystander

calmed-down capable captivated captive cared-about carefree careful careless caring carried-away cast-out cautious censored certain changed chained challenged chaotic charismatic charitable charmed charming cheap cheeky cheerful cheated cherished claustrophobic clueless clumsy chicken childish chilled choked-up clean cleansed clever clingy close closed-in clueless clumsy cocky coerced cold cold-hearted collected comatose combative comfortable committed common communicative compared-to compassionate compatible compelled competent competitive complacent complete complex compromised compulsive concerned condemned confident confined confused conned conquered conscientious conservative considerate consistent consoled conspired-against constrained contemplative controlled convinced cooperative coping copied cornered correct courageous courteous cowardly coy cosy crafty cramped cranky crap crazy criminal crippled critical cross crushed curious cursed cut-down cut-off cynical

Damaged dared daring dammed dangerous daring dark daunted dazed dead dear debased deceitful deceived decent deceptive decimated dedicated defeated defective defenceless defensive defiant deflated deformed degraded dehumanised dejected delicate delighted delinquent delirious deluded demanding demeaned demolished demonized demoralized demoted dependent depended-upon depleted depreciated depressed deprived deserving deserted desired despairing desperate destitute destroyed detached deteriorated determined detested devastated devious devoted dim different difficult dirty disabled disaffected disappointed disapproving disbelieving discarded disciplined disconnected discounted discouraged discriminated against discriminating disgraced disgruntled disgusted disgusting disheartened dishonest disliked disloyal dismal dismayed disobedient disorganised disposable disregarded disrespected disruptive dissatisfied distant distorted distracted distressed distrusted distrustful disturbed divided divorced from docile dominant dominated doomed double-crossed doubted down drained dread dreadful dreamy driven dropped drowning drunk dubious dull dumb dumbfounded dumped-on dwarfed dynamic dysfunctional

Eager easy easy-going eccentric ecstasy edgy educated effeminate efficient egotistic elevated electrified elegant eloquent embarrassed emotional emotionless empathic empowered empty elated elusive emancipated embittered enchanted enclosed encouraged encroached upon energetic energised elated engulfed enhanced enigmatic enlightened enraged enriched enslaved entangled entertained enthralled enthusiastic entombed entranced envied envious equal equipped established euphoric evasive evicted evil examined exasperated excellent excited excluded exhausted exhilarated exonerated experienced exploited explosive exposed extraordinary extravagant extreme extroverted exuberant

Fabulous faint fair faithful fake fallible famous fanatical fantastic fascinated fashionable fatigued favoured fazed fear feared fearless fed-up feeble feisty feminine festive fettered fickle fidgety fierce fiery filthy fine finished fired firm first-class fit flat flattered flexible flippant flirtatious floored flustered focused foggy foolish forgiven forgotten forced forceful fortunate framed fraudulent freaked-out freaky free frenzied fresh friendless friendly frightened frustrated frustration fulfilled full fuming fun funny furious fussy

Gagged galvanised gay generous gentle genuine ghastly giddy gifted giggly giving glad glamorous gleeful gloomy glorious glowing glum good good-looking gorgeous grateful great greedy grey grief grim grouchy gross grown-up grumpy guarded guilty guiltless gullible gutted

Hammered hampered handicapped happy happy-go-lucky harassed hard hard-working harmless hasty hated hateful haunted headstrong healthy heartbroken heart-ened heartless helped helpful helpless heroic hesitant hideous high hollow homesick honest honoured hopeful hopeless hormonal horny horrendous horrible horrified horror hospitable hostile hot hot-tempered hounded huge humble humiliated humoured humorous hungry hunted hurried hurt hyped-up hyperactive hypocritical hysterical

Idealistic idiotic idle idolised ignorant ignored ill ill-at-ease imaginative immature immoral immortal immune impartial impatient impelled imperfect impervious impetuous implacable impolite important imposed-upon impotent impressed imprisoned impulsive inattentive insecure in-a-stew in-control incapable incensed incoherent incompetent incomplete indebted indecent indecisive independent indifferent indignant indiscreet indoctrinated indolent indulgent ineffective inefficient infatuated infected inferior inflexible influential informed infuriated ingenious innovative insignificant insane insightful insincere insistent insolent inspired insulted intact intellectual intelligent intense interested interesting interfered-with interrogated in the dumps intimate intimidated intolerant in-touch intrepid introspective intruded-upon intuitive invalidated inventive invigorated invisible invited involved irate irrational irresistible irritated

Jaded jealous jeopardised jinxed jittery jolly jolted joy jubilant judged judgemental jumbled-up jumpy just justified joyless joyous jubilant

Keen kept kept-out kicked-around kind knocked-down knotted knowledgeable known

Labelled laid-back late laughable laughed at lazy led astray leaned on lectured left out let down lethargic liberated lied to lifeless lifted light likable liked listened to listless loathing logical lousy love lovely loving low loyal luckless lucky lustful

Macho mad made fun of magical magnificent malleable malicious malignant maligned manageable maniac manipulated manipulative marginalised marvellous masochistic materialistic maternal mature mean mechanical mediocre meditative melancholy mellow menacing merciful merry mesmerised messed-around messed-up methodical meticulous miffed mighty militant minimised mischievous miserable miserly misinformed misinterpreted misled missed missed out mistaken mistreated mistrustful misunderstood misused mocked molested monitored monopolised moody moralistic morbid mortified mothered motherly motivated mournful moved muddled mystified

Naive nasty needed needy negative neglected nervous neutral neurotic nonchalant non-existent normal nostalgic nosy nothing noticed nourished nullified numb

Obedient obeyed obliged obliterated obnoxious obscene observant observed obsessed obstinate obstructed odd off off-the-hook offended okay old omnipotent open opinionated opportunistic opposed oppositional oppressed optimistic organised ostracised ousted out-of-control out-of-place out-of-touch outdone outraged outrageous over-controlled over-protected overanxious overcome overjoyed overloaded overlooked oversensitive overwhelmed overworked overweight overzealous

Pain pampered panicked paralysed paranoid passionate passive paternal pathetic patient patronised peaceful peculiar peeved penetrated pensive perfect peripheral perky perplexed persecuted persevering pessimistic persistent pestered persuaded persuasive petrified petty phlegmatic phony picked-on pissed-off pitiful placated placid playful pleading pleasure pleased pliable poised polite popular porous poor possessed possessive positive powerful powerless practical pragmatic preached-to precarious preoccupied pressed pressured pretty private privileged prized productive promiscuous protected protective proud provocative provoked psychopathic pulled apart pulled in punished pushy puzzled

Qualified quarrelsome queasy queer questioned questioning quiescent quiet quirky quizzed

Radiant radical rage rancid raped rapture rare rash rated rational rattled raunchy ravenous ravishing raw re-energised reactive ready real realistic reasonable reassured rebellious reborn rebuffed rebuked receptive reckless reclusive recognised reconciled re-enforced released reunited redeemed red-hot reduced reflective refreshed refuelled regimented regret rejected rejecting rejuvenated relaxed reliable relieved religious reluctant remorse repelled replaced replenished repressed reproached repugnant repulsive rescued resented resentful resigned resilient resistant resolute resourceful respected respectful responsible rested restful restless restrained restricted retaliatory retarded reticent reunited revealed revengeful revered reverent revived revolted rewarded rich ridiculed ridiculous right righteous rigid riled riveted robbed robot-like robust romantic rotten rough rowdy rude ruffled ruined run-down rushed ruthless

Sabotaged sacrificed sad sadistic safe sane satisfied saucy saved scapegoated scared scarred scattered second-best secure sedate seduced seductive seething self-absorbed self-assured self-centred self-confident self-conscious self-destructive self-hatred self-pitying self-reliant self-sacrificing selfish selfless sensational sensible sensitive sentimental sensual sentenced separated serene serious servile set-up settled sexy skilful shaken shallow shamed shaken sharp shattered sheepish sheltered shocked shook-up short-changed shot-down shouted-at shunned shut-out shy sick silenced silly simple sincere singled-out sinking slaughtered slap-happy sluggish slutty small smarmy smart smothered snapped-at snobbish snubbed sceptical social soft-hearted solemn solid solitary sombre soothed sophisticated sore sorrow sorry sour sparkling special spirited spiteful squashed stalked startled starved stepped-on stereotyped sterile stewing stiff stifled stigmatised stimulated strained strangled strengthened stretched stressed strict strong stubborn stuck stuck-up studious stunned stunning stupid stylish subdued submissive subordinate successful suicidal suffocated sulky sullen sunny superior supported sure surly surprised suspicious sympathetic

Tacky tactful talented talkative tame tarnished tearful teased tenacious tender tense tepid terrible terrific terror tested thankful thoughtful threatened thrilled thuggish timid tired together tormented torn tortured tough tragic tranquil transformed trapped treasured trembly tremendous tricked triumphant troubled trusted

Ugly unaccepted unappreciated unbalanced unbearable unbelieving uncertain uncomfortable undecided understood uneasy unhealthy unguarded unpopular unreal upbeat urgent

Vacant vague vain valid valued vengeful vexed vicious victimised victorious violated virulent vivid void vulnerable

Wacky warlike warm warm-hearted warned wary wasted wavering weak wealthy weary weird well whole wicked wild wilful wise wishful witty wonderful worried worse worthy wounded wrong wronged

XYZ xenophobic yellow yielding young youthful yucky zany zealous zest zombie-like

REFERENCES

Attwood, T. (1993) *Why Does Chris Do That?* London: National Autistic Society.

Axline, V. (1964) *Dibs: In Search of Self.* London: Penguin.

Axline, V. (1989) *Play Therapy.* London: Churchill Livingstone.

Barrineau, P. and Bozarth, J.D. (1989) 'A Person-centred Research Model', *Person-centred Review*, 4: 465–74.

Bayne, R., Horton, I., Merry, T. and Noyes, E. (1994) *The Counsellor's Handbook: A Practical A–Z Guide to Professional and Clinical Practice.* London: Chapman and Hall.

BBC (2008) 24 April. Internet source: http://news.bbc.co.uk/go/pr/fr/-/hi/health/7363332.stm

Berman, L. (1993) *Beyond the Smile: The Therapeutic Use of the Photograph.* London: Routledge.

Berman, M. and Brown, D. (2000) *The Power of Metaphor: Story Telling and Guided Journeys for Teachers, Trainers and Therapists.* Carmarthan: Crown House Publishing Ltd.

Biermann-Ratjen, E. (1998) 'On the Development of the Person in Relationship', in B. Thorne and E. Lambers (eds) *Person-centred Therapy: A European Perspective.* London: Sage Publications.

Boeree, C.G. (2006) 'Personality Theories: Carl Rogers (1902–1987)', internet source: www.webspace.ship.edu/cgboer/rogers.html

Bohart, A.C., Elliott, R., Greenberg, L.S. and Watson, J.C. (2002) 'Empathy', in J.C. Norcross (ed.) *Psychotherapy Relationships that Work: Therapist Contributions and Responsiveness to Patients.* Oxford: Oxford University Press.

Bond, T. and Sandhu, A. (2005) *Therapists in Court: Providing Evidence and Supporting Witnesses.* London: Sage Publications.

Bondi, L. (2006) *The Effectiveness of Counselling: COSCA's Review and Comments.* Stirling: Counselling and Psychotherapy in Scotland, available at: www.cosca.org.uk

Bozarth, J.D. (1997) 'Research and Psychotherapy and the Person-centered Approach', internet source: www.personcentered.com/research.html

Bozarth, J.D. (1998) *Person-centred Therapy: A Revolutionary Paradigm.* Ross-on-Wye: PCCS Books.

Bozarth, J.D. and Wilkins, P. (2001) *Rogers' Therapeutic Conditions: Evolution, Theory and Practice – Unconditional Positive Regard.* Ross-on-Wye: PCCS Books.

Bradway, K. and McCoard, B. (1997) *Sandplay: Silent Workshop of the Psyche.* London and New York: Routledge.

Brazier, D. (ed.) (1993a) *Beyond Carl Rogers: Towards a Psychotherapy for the 21st Century.* London: Constable.

Brazier, D. (1993b) 'Occasional Paper: Congruence', Amida Trust. Internet source: www.amidatrust.com/article_congruence

British Association for Counselling and Psychotherapy (BACP) (2007a) *Ethical Framework for Good Practice in Counselling and Psychotherapy.* Lutterworth: BACP.

British Association for Counselling and Psychotherapy (BACP) (2007b) *Confidentiality Guidelines on Reporting Child Abuse for College Counsellors and Psychotherapists.* Lutterworth: BACP.

British Association for Counsellors and Psychotherapists (BACP) (2009) *Good Practice Guidelines for Counsellors in Schools*, 4th edn. Lutterworth: BACP.

British Psychological Society (2006) *Code of Ethics and Conduct.* Leicester: BPS.

Brodley, B.T. (1993) 'The Therapeutic Clinical Interview: Guidelines for Beginning Practice', *Person-Centred Practice*, Vol. 1(2). (Reprinted in T. Merry (ed.) (2000) *Person Centred Practice: The BAPCA Reader.* Ross-on-Wye: PCCS Books.)

Bryant-Jefferies, R. (2004) *Counselling Young People: Person-Centred Dialogues.* Oxford: Radcliffe Medical Press.

Buber, M. (1923) *I and Thou.* New York: Charles Scribner's Sons.

Buchanan, L. and Hughes, R. (2000) *Experiences of Person-centred Counselling Training.* Ross-on-Wye: PCCS Books.

Campion, J. (1991) *Counselling Children.* London: Whiting & Birch.

Carroll, J. (1998) *Introduction to Therapeutic Play.* Oxford: Blackwell Science.

Clarke, G. (2008) 'The Risks and Costs of Learning to Trust the Client's Process When Working with Vulnerable Young People', in S. Keys and T. Walshaw (eds) *Person-centred Work with Children and Young People: UK Practitioner Perspectives.* Ross-on-Wye: PCCS Books.

Cohen, D. (1997) *Carl Rogers: A Critical Biography.* London: Constable.

Cooper, M. (2006) *Counselling in Schools Project, Glasgow, Phase 2: Evaluation Report.* Glasgow: University of Strathclyde.

Cooper, M. (2007) 'The Effectiveness of Counselling in Schools: Key Findings from the Evaluation of the Second Phase of the "Glasgow Counselling in Schools Project"', paper presented at the 13th Annual BACP Research Conference, York.

Cooper, M., O'Hara, M., Schmid, P. and Wyatt, G. (eds) (2007) *The Handbook of Person-centred Psychotherapy and Counselling.* Basingstoke: Palgrave Macmillan.

Corey, M.S. and Corey, G. (1989) *Becoming a Helper.* Pacific Grove, CA: Brooks/Cole Publishing Company.

Crompton, M. (1992) *Children and Counselling.* London: Edward Arnold.

Dalley, T. (ed.) (1984) *Art as Therapy: An Introduction to the Use of Art as a Therapeutic Technique.* London and New York: Routledge.

Daniels, D. and Jenkins, P. (2000) *Therapy with Children: Children's Rights, Confidentiality and the Law.* London: Sage Publications.

D'Ardenne, P. and Mahtani, A. (1989) *Transcultural Counselling in Action.* London: Sage Publications.

Davies, M. (2007) *Boundaries in Counselling and Psychotherapy.* London: Athena Press.

Davis, T. and Osborn, C. (2000) *The Solution-Focused School Counsellor.* Philadelphia, PA: Accelerated Development.

Department of Health (2005) *National Healthy School Status: A Guide for Schools.* London: DoH.

DfES (2001) *Promoting Mental Health in Early Years and School Settings.* London: DfES.

Dorfman, E. (1951) 'Play Therapy', in C. Rogers (ed.) *Client-centred Therapy.* London: Constable.

Dryden, W. and Thorne, B. (1991) *Training and Supervision for Counselling in Action.* London: Sage Publications.

Elliott, R. (2007) 'Person-centred Approaches to Research', in M. Cooper, M. O'Hara, P. Schmid and G. Wyatt (eds) *The Handbook of Person-centred Psychotherapy and Counselling.* Basingstoke: Palgrave Macmillan. pp. 327–40.

Everall, R.D. and Paulson, B.L. (2002) 'The Therapeutic Alliance: Adolescent Perspectives', *Counselling and Psychotherapy Research*, 2(2): 78–87.

Eysenck, H.J. (1952) 'The Effects of Psychotherapy', *J Consult. Psychol*, 16: 319–24.

Faber, A. and Mazlish, E. (1980) *How to Talk So Kids Will Listen and Listen So Kids Will Talk*. New York: Rawson Wade Publishers.

Feltham, C. (1999) *Understanding the Counselling Relationship*. London: Sage Publications.

Feltham, C. and Dryden, W. (1993) *Dictionary of Counselling*. London: Whurr Publishers.

Frankl, V.E. (1959) *Man's Search for Meaning*. Boston, MA: Beacon Press.

Freeth, R. (2007) 'Working within the Medical Model', *Therapy Today*, November 18(9).

Freire, E.S., Hough, M. and Cooper, M. (2007) 'Counselling in Schools: An Evaluation', paper presented at the 13th Annual BACP Research Conference, York.

Garner, R. (2008) 'The Anxiety Epidemic: Why Children are so Unhappy', *The Independent*, Tuesday 11 March.

Gaylin, N.L. (1996) 'Reflections on the Self of the Therapist', in R. Hutterer, G. Pawlowsky, P.E. Schmid and R. Stipsits (eds) *Client-centred and Experiential Psychotherapy: A Paradigm in Motion*. Frankfurt-am-Maine: Peter Lang.

Geldard, D. (1998) *Basic Personal Counselling*. London: Free Association Books.

Geldard, K. and Geldard, D. (1997) *Counselling Children: A Practical Introduction*. London: Sage Publications.

Gibbard, I. and Hanley, T. (2008) 'A Five-year Evaluation of the Effectiveness of Person-centred Counselling in Routine Clinical Practice in Primary Care', *Counselling and Psychotherapy Research*, 8(4) December.

Ginott, H. (1965) *Between Parent and Child*. New York: Macmillan.

Ginott, H. (1969) *Between Parent and Teenager*. New York: Macmillan.

Ginott, H. (1972) *Teacher and Child*. New York: Macmillan.

Glasser, W. (1965) *Reality Therapy: A New Approach to Psychiatry*. New York: Harper and Row.

Glasser, W. (1969) *Schools Without Failure*. New York: Harper & Row.

Glasser, W. (1990) *The Quality School: Managing Students Without Coercion*. New York: Harper Perennial.

Gottman, J. (1997) *The Heart of Parenting: How to Raise an Emotionally Intelligent Child*. London: Bloomsbury.

Grant, B. (1990) 'Principled and Instrumental Non-directiveness in Person-centred and Client-centred Therapy', *Person-centred Review*, 5(1): 77–88. (Reprinted in D.J. Cain (ed.) (2002) *Classics in the Person-centred Approach*. Ross-on-Wye: PCCS Books. pp. 371–7.)

Greenberg, L.S. and Paivio, S.C. (2003) *Working with Emotions in Psychotherapy*. New York: Guilford Press.

Hamblin, D. (1974) *The Teacher and Counselling*. Oxford: Basil Blackwell.

Harrington, J. (2001) '*Self-disclosure: Temptations and Alternatives*', paper delivered at the SACES Idea Exchange, Alabama.

Haugh, S. (2001) 'A Historical Review of the Development of the Concept of Congruence in Person-centred Theory', in G. Wyatt (ed.) *Rogers' Therapeutic Conditions: Evolution, Theory and Practice – Congruence*. Ross-on-Wye: PCCS Books.

Haugh, S. and Merry, T. (2001) *Rogers' Therapeutic Conditions: Evolution, Theory and Practice – Empathy*. Ross-on-Wye: PCCS Books.

Hawkins, J.M. and Allen, R. (eds) (1991) *The Oxford Encyclopaedic English Dictionary*. Oxford: Clarendon Press.

Hazzard, A.J. (1995) 'Measuring Outcome in Counselling: A Brief Exploration of the Issues', *British Journal of General Practice*, 45(392): 118–19.

Holden, A. (1971) *Counselling in Secondary Schools*. London: Constable.

Hough, M. (1996) *Counselling Skills*. Harlow: Longman.

Howe, D. (1993) *On Being a Client: Understanding the Process of Counselling and Psychotherapy*. London: Sage Publications.

Humphrey, G.M. and Zimpfer, D.G. (1996) *Counselling for Grief and Bereavement*. London: Sage Publications.

Jacobs, M. (1988) *Psychodynamic Counselling in Action*. London: Sage Publications.

Jenkins, P. (2007) *Counselling, Psychotherapy and the Law*, 2nd edn. London: Sage Publications.

Jewish Virtual Library (2008) 'Martin Buber', internet source: www.jewishvirtuallibrary.org/jsource/biography/Buber

Jones, A. (1970) *School Counselling in Practice*. East Grinstead: Ward Lock Educational.

Jones, A. (1977) *Counselling Adolescents in School*. London: Kogan Page.

Keating, M. (2007) 'A Place to Hide and Heal', *The Guardian*, Tuesday 13 November.

Keys, S. (2003) *Idiosyncratic Person-centred Therapy*. Ross-on-Wye: PCCS Books.

Khan, M. (1997) *Between Therapist and Client: The New Relationship*. New York: W.H. Freeman and Company.

Kindlan, D. and Thompson, M. (2000) *Raising Cain: Protecting the Emotional Life of Boys*. New York: Ballantine Books.

Kirschenbaum, H. (2007) *The Life and Work of Carl Rogers*. Ross-on-Wye: PCCS Books.

Kirschenbaum, H. and Henderson, V.H. (eds) (1990) *The Carl Rogers Reader*. London: Constable.

Kopp, B.M. (1998) 'Using Metaphors in Creative Writing', internet source: http://owl.english.pudue.edu/handouts/general/gl_metaphor.html

Kutner, L. (2008) 'Insights for Parents: How Children Develop Empathy', internet source: www.drkutner.com/parenting/articles/develop_empathy.html

Lago, C. (2007) 'Counselling Across Difference and Diversity', in M. Cooper et al. (eds) *The Handbook of Person-centred Psychotherapy and Counselling*. Basingstoke: Palgrave Macmillan.

Lambers, E. (2007) 'A Person-centred Perspective on Supervision', in M. Cooper, M. O'Hara, P. Schmid and G. Wyatt (eds) *The Handbook of Person-centred Psychotherapy and Counselling*. Basingstoke: Palgrave Macmillan.

Langridge, G. (2007) 'The Counselling Relationship', internet source: www.creativecounselling.org.uk/relationship.html

Levitt, B.E. (2005) *Embracing Non-directivity: Reassessing Person-centred Theory and Practice in the 21st Century*. Ross-on-Wye: PCCS Books.

Lietaer, G. (1984) 'Unconditional Positive Regard: A Controversial Basic Attitude in Client-centred Therapy', in R. Levant and J. Shlien (eds) *Client-centred Therapy and the Person-centred Approach*. New York: Praeger. pp. 41–58.

Lietaer, G. (2001) *'Being Genuine as a Therapist: Congruence and Transparency'*, in G. Wyatt (ed.) *Rogers' Therapeutic Conditions: Evolution, Theory and Practice*. Ross-on-Wye: PCCS Books.

Luczaj, S. (2007) 'How Useful are Therapeutic Boundaries?', internet source: http://counsellingresource.com/features/2007/12/10/boundaries-therapy-person-centred/

McLeod, J. (1993) *An Introduction to Counselling*. Buckingham: Open University Press.

McLeod, J. (1994) *Doing Counselling Research*. London: Sage Publications.

McLeod, J. (2008) 'Outside the Therapy Room', *Therapy Today*, 19(4): 14–18.

McLoughlin, B. (1995) *Developing Psychodynamic Counselling*. London: Sage Publications.

Maslow, A.H. (1968) *Toward a Psychology of Being*. New York: Wiley.

Masson, J. (1992) *Against Therapy*. London: Fontana.

Mayhall, C. and Mayhall, T. (2004) *On Buber*. Belmont, CA: Wadsworth Publishing.

Mearns, D. (1994) *Developing Person-centred Counselling*. London: Sage Publications.

Mearns, D. (1996) 'Working at Relational Depth with Clients in Person-centred Therapy', *Counselling*, 7(4): 306–11.

Mearns, D. (1997) *Person-centred Counselling Training*. London: Sage Publications.

Mearns, D. and Cooper, M. (2005) *Working at Relational Depth in Counselling and Psychotherapy*. London: Sage Publications.

Mearns, D. and McLeod, J. (1984) 'A Person-centred Approach to Research', in R.F. Levant and J.M. Shlein (eds) *Client-centred Therapy and the Person-centred Approach: New Directions in Theory, Research and Practice*. Eastbourne: Praeger. pp. 370–89.

Mearns, D. and Thorne, B. (1988) *Person-centred Counselling in Action*. London: Sage Publications.

Mearns, D. and Thorne, B. (2000) *Person-centred Therapy Today: New Frontiers in Theory and Practice*. London: Sage Publications.

Merry, T. (1995) *Invitation to Person-centred Psychology*. London: Whurr Publishers.

Merry, T. (1997) 'Counselling and Creativity: An Interview with Natalie Rogers', *British Journal of Guidance and Counselling*, 25(2): 263–73.

Merry, T. (1999) *Learning and Being in Person-centred Counselling*. Ross-on-Wye: PCCS Books.

Merry, T. (ed.) (2000) *The BAPCA Reader*. Ross-on-Wye: PCCS Books.

Milner, P. (1974) *Counselling in Education*. London: J.M. Dent and Sons.

Mulhauser, G. (2006) 'The Heart & Soul of Change: Book Review', internet source: http://counsellingresource.com/books/what-works

National Office for Statistics (2004) *Mental Health of Children and Young People*. London: National Office for Statistics.

Nelson-Jones, R. (1993) *Practical Counselling and Helping Skills*. London: Cassell.

Nichols, K.A. and Jenkinson, J. (1991) *Leading a Support Group*. London: Chapman and Hall.

Noonan, E. (1983) *Counselling Young People*. London: Methuen and Co. Ltd.

Oaklander, V. (1989) *Windows to Our Children: A Gestalt Therapy Approach to Children and Adolescents*. Moab, UT: Real People Press.

Oaklander, V. (2006) *Hidden Treasure: A Map to The Child's Inner Self*. London: Karnac Books.

O'Connell, B. (1998) *Solution-Focused Therapy*. London: Sage Publications.

Patterson, C.H. (1962) *Counselling and Guidance in Schools*. New York: Harper & Row.

Pattison, S., Rowland, N., Cromarty, K., Richards, K., Jenkins, P.L., Cooper, M. et al. (2007) *Counselling in Schools: A Research Study into Services for Children and Young People in Wales*. Lutterworth: BACP.

Prochaska, J. and Norcross, J. (1994) *Systems of Psychotherapy: A Transtheoretical Analysis*. Pacific Grove, CA: Brooks/Cole Publishing.

Procter, G., Cooper, M., Sanders, P. and Malcolm, B. (2006) *Politicising the Person-centred Approach: An Agenda for Social Change*. Ross-on-Wye: PCCS Books.

Reber, A. and Reber, S. (2001) *The Penguin Dictionary of Psychology*. Harmondsworth: Penguin Books.

Rhodes, J. and Ajmal, Y. (1995) *Solution Focused Thinking in Schools*. London: BT Press.

Rice, L.N., Greenberg, L.S. and Elliott, R. (1996) *Facilitating Emotional Change*. New York: Guilford Press.

Rogers, C.R. (1939) *The Clinical Treatment of the Problem Child*. Boston: Houghton Mifflin.

Rogers, C. (1951) *Client-centred Therapy*. London: Constable.

Rogers, C.R. (1957) 'The Necessary and Sufficient Conditions for Therapeutic Change', *Journal of Consulting Psychology*, 21: 95–103.

Rogers, C. (1967) *On Becoming a Person: A Therapist's View of Psychotherapy*. London: Constable.

Rogers, C.R. (1969) *Freedom to Learn: A View of What Education Might Become*. Columbus, OH: Charles Merrill.

Rogers, C. (1977) *On Personal Power*. New York: Delacorte Press.

Rogers, C. (1978) *Carl Rogers on Personal Power: Inner Strength and its Revolutionary Impact*. London: Constable.

Rogers, C. (1980) *A Way of Being*. Boston: Houghton Mifflin.

Rogers, C.R. (1983) *Freedom to Learn for the 80's*. Columbus, OH: Charles Merrill.

Rogers, C. (1986) 'Reflection of Feelings', *Person-centred Review*, 1(4): 125–40.

Rogers, C. (1987) 'Comment on Schlien's Article: A Countertheory of Transference', *Person-centred Review*, 2(2). (Reprinted in T. Merry (ed.) (1995) *Invitation to Person-centred Psychology*. London: Whurr Publishers.

Rogers, C. and Russell, D.E. (2002) *Carl Rogers the Quiet Revolutionary: An Oral History*. Roseville, CA: Penmarin Books.

Rogers, C. and Stevens, B. (1967) *Person to Person: The Problem of Being Human*. Boulder, CO: Real People Press.

Rogers, N. (2000) *The Creative Connection: Expressive Arts as Healing*. Ross-on-Wye: PCCS Books.

Rowland, N., Bower, P., Mellor-Clark, J., Heywood, P. and Hardy, R. (2000) 'Counselling in Primary Care: A Systematic Review of the Research Evidence', *British Journal of Guidance and Counselling*, 28(2): 215–31.

Sanders, P. (2004) *The Tribes of the Person-centred Nation: An Introduction to the Schools of Therapy Related to the Person-centred Approach*. Ross-on-Wye: PCCS Books.

Selekman, M. (1993) *Pathways to Change: Brief Therapy with Difficult Adolescents*. London and New York: Guilford Press.

Silverstone, L. (1997) *Art Therapy the Person-centred Way: Art and the Development of the Person*. London: Jessica Kingsley Publishers.

Smith, E.M.J. (1985) 'Ethnic Minorities: Life Stress, Social Support and Mental Health Issues', *The Counselling Psychologist*, 13(4): 537–79.

Stewart, W. (1997) *An A–Z of Counselling Theory and Practice*. Cheltenham: Stanley Thornes Publishers Ltd.

Straus, M. (1999) *No-talk Therapy for Children and Adolescents*. New York: W.W. Norton and Company.

Sunderland, M. (2000) *Using Story Telling as a Therapeutic Tool with Children*. Bicester: Winslow Press Ltd.

Sutton, J. and Stewart, W. (2002) *Learning to Counsel: Develop the Skills You Need to Counsel Others*. Oxford: How To Books.

Thorne, B. (1991) *Person-centred Counselling: Therapeutic and Spiritual Dimensions*. London: Whurr Publishers.

Thorne, B. (1992) *Key Figures in Counselling and Psychotherapy: Carl Rogers*. London: Sage Publications.

Thorne, B. (2005) *Love's Embrace: The Autobiography of a Person-centred Therapist*. Ross-on-Wye: PCCS Books.

Thorne, B. and Lambers, E. (1998) *Person-centred Therapy: A European Perspective*. London: Sage Publications.

Tolan, J. (2003) *Skills in Person-centred Counselling and Psychotherapy*. London: Sage Publications.

Tolan, J. (2007) *Skills in Person-centred Counselling and Psychotherapy*, 2nd edn. London: Sage Publications.

Truax, C. (1971) 'Self-disclosure, Genuineness, and the Interpersonal Relationship', *Counsellor Education and Supervision*, 10(4): 351–4.

Tudor, K. (2007) 'Training in the Person-centred Approach', in M. Cooper et al. (eds) (2007) *The Handbook of Person-centred Psychotherapy and Counselling*. Basingstoke: Palgrave Macmillan.

Tudor, L., Keemar, K., Tudor, K., Valentine, J. and Worrall, M. (2004) *The Person-centred Approach: A Contemporary Introduction*. Basingstoke: Palgrave Macmillan.

Tudor, K. and Worrall, M. (2004) *Freedom to Practice: Person-centred Approaches to Supervision*. Ross-on-Wye: PCCS Books.

Tudor, K. and Worrall, M. (2006) *Person-centred Therapy: A Clinical Philosophy*. London and New York: Routledge.

Vaknin, S. (2008) 'On Empathy', internet source: www.samvak.tripod.com/empathy.html

Vincent, S. (2005) *Being Empathic: A Companion for Counsellors and Therapists*. Oxford: Radcliffe.

Walshaw, T. (2008) 'Creative Discernment: The Key to the Training and Practice of Person-centred Play Therapists', in S. Key and T. Walshaw (eds) *Person-centred Work with Children and Young People: UK Practitioner Perspectives*. Ross-on-Wye: PCCS Books.

Warren, B. (1984) *Using the Creative Arts in Therapy*. London and New York: Routledge.

Webb, S.B. (1997) 'Training for Maintaining Appropriate Boundaries in Counselling', *British Journal of Guidance and Counselling*, 25(2): 175–88.

Welsh Assembly Government (2008) *School-based Counselling: A National Strategy*. Available at: www.welsh.gov.uk

Wilkins, P. (1997) 'Towards a Person-centred Understanding of Consciousness and the Unconscious', *Person-centred Practice,* 5(1). (Reprinted in T. Merry (ed.) (2000) *The BAPCA Reader*. Ross-on-Wye: PCCS Books.)

Wilkins, P. (1999) 'The Relationship in Person-centred Counselling', in C. Feltham (ed.) *Understanding the Counselling Relationship*. London: Sage Publications.

Wilkins, P. (2001) 'Unconditional Positive Regard Reconsidered', in J.D. Bozarth and P. Wilkins (eds) *Rogers' Therapeutic Conditions: Evolution, Theory and Practice – Unconditional Positive Regard*. Ross-on-Wye: PCCS Books. (First published in *British Journal of Guidance and Counselling*, 28(1) (2000): 23–36.)

Williams, K. (1973) *The School Counsellor*. London: Methuen.

Wilson, A. (1983) *The Collected Stories of Elizabeth Bowen*. Harmondsworth: Penguin.

Wood, J.K. (1996) 'The Person-centred Approach: Toward an Understanding of its Implications', in R. Hutterer, G. Pawlowsky, P.F. Schmid and R. Stipsits (eds) *Client-centred and Experiential Psychotherapy: A Paradigm in Motion*. Frankfurt-am-Main: Peter Lang.

Woodhouse, J. (2008) 'Sandplay: "Growing Ground" in Person-centred Play Therapy', in S. Keys and T. Walshaw (eds) *Person-centred Work with Children and Young People: UK Practitioner Perspectives*. Ross-on-Wye: PCCS Books.

Wyatt, G. (2001) *Rogers' Therapeutic Conditions: Evolution, Theory and Practice. Volume 1: Congruence*. Ross-on-Wye: PCCS Books.

Yalom, I. (1980) *Existential Psychotherapy*. New York: Basic Books.

Yalom, I. (2001) *The Gift of Therapy: Reflections on Being a Therapist*. London: Piatkus.

Zur, O. and Nordmarken, N. (2009) 'To Touch or Not to Touch: Exploring the Myth of Prohibition Touch in Psychotherapy and Counselling', internet source: www. zurinstitute. com/touchintherapy.html

USEFUL ORGANISATIONS

The Association for the Development of the Person-Centred Approach (ADPCA)
www.adpca.org

The British Association of Art Therapists
www.baat.org

The British Association for Counselling and Psychotherapy (BACP)
BACP House, 15 St John's Business Park, Lutterworth, Leicestershire, LE17 4HB.
Tel. 01455 883300
www.bacp.co.uk
Counselling Children and Young People (CCYP) is a Division of BACP

The British Association of Dramatherapists
www.badth.org.uk

The British Association for the Person-Centred Approach (BAPCA)
BAPCA, PO Box 143, Ross-on-Wye, HR9 9AH.
Tel. 01989 763 863
www.bapca.org.uk

The British Association of Play Therapists
www.bapt.info

Network of the European Associations for Person-Centred and Experiential Psychotherapy and Counselling (NEAPCEPC)
www.pce-Europe.org

PCCS Books
2 Cropper Row, Alton Road, Ross-on-Wye, HR9 5LA.
Tel. 01989 763 900
www.pccs-books.co.uk

Person–Centered International
www.personcentered.com/research

Play Therapy UK
www.playtherapy.org.uk

World Association for Person-Centred and Experiential Psychotherapy and Counselling
www.pcc-world.org

INDEX

abuse, 10, 13, 25, 36, 123
acceptance, 21, 95, 141, 171
accurate understanding, 116
actualising tendency, 15, 22–4
    case study, 23–4
ADHD, 55
adult and child connecting, 11
Adler, Alfred, 33
alienation, overcoming, 118
analysis, 11
anger, 28, 34
anxiety, 36, 51, 55, 61, 152, 168
art therapy, 131–2
'as if' quality, 28, 108, 115, 116
attachment theory, 33
authority and control, 57
autism, 114
Axline, Virginia, 34, 132

behaviourism, 20, 23, 33
Behr, Michael, 31
bereavement, 23, 36, 104
bibliotherapy, 137
boundaries, 38, 44–5, 174
    case study, 37
    challenge to the orthodoxy, 44
    and supervision, 170
Bowlby, John, 33
British Association for Counselling and
    Psychotherapy, 35, 39, 41, 151, 169
    counselling children and young people
        division, 10, 35
British Association of Art Therapists, 131
British Association of Play Therapists, 135
British Psychological Society, 39
Buber, Martin, 30
bullying, 36

CAMHS, 10, 56
causation, rejection of, 20

challenging, 146–7
checking understanding, 111
child-centredness, 121
childhood, knowledge of, 11
children,
    abused, 154
    angry, 155
    bullying of, 154
    in care, 36
    creativity, inclination toward, 124
    dependency of, 11
    different to work with adults, 11–14, 123
    and discrimination, 154, 156
    and empathy, 114
    empowerment of, 156, 157, 174
    experiences of adults, 28
    feeling listened to, 12
    finding own solutions to problems, 22, 57
    freedom when working with, 44
    interventions, 12
    mental health of, 10
    and poverty, 154
    rewards of working with, 11, 173
    rights, 152, 156
    self-blame, 11
    and silence, 147
    training to work with, 167–8
    views of the world, 20
    and violence, 154
child protection, 41, 42, 167
children's workforce, 10
cognitive-behavioural approaches, 11, 15, 78
conditions of worth, 25–6, 58–9, 91, 146, 155
    case studies, 25–6
    and challenging, 146
    parental approval, 26
    and supervision, 170
confidentiality, 39–40, 152, 167
confrontation, 146
confusion, 28

congruence, 28, 66, 97–105, 141
  case studies, 99
  communication of, 102
  counsellor, 171
  definition of, 98
  importance of, 103–5
  and self-awareness, 102, 103
  and trust, 103
content, reflection of, 83
Cooper, Mick, 31
CORE, 50
core conditions, 9, 27–9, 52–3, 63, 70,
    138, 152, 159
  and challenging, 146, 147
  necessary and sufficient, 27, 52, 125, 140, 171
  and presence, 143
  and relational depth, 118
  relationship between, 118
  and supervision, 171
  and training, 165
counselling
  and creativity, 120
  effectiveness of, 48–53
  ethical, 151, 167
  and friendship, 45
  growth of, 10
  and helping, differences between, 4
  models of, 11, 15
  non-specialist, 6
  open-ended, 15
  settings, 6, 12, 36
  skills, 6, 13, 19, 139, 140, 141, 142, 165
  time-limited, 16
  touch in, 42
  values, 151
  voluntary nature of, 70–1
  voluntary nature of, case study, 71
  with children as a growth area, 10
  why different with children, 11–12
counsellor
  attitudes, 152
  burnout, 173
  as a person, 6, 21, 142
  prejudices of, 161
  professional roles, 7
  qualities, 151
  self-criticism, 174
  stress, 173
  well-being, 173–4
counter-transference, 157
  and supervision, 172
creativity, 120–38
  case studies, 121–3, 128–9
culture, 162

defences, 62–3, 125, 157
  case study, 62
depression, 36, 47, 51, 55, 61, 168
diagnosis, avoidance of, 6
diversity and difference, 160, 162
divorce and separation, 36, 115
domestic violence, 36
drama therapy, 136
drug treatment, 55
dual roles, 39

Ellis, Albert, 34
'embedded' counselling roles, 6
emotional literacy, 81, 114
emotion-focused therapy, 83
emotions, 78, 83, 124, 166
  and autism, 114
  counsellor's, 161
  and empathy, 115
  and music, 135
  and the unconscious, 157
empathy, 21, 22, 28, 66, 84, 99, 107–19, 141, 152
  advanced, 113
  case studies, 109–11, 113
  and challenging, 146
  communicating, 108, 111
  dangers associated with, 116
  definition of, 107
  development of, 114
  and drama therapy, 136
  and frames of reference, 143
  importance of, 116
  levels of, 113
  and listening, 111
  and other approaches, 113
  permeating nature of, 116
  power of, 116, 118
  and sympathy, 109
  teaching about, 114
Erikson, Erik, 33
Ethical Framework for Good Practice in Counselling
    and Psychotherapy, 39, 43, 151
Every Child Matters, 10, 35, 40
existentialism, 15, 19
experience,
  as authority, 15
  learning through, 167
  as opposed to theory, 15
expertise, 6, 57
expressive arts therapy, 128
expressive therapies, 125
  art, 124, 128, 131–2
  collage, 125, 128, 131
  drama, 124, 125, 136

expressive therapies *cont.*
  music, 124, 129, 135
  sculpture, 125, 128, 131
  voice work, 125, 136
  writing, 124, 125, 136
external frame of reference, 143
external validation, 25
Eysenck, H.J., 49

Faber, Adele, 3
feelings, 78, 118, 137, 166
  boy's, 82
  children's, 81–2
  and congruence, 104–5
  counsellor's, 161
  and creativity, 126, 131
  and drama, 136
  expression of, 79–81, 123
  and music, 135
  reflection of, 82, 83–5
  teaching about, 81
  thoughts, compared to, 78, 83
  unconscious, 159
  and understanding, 107
  vocabulary, 80–2
film therapy, 137
frames of reference, 82, 84, 115, 118, 119, 143, 146, 158
Frankl, Victor, 30, 33
Freud, Anna, 30
Freud, Sigmund, 33, 157, 159
Fromm, Eric, 31, 33
fully functioning person, 29

gay and lesbian young people, 36
Gestalt, 30
Ginott, Haim, 30
Glasser, William, 31, 34
Gottman, John, 30
grief, 25, 47, 121
group experience, 166
growth, 116, 165
guilt, 98

Hamblin, Douglas, 34
Haugh, Sheila, 31
helper, role of, 4, 6, 7
  limits to experience, 13
'helping alliance', 68
'here-and-now', 144, 168
hierarchy of needs, 23
Holden, Alick, 34
holistic working, 126, 166
homophobia, 36

humanistic approach, 19, 34, 57
humanity, 22, 174

ideal self, 26
immediacy, 144–5
incongruity, 26, 60, 62, 100
  case study, 60
intellectualisation, 79
interpretation, 112
isolation, 67
'I-Thou' relationship, 30

Jaspers, Carl, 113
Jones, Anne, 34
journal work, 136
Jung, Carl, 33

Keys, Suzanne, 31
Khan, Michael, 69, 70
Klein, Melanie, 33
knowledge, 167
knowledge, cultural, 162
Kohut, Heinz, 113

labelling children, 28, 36, 58
learning through experience, 165
Levitt, Brian, 31
'living in the moment', 29
locus of control, 61
loss, 36, 115, 160
love, 72–3, 133
  parental, 26
Lowenfeld, Margaret, 33

Maslow, Abraham, 23, 33
May, Rollo, 30, 33
Mazlish, Elaine, 30
mental health, 35, 36, 55
  case study, 56
medical model, 57
Mental Health Foundation, 10, 36
mentor, 13
metaphor, 129, 137, 149–50
  relationship to simile, 149
Milner, Patricia, 34
MIND, 10
Moreno, Jacob, 113
Moustakas, Clark, 31
multi-cultural, 161
music therapy, 135

National Healthy Schools Status, 35
non-directivity, 93–4,
  and creativity, 126

non-directivity *cont.*
    and play therapy, 132
non-judgementalism, 22, 88, 94, 96, 134, 152, 161
Noonan, Ellen, 34

Oaklander, Violet, 34
obsessive-compulsive disorders, 55, 56
offering solutions, 112
openness, 12
openness to experience, 29, 127
organismic self, 60, 61
organismic valuing process, 24–6
outcomes, 47–8
    case study, 47
    and empathy, 117
    emphasis on, 10
over-identification, 116, 168, 173

pastoral care in schools, 34
Patterson, C.H., 34
Perls, Fritz, 30, 34
personal development, 6, 166
personal therapy, 167
person-centred approach,
    and analysis, 116
    case study, 12–13
    criticisms of, 14–15, 121
    and education, 165
    essence of, 21
    expertise, in contrast to, 57
    faith and belief in the process of, 4, 25, 53
    feelings, importance of, 78
    and growth, 27
    and immediacy, 144
    and open-endedness, 16
    optimistic nature of, 15, 59
    philosophy of, 15, 17
    and politics, 154
    and presence, 143
    principles, not losing sight of, 126
    and psychodynamic theory, 159
    purist approaches to, 29, 138
    and relationships, 27
    and supervision, 170
    theoretical basis, 14
    and training, 165
    and transference, 158
    and the unconscious, 157
phenomenology, 19–20, 155
phobias, 55
photographs, using, 137
pictures and images, using, 137
play therapy, 33, 132–5
positive regard, 26
    conditional, 26

poverty, 36
power differentials, 27, 168
presence, 142–3, 159
psychiatric services, 13
psychodynamic theory, 15, 22, 157, 158
    approaches, 49
    and supervision, 172
psychological contact, 27
psychologically safe environment, 130, 152
psychosomatic symptoms, 62

questions, use of, 112, 139

racism, 36, 161, 162
rational emotive behaviour therapy, 32, 34
realness, 104
real self, 26
refugees and asylum-seekers, 36
rejection, feelings of, 91
relational depth, 118
    and relational depth, 144
relationships, 6, 11, 17, 28, 29, 57, 65–6, 85, 100,
        103, 123, 140, 141, 143, 148, 158, 173
    case studies, 67–8
    and core conditions, 118
    cultural dimensions, 162
    and empathy, 115, 117, 150
    and silence, 147
    trust in, 71–2
    views of young people, 65–7
    why so important, 67–70
'rescuing', 148
resilience, 22, 23, 24
Rogers, Carl, 5, 8
    and actualising tendency, 23
    biographical details, 8–9
    challenge to psychological orthodoxy, 9
    and conditions of worth, 59
    and congruence, 28, 100
    and core conditions, 27
    and creativity, 125, 127
    and diagnosis, 57
    and education, 9, 165
    and empathy, 28, 108, 116
    and expertise, 117
    and feelings, 78–80
    and fully functioning person, 29
    on importance of experience over theory, 15
    influence of, 9, 27, 35
    and locus of control, 61
    and love, 72–3
    and openness to experience, 29
    politicisation, 155–6
    and the private perceptual world of the
        client, 108

Rogers, Carl *cont.*
and psychological freedom, 127
and psychological safety, 127
and relationships, 68
and research, 50–1
as revolutionary, 155
and use of techniques, 140–1
views on transference, 158
and unconditional positive regard, 28, 88–9
Rogers, Natalie, 125, 128–31
role-play, 167

Samaritans, 10, 36
sand play, 134
Schmid, Peter, 31
school counselling, 34, 35, 50, 168, 173
and supervision, 168
self-actualisation, 22, 59, 131
self-awareness, 102, 130
and empathy, 114
and immediacy, 145
and training, 166
when working with children, 168
self-concept, 59, 60, 62, 91, 114
self-defeating cycles, 91
self-defending tendency, 62
self-disclosure, 41–2
and congruence, 102, 104
self-harm, 160, 168
self-worth, 59, 63
sense of humour, 152
shame, 13, 98
silence, 121, 147–9
Silverstone, Liesl, 131–2
Social Emotional Aspects of Learning, 35
solution-focused therapy, 11, 56
'spontaneous recovery', 49
stereotyped responses, 85
storytelling, 136–7
story writing, 136
subjective experience, 53, 107
suicidal clients, 168, 173
Sunderland, Margot, 136–7
supervision, 71, 146, 169–73
feelings of inadequacy and insecurity in
counsellor, 141
and over-identification, 116
reasons for, 169, 170
and self-doubt, 19

supervision *cont.*
therapy, compared with, 171
types of, 169
supervisor, experience of, 171
sympathy, 83–4, 106, 109
case studies, 109–11
and pity, 109

talk, 123
Targeted Mental Health in Schools Project, 35
technique, avoidance of, 116, 139–42
'tentativeness', 111, 144, 145
theory, 15, 17–19
definition of, 18
and experience, 15
and training, 167
therapeutic alliance, 113
training, 6, 20–1, 139, 160, 164–8
transference, 157
and supervision, 172
transparency, 104
and immediacy, 144
trust, 71–2, 103, 152
in the individual, 156

unconditional positive regard, 22, 28, 86–96, 100
and acceptance, 95
case studies, 86–7, 91
and challenging, 146
conditions of worth, relationship to, 91
and empathy, 112
and 'liking', 92–3
why therapeutic, 90–2
unconscious, 22, 126, 157–60
understanding, preoccupation with, 143
unhappiness, causes of, 54–63, 83–4

voluntary sector, 7, 40, 49, 167, 169

Warner, Margaret, 31
warmth, 12, 16, 152
Williams, Ken, 34
Winnicott, Donald, 33
World Association for Person-centred and
Experiential Psychotherapy and
Counselling, 31

Yalom, Irving, 69
Young Minds, 10, 36

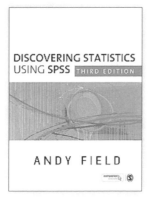
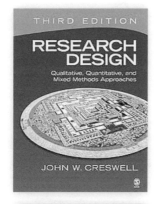
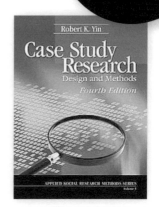

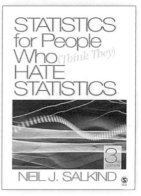
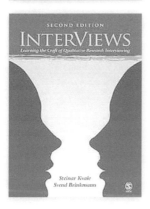
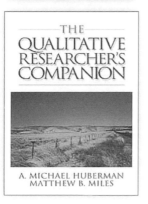

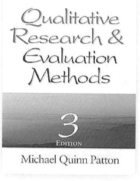
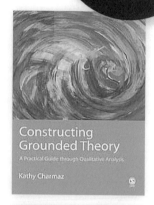
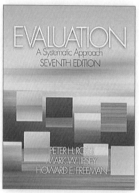
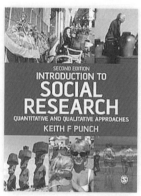
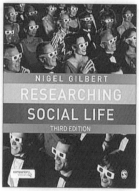

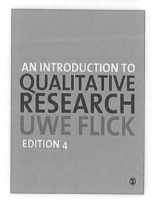

The Qualitative Research Kit

Edited by Uwe Flick

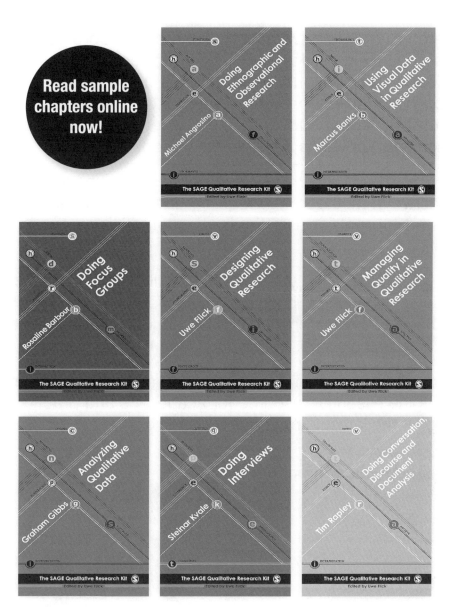

Read sample chapters online now!

Michael Angrosino — Doing Ethnographic and Observational Research — The SAGE Qualitative Research Kit — Edited by Uwe Flick

Marcus Banks — Using Visual Data in Qualitative Research — The SAGE Qualitative Research Kit — Edited by Uwe Flick

Rosaline Barbour — Doing Focus Groups — The SAGE Qualitative Research Kit — Edited by Uwe Flick

Uwe Flick — Designing Qualitative Research — The SAGE Qualitative Research Kit — Edited by Uwe Flick

Uwe Flick — Managing Quality in Qualitative Research — The SAGE Qualitative Research Kit — Edited by Uwe Flick

Graham Gibbs — Analyzing Qualitative Data — The SAGE Qualitative Research Kit — Edited by Uwe Flick

Steinar Kvale — Doing Interviews — The SAGE Qualitative Research Kit — Edited by Uwe Flick

Tim Rapley — Doing Conversation, Discourse and Document Analysis — The SAGE Qualitative Research Kit — Edited by Uwe Flick

www.sagepub.co.uk

Supporting researchers for more than forty years

Research methods have always been at the core of SAGE's publishing. Sara Miller McCune founded SAGE in 1965 and soon after she published SAGE's first methods book, *Public Policy Evaluation*. A few years later, she launched the Quantitative Applications in the Social Sciences series – affectionately known as the 'little green books'.

Always at the forefront of developing and supporting new approaches in methods, SAGE published early groundbreaking texts and journals in the fields of qualitative methods and evaluation.

Today, more than forty years and two million little green books later, SAGE continues to push the boundaries with a growing list of more than 1,200 research methods books, journals, and reference works across the social, behavioural, and health sciences.

From qualitative, quantitative and mixed methods to evaluation, SAGE is the essential resource for academics and practitioners looking for the latest in methods by leading scholars.

www.sagepublications.com